W9-BRX-383

A SAFEWAY IN ARIZONA

A SAFEWAY
IN ARIZONA

TOM ZOELLNER

**WHAT THE GABRIELLE GIFFORDS SHOOTING
TELLS US ABOUT THE GRAND CANYON STATE
AND LIFE IN AMERICA**

VIKING

VIKING

Published by the Penguin Group

Penguin Group (USA) Inc., 375 Hudson Street, New York, New York 10014, U.S.A. • Penguin Group (Canada), 90 Eglinton Avenue East, Suite 700, Toronto, Ontario, Canada M4P 2Y3 (a division of Pearson Penguin Canada Inc.) • Penguin Books Ltd, 80 Strand, London WC2R 0RL, England • Penguin Ireland, 25 St. Stephen's Green, Dublin 2, Ireland (a division of Penguin Books Ltd) • Penguin Books Australia Ltd, 250 Camberwell Road, Camberwell, Victoria 3124, Australia (a division of Pearson Australia Group Pty Ltd) • Penguin Books India Pvt Ltd, 11 Community Centre, Panchsheel Park, New Delhi – 110 017, India • Penguin Group (NZ), 67 Apollo Drive, Rosedale, Auckland 0632, New Zealand (a division of Pearson New Zealand Ltd) • Penguin Books (South Africa) (Pty) Ltd, 24 Sturdee Avenue, Rosebank, Johannesburg 2196, South Africa

Penguin Books Ltd, Registered Offices:
80 Strand, London WC2R 0RL, England

First published in 2011 by Viking Penguin,
a member of Penguin Group (USA) Inc.

10 9 8 7 6 5 4 3 2 1

LIBRARY OF CONGRESS CATALOGING IN PUBLICATION DATA
Zoellner, Tom.
A Safeway in Arizona : what the Gabrielle Giffords shooting tells us about the Grand Canyon State and life in America / Tom Zoellner.
p. cm.
Includes bibliographical references.
ISBN 978-0-670-02320-2
1. Giffords, Gabrielle D. (Gabrielle Dee), 1970– —Assassination attempt, 2011.
2. Giffords, Gabrielle D. (Gabrielle Dee), 1970– 3. Arizona—Politics and government—21st century. 4. Arizona—Social conditions—21st century. 5. Arizona—Economic conditions—21st century. 6. Arizona—Civilization—21st century. 7. Political culture—Arizona. 8. Political culture—United States. I. Title.
E901.1.G54Z64 2012
328.73'092—dc23
[B]   2011031521

Printed in the United States of America
Set in Adobe Garamond Pro with Aldus LT Std
Designed by Daniel Lagin

This book is for the victims of January 8, 2011.

All of them, all except Phineas, constructed at infinite cost to themselves these Maginot Lines against this enemy they thought they saw across the frontier, this enemy who never attacked that way—if he ever attacked at all; if he was indeed the enemy.

—John Knowles, *A Separate Peace*

AUTHOR'S NOTE

This book is an attempt to make sense of a fundamentally baffling event. I have used the tools of journalism to arrive at a few conclusions. Several personal biases—explained within the text—make this not a work of objective journalism in the traditional sense, though I have striven to be fair to all concerned.

A Safeway in Arizona

ONE

THE SAFEWAY

On the morning of January 8, 2011, a cluster of people began to come together under the brick facade of a Safeway supermarket, where U.S. Representative Gabrielle Giffords was supposed to stand for a few hours and meet with anyone who wanted to talk with her.

The Safeway is known within the company as Store #1255, and it serves as the anchor of a retail plaza called La Toscana Village in the unincorporated northern suburbs of Tucson, Arizona. Three brick arches out front were designed as an homage not to Tucson but to the Tuscany region of Italy. Their bricks are maroon-colored and coarse. The columns are smooth white concrete.

The idea to do these supermarket events didn't come from Gabrielle. It was from Rahm Emanuel, now mayor of Chicago, who had served in Congress himself for three terms before becoming chief of staff to President Barack Obama. He used to run these events from plazas around his Chicago district, reasoning that grocery shopping was a universal activity in a car-based society and that the visibility would be high.

Gabrielle, a forty-year-old with short chestnut-colored hair, pulled into La Toscana Village at 9:58 A.M. in her green Toyota 4Runner. Before getting out, she reached for her iPad to put out a message on Twitter, which she had been using liberally for the last several months.

> My 1st Congress on Your Corner starts now,

she wrote,

> Please stop by to let me know what is on your mind or tweet me later.

The air was a little cold for a January afternoon, and she was wearing a short black skirt, black stockings, and a red blouse. No coat. The temperature that morning had been slightly above freezing after sunup at 7:25 A.M., and would gradually warm up throughout the day to an eventual high of fifty-nine degrees, gentle enough for a golf shirt and shorts. The air was desert-crisp and the sky was a bright blue. "No significant weather was observed" was the summary of the National Weather Service on that day's meteorological activity in Tucson.

That same day in Wilmington, Ohio, the thermometer reached a high of twenty-two degrees, with light snow and fog cluttering the air. Portland, Oregon, reported a high of forty-four with heavy rain and Albany, New York, checked in at twenty-five degrees and clear. It was, in short, the kind of day on which the economic foundations of Arizona had been built.

Gabrielle got out of the vehicle and walked toward the three arches of the Safeway front, where her staff was busy setting up the temporary event. "Good morning, Mr. Kimble!" she said to her press aide, a longtime friend named Mark Kimble who used to write a column for a local newspaper. A banner hung from the dark bricks proclaiming her in block letters: GABRIELLE GIFFORDS. UNITED STATES CONGRESS. Under it: a line of chairs, a rope, posts, creating a strong psychological cue for people to form up in a line to see her. A folding table to suggest a bar of office. An American flag. An Arizona flag. Portable ceremony. Prosecutors would later come up with a judicial theory that Gabrielle's physical presence and the temporary reception line meant that the front of Safeway #1255 had been transformed, for a morning, into the halls of Congress.

Gabe Zimmerman had brought the folding tables and blue-padded chairs from the district office, and was busy setting them up. He was thirty years old, recently engaged to be married, a dark-haired graduate of Arizona State University's graduate program in social work whose tranquil demeanor with the occasional pissed-off people who called the office earned him the nickname "The Constituent Whisperer." He had worked for Gabrielle for four years—her entire time in Congress—and in that span had accumulated a thick file of phone contacts within the Veterans Administration, the State Department, the Agriculture Department—all the alcoves and inlets within the federal system that had to be pumped for information about lost benefits and delayed passports and the daily panoply of frustrations associated with getting things out of the government. Gabe's earnestness had earlier earned him the nickname "The Beav," as in *Leave It to Beaver*.

Pam Simon asked him if she could get him some hot cocoa from the Safeway, and he declined but told her to ask Daniel Hernandez, who had worked as an intern for Gabrielle for the past five days. Hernandez grew up in a bilingual household and had attended a certified nursing assistant program at Sunnyside High School. His current ambition was to win office himself, in the student government at the University of Arizona. Today he was wearing a green argyle sweater over his portly middle. Simon and Kimble went into the Safeway.

The lights are muted inside the air-conditioned cavern, and the first thing that commands a visitor's attention is the flower section. Cones of daffodils and roses and racks of potted geraniums are arranged under lettering on the wall that announces POETRY IN BLOOM. Beyond that and to the left is the produce section, where bins of asparagus, tomatoes, bagged lettuce, and avocados are gathered in square bins and tilted up at an appealing angle. Oranges shine under lamps hanging from metal wires. This Safeway is of a type called the Lifestyle Store, which puts an emphasis on prepared food, such as deli subs and sushi, and has earthen interior colors instead of bright lights and linoleum. In the front is a tiered rack of coin-op machines for children. One is full of colored gumballs. Another is "Spy Undercover," dispensing miniature plastic handcuffs, and yet another is "Gun Collection," which displays a logo featuring a gun barrel pointing directly at the viewer; the game has a square carafe holding dozens of transparent spheres, each containing a small metal pistol with a keychain loop.

Congress on Your Corner began exactly on schedule, at 10:00 A.M. About twenty people were lined up. Forty-three-year-old Matthew Laos was the first to be seen. He wanted to show her an award he had won and chat with her about his service. He told her he was proud of her for winning her last election, then started to feel embarrassed that he was hogging her time. He got his picture taken with Gabrielle, then left.

Almost no one who came up to Gabrielle at these events during her previous term had approached her with anger or disquiet. The ceremonial aspect, even at grocery stores, seemed to put people on their good behavior. During the lead-up to the contentious health-care vote in 2009—a proposition she ultimately voted for—two young men got in one of these Congress on Your Corner lines wearing T-shirts with nasty slogans and a look set for battle on their faces, and every staff member who saw them did an eye roll. Their turn came, and they laid into her, but instead of leaning away from the spittle she had stepped forward and put a friendly hand on one of their arms as she listened to them go on about a range of issues. "I understand where you're coming from," she kept saying. "My staff is here to help you." This confused them and they left quietly.

That was around the time of the Corner done at the Safeway down in Douglas, a usually moribund town on the Mexican border. Members of a local Tea Party chapter had sent out e-mails suggesting that Gabrielle's event was more like a "town hall meeting" where they should show up and protest. The Safeway parking lot was jammed with people carry-

ing signs saying DON'T TREAD ON ME and attacking the health insurance reform they loathed and called Obamacare. The staff had no choice
but to hold the event. Gabrielle wouldn't speak to them as a group, but
she would speak to them one-on-one, and it took hours. Near the end of
it a man waiting in line who had been shouting along with the rest of the
crowd bent over to pick something up off the ground and a pistol fell
out of his pants pocket, clattering on the asphalt. Police were called, but
there were no arrests. "When you represent a district that includes the
home of the O.K. Corral and Tombstone, 'the town too tough to die,'
nothing's a surprise out in Cochise County," she told the editorial board
of *The Arizona Republic*. It was a public way to laugh it off.

Even so, nobody felt it necessary to have police officers standing by
in Tucson today to keep the peace.

A young man in a dark blue, hooded sweatshirt came up at 10:07
A.M. His head was covered by the hood, but he was nearly bald, as though
he had just shaved himself to the scalp. "Is Giffords here?" he asked, and
Alex Villec, an intern, directed him to the back of the line.

He wandered off into the parking lot, seeming to lose interest.

Dorwan and Mavanell Stoddard were near the front of the line
to meet Gabrielle. The couple had been grade school friends, married
others, and then married each other after losing their respective spouses.
He used to own a hot dog stand in Ash Springs, Nevada, and now did a
lot of fix-it work for their church, Calvary Chapel East. They were planning to have breakfast at the Coco's restaurant nearby and dropped by
to thank Gabrielle for speaking out about the safety of ranchers near the
Mexican border. It was a relevant topic for Dorwan, who grew up in a
ranching family.

A woman named Anna Ballis came over and saw that the line was
too long for her. She started to go into the Safeway to buy a can of beef
broth for that night's roast. "Don't go away," called Ron Barber, Gabrielle's
district director. "Come back and see us when you're done shopping."

John Roll, sixty-three, also came up to say hello. He was the chief federal judge for Arizona and had just come from morning Mass, where he went without fail every day. He had worked with Gabrielle to secure funding for a new courthouse in Yuma. Barber told the judge much the same cheerful thing he had just told Ballis: "Don't go away, Gabby would love to see you."

Roger Salzberger and his wife, Faith, were standing about fourth in line. He had owned a cactus and succulent nursery in Tucson for more than three decades. Gabrielle had seemed too conservative for him at first, but he had been won over by the warmth of her personality and her conviction that pragmatic solutions were necessary in a divided town like Tucson. He had knocked on thousands of doors for her in the last campaign. He had come wearing a John Deere tractor cap, and Gabe Zimmerman, whom he had not met yet, asked him a friendly question about it. And they talked tractors.

At about this moment, Gabrielle's photographer, Sara Hummel Rajca, snapped a photo of Gabrielle talking to a couple named Jim and Mary Tucker. She is facing Mary Tucker with her hands clasped, her eyes calm. Dim reflections of people can be seen in the glass wall of the grocery store. There was now a cluster of people around Gabrielle, as there often was when she appeared in public. Beaming up at her was Christina-Taylor Green, a nine-year-old girl with dark hair. She had come in the company of a neighbor, Suzi Hileman, who had received a recorded phone invitation to the event the day before. Christina had been born on September 11, 2001, and her picture was included in a book called *Faces of Hope* about babies born on that day. She was the only girl on her Little League baseball team and had just been elected to the student council at Mesa Verde Elementary School.

The young man in the blue-hooded sweatshirt seemed to make a decision at that moment. He moved forward from his place in line toward Gabrielle and the judge with a look of cold intent that witnesses described as "stone-faced" and "determined." He was wearing earplugs. Only three feet separated him from the congresswoman from the Eighth District.

Without speaking a word, he raised a Glock Safe Action Pistol, painted black. The photographer watched with disbelief as it came upward. The gun looked so small, she thought. It was practically enveloped by his hand, looking more like flesh than metal.

The exact angle of his arm at this moment would be of great importance. Had the horizontal line been different by even a millimeter—a twinge from a humerus muscle, a slight recalculation of where he was pointing, even just an imperceptible, nervous shake—the course of the future would have been very different.

The man holding the gun squeezed its trigger. The bullet traveled three feet in one twenty-thousandth of a second and struck Gabrielle on the left side of her forehead, an inch and a half over her eye. She slumped to the cement in front of the Safeway, blood seeping from her brow and from a hole made in the back of her head. She did not make a sound.

Hummel Rajca, unhurt and completely stunned, held on to her camera and sprinted away from the raised gun and toward her car to call the police as two bullets punched holes through the glass front windows of the Safeway. One of the copper-jacketed rounds was later found lying in the meat department near the back of the store. The other punctured a plastic bottle of 7-Up that had been stacked in a display at the front. Soda sputtered out onto the fake wood linoleum.

"Get down!" yelled somebody.

A Saturday morning at the Safeway, enlivened by the presence of a local celebrity, had turned into an American iconography that everyone understood and dreaded: the shooting rampage. They had been ordinary people up until this moment. Now their names and movements were being written in red pen.

There was a scream and ducking and cowering; paralyzed indecision and instantaneous fight-or-flight reflexes. Gabe Zimmerman turned toward the popping noises. He took a step forward. The man with the gun turned to him and shot him once in the head at close range. Gabe died instantly, the look on his face one of perfect stillness.

Gabrielle's aide Pam Simon, age sixty-three, was shot in the wrist and in the chest. She fell down face-first.

The gunman shifted his aim and shot Ron Barber twice, once across the cheek and once in the groin. Judge John Roll lunged to push Barber out of the way and a bullet hit him in the back.

The Glock Safe Action Pistol was originally designed in 1981 for the Austrian military. The frame is made out of a synthetic polymer, which led some gunmetal purists to deride it as "tactical Tupperware" when the first models began to show up in the American market. It has only thirty-three separate parts, can be easily fieldstripped, and its durability is greater than that of most guns with metal frames. Some owners have been known to clean them by throwing the parts in the dishwasher. Glocks have been shown to work dependably after being tossed from the roof of twenty-story buildings, frozen in a block of ice, soaked in mud puddles, and run over with armored personnel carriers. About two thirds of the police departments and sheriffs' offices in the nation issue Glocks to their officers.

Though expensive, at about five hundred dollars, it is considered a forgiving weapon to an amateur. The trigger on a Glock 19 requires about five and a half pounds of pressure before it will fire. That is slightly less than the equivalent of picking up a full plastic gallon jug of milk with one's index finger. A bullet is automatically rechambered with every shot. About two can be fired per second.

The man with the gun turned from Roll's falling body and methodically started to execute the total strangers sitting in the padded chairs who had been waiting to see their congresswoman.

A bullet came for Christina-Taylor Green, age nine, and struck her in the chest.

Three bullets struck Suzi Hileman, age fifty-eight, who had thought that Christina would enjoy the event and find it inspiring.

These bullets passed all around Roger and Faith Salzberger but none struck them. Roger hit the pavement. Faith dived over a row of chairs and landed hard, breaking five of her ribs.

The gunman turned his eyes to Bill Badger, age seventy-four, a retired army colonel, and Badger could see nothing but blankness in them. Then a reflex: He ducked. A burning sensation stung his scalp as he hit the ground and put his arms over his head.

Dorwan Stoddard tried to push his wife out of the way and was shot three times. The former hot-dog-stand owner from Nevada started to bleed uncontrollably. "I love you, I love you," his wife kept saying to him as he lay dying.

The western outer wall of the Safeway and the Italian-style arches created a boxed-in passage, and there was little room for anyone to maneuver. To some the sound of the Glock was unmistakably that of a handgun. To others, mysterious pops, like a string of firecrackers. "It was surreal," said Dr. Stephen Rayle, a hospice doctor who happened to be at the scene to meet Gabrielle. "Gunshots sound less real in person. I thought someone was staging a protest."

Two bullets came for George and Dorothy Morris, who were standing together, high school sweethearts who had been married for more than half a century. He reached to throw her to the ground and was wounded in the chest. She was hit in the head and died in his arms.

Kenneth Dorushka, age sixty-three, also threw his wife, Carol, to the ground and shielded her head with his arm. He received a bullet in that same arm. Eric Fuller, age sixty-three, was shot in the knee. Randy Gardner, a sixty-year-old retired mental health therapist who had been among the crowd of students who was unhurt during the Kent State University shootings in 1970, was shot in his foot and started crawling toward the safety of his car. "All I could think was, 'Okay, I'm going to try to get out of this situation,'" he said. He had just been chatting with Phyllis Schenk, a retiree from New Jersey who collected ceramic snails because her last name means "snail" in German. A bullet struck her in the head and she was killed instantly.

Three more bullets hit Mary Reed, fifty-two, who threw her daughter, Emma, up against the wall to shield her. "He was literally going to have to go through me, and that wasn't going to happen," she told a reporter. Jim Tucker, fifty-eight, was hit in the collarbone and the knee. He had come to thank Gabrielle for her courage in asking Congress to take a 5 percent pay cut, and he was pictured in the last photo to be taken of her before she was shot. Kenneth Veeder, seventy-five, a retired Vietnam veteran, was grazed in the leg.

The Glock held thirty-two rounds of 9 millimeter bullets, each one a slug of lead covered by a jacket of copper and weighing about five nickels. They were lined up vertically in a grotesquely long clip called an "extended magazine," which protruded from the barrel of the Glock like a prosthetic limb. The sale of these types of magazines had been illegal from 1994 to 2004 under a now-expired law known as the Violent Crime Control and Law Enforcement Act. But now they were available at Walmart, which is where this one had been purchased.

The huge clip empty, the gunman paused to reload. He pulled another magazine out of his pocket with his left hand.

When he heard the shooting stop, Bill Badger got to his feet. He was in a complete daze. The bullet fired at him had made a two-inch groove in his scalp but had not penetrated his skull.

Roger Salzberger made a similar decision to stand up, though he realized later that this could have gotten him killed.

A woman named Patricia Maisch had been lying on the pavement. "I was wondering what a bullet would feel like because I was certain I was going to get hit," she would say to a reporter later. Maisch and her husband owned Oro Valley Heating & Cooling, an air-conditioning business, and she had come by to thank Gabrielle for her vote for the stimulus package that Congress had approved the previous year. Now she watched the gunman's feet walk right past her.

Bill Badger saw someone in the melee—it has not been disclosed who—pick up a folding chair and bring it down in a glancing blow on the back of the gunman's head, breaking his stride. Badger then lunged for the gunman, striking him with an open hand. His body turned out to be light and almost fragile, and he crumpled immediately, offering no resistance. The move wasn't a professional jab, said Badger, but it had as much force behind it as he could muster. "In the military," he said, "we were taught to react."

At the same time, Roger Salzberger tackled the gunman from the opposite direction. The three of them went down to the cement, the gunman landing hard on the pavement on his right shoulder. With his free left hand, he blindly grasped for the clip of ammunition that he'd dropped.

Without thinking, Patricia Maisch snatched it away from him.

Bill Badger then grabbed the struggling gunman by his free left hand and twisted it around his back. Blood from his scalp wound was freely trickling down his neck and arm and all over the suspect, but he barely noticed. Salzberger pressed his knee down and put the full weight of his 170 pounds on the suspect's neck. The gun left his grip and was kicked away.

The gunman was separated from his gun; it was over. The entire assault had taken approximately fifteen seconds from start to finish.

Daniel Hernandez, the twenty-year-old intern, rushed toward Gabrielle. His high school medical training program had inured him to the sight of gore. He sat her up against the Safeway wall so she would not choke on her blood. Then he put a hand over the wound in her head. "I would ask her a question and then ask her to squeeze my hand," he told a reporter later. Her other hand lay twitching in a pool of blood.

"Oh, my arm!" cried the gunman from down on the sidewalk, as Salzberger dug his knee into him. "You're breaking my arm!"

The pressure on his neck from Salzberger's knee was on the carotid artery slightly behind the ear.

"It was a 'Say uncle' thing except it was a little more than that," said Salzberger.

Furious and full of adrenaline, he balled his hand into a fist and dealt the gunman five sharp blows to the left side of his face.

A man who had been wounded in the leg, identified by a witness as Ken Veeder, picked up the pistol that the gunman had been using.

It was at this point that Joseph Zamudio, twenty-four, emerged from the Walgreens check-out lane, where he had been buying a pack of cigarettes. He had heard the *pop-pop-pop* of the Glock and then the screams, "Shooter! Get down!" He routinely carries a Ruger P95 pistol, and his hand was down his jacket pocket, a finger on the trigger and the safety off.

Zamudio saw an older man standing there amid the carnage, holding a gun in the air.

In the confusion of the moment, Zamudio almost decided to shoot him. But instead he noticed that the slide on the other man's gun was open and back, which meant it was temporarily disabled and unable to fire. "I decided that I wasn't the one to kill him," said Zamudio. Bystanders immediately began yelling that he had the wrong guy, that the real shooter was already restrained. Badger said he yelled to Veeder: "Drop the gun quick, somebody's going to kill you!"

The man identified as Veeder dropped the gun to the ground and put his foot squarely on top of it, securing it in place.

Salzberger had wanted to choke the gunman to death on the spot. But the frenzied exchange with Veeder and the possibility of a second shooting had calmed him down. "It was a wake-up call," he said later. "Let's not do anything even more crazy."

The gunman twitched and Badger twisted his arm back harder. Three more magazines had spilled out of his pockets. They were not the grotesquely long variety but normal size, enough to hold ten bullets each.

"If you move," said Badger, "I'm going to choke you." Zamudio came and lay down on top of the gunman's legs. He was joined by Dr. Stephen Rayle. "Honestly, it was a matter of seconds," said Zamudio. "Two, maybe three seconds between when I came through the doorway and when I was laying on top of [the gunman], holding him down. So, I mean, in that short amount of time I made a lot of really big decisions really fast."

Anna Ballis had ducked behind one of the cast-concrete pillars and fell to the ground when the shots started. Now she crawled out and went over to the man who had called to her not to go away, Ron Barber. She put pressure on his wounds, then gave her coat to Daniel Hernandez, who put it behind Gabrielle's head to keep it from resting directly against the Safeway's outer wall. His sweater and his name tag were smeared with her blood.

"What's going on?" asked Christina-Taylor Green. She was lying on the ground, bleeding uncontrollably from the chest. He eyes were confused and panicked. Suzi Hileman looked at her in the eyes and said sternly, in her New York accent: "Christina-Taylor Green, don't you die on me!" The girl was already going into cardiac arrest, and Hileman thought she could see light going out of her eyes.

"Why in the world would you do something like that?" Badger asked the gunman. But he received no reply.

The first Pima County sheriff's deputy arrived with lights and sirens at 10:14, three minutes after the shooting commenced, and figured out quickly that the gunman was pinned to the sidewalk and the killing was effectively over. Blood was everywhere; witnesses were crying. The first ambulance and fire engine from Northwest Fire Rescue District arrived five minutes after that, and at just before 10:23, as the parking lot was becoming a flashing sea of emergency vehicles, the sheriff's deputies gave the paramedics clearance to go in and treat the wounded. The delay felt "like an eternity," according to a witness, but this is standard procedure at scenes of mass shootings, where an unrestrained gunman might treat the EMTs as new targets.

The Safeway was bizarrely peaceful after that. A number of people at the scene later commented on the sudden calm, as though the gunfire had been like a crack of lightning from a storm that had passed quickly. The medical personnel bent, murmuring, to their tasks. The American flag lay tipped over on the pavement, streaked with blood. Police lights flashed all around in revolving cadence, though silently. None of the victims were screaming or crying.

James Palka said he clearly heard birds chirping.

"It was like a little vortex, where some lives were saved but others weren't," he said.

Christina-Taylor Green died of cardiac arrest and was pronounced dead at University Medical Center. Gabe Zimmerman was dead at the scene. So were Dorwan Stoddard and Phyllis Schenk and John Roll and Dorothy Morris. Gabrielle was loaded onto an ambulance within ten minutes and rushed to the same hospital, where she underwent immediate surgery. The bullet had passed through the left temporal lobe of her brain, cutting through the regions of the cortex that affect speech and logical tasks. The surgery took less than half an hour, and she would remain effectively in a coma for the next six days.

Pima County sheriff's deputy Thomas Audetat took over the custody of the gunman from Badger and Salzberger, driving his knee into the young man's back as he fitted him with plastic handcuffs, then pulling him to his feet. An Arizona driver's license in his back pocket identified him as Jared Lee Loughner, age twenty-two. Deputy Audetat took him to the back of a sheriff's car and loaded him in.

"I plead the Fifth," said the cuffed suspect from the back of the car.

Drive west from the Safeway about five miles, turn north on Oldfather Road, and you come into a working-class subdivision of detached family homes called Orangewood Estates, built in the midseventies. On a street called North Soledad, Spanish for "solitude," one house has a screen of tall prickly pear planted out in the front, with leaves the size of serving plates. The yard is carefully swept, and there is a set of high, narrow windows in the garage. This is the home to which Jared Lee Loughner was brought as an infant in 1988, and where he had been living until the morning of January 8, 2011, when he had one final argument with his father and then ran off to phone for a taxi to take him to Safeway to kill Gabrielle Giffords.

Within hours of the shooting, a division of the international army of the media had quickly set up a camp outside the Loughner home and waited for any chance to take shots of the parents. Reporters were also scrambling to find anyone who was acquainted with Jared Loughner—"the shooter," as he became known. Photographers went over the wall in back of the home on North Soledad and found a skull surrounded with candles.

Loughner appeared before a judge the next day, showing a black eye from one of the blows that Salzberger had dealt him. "Tell me what he looked like," a local television anchor asked the reporter who had been in the courtroom, "what he was wearing, where his eyes were darting. Anything you can say?"

His public biography quickly took shape. He was an unemployed former fast-food employee, the only son of Randy Loughner, a freelance construction handyman, and Amy Loughner, the manager of a county park called Agua Caliente. Jared had been shy in elementary school and was teased in junior high for his bowl-cut mop of hair. He worked hard at playing the saxophone, and his mother religiously drove him to lessons. Charlie Parker was an idol. His iPod was stuffed with jazz. But things took a chemical turn in the middle of his time at Mountain View High School. One day in May 2006 he drank a third of a bottle of vodka raided from his parents' liquor cabinet and had to be taken to the emergency room for alcohol poisoning. He was upset, he told officers, that his father had yelled at him. His eyes were red and miserable.

The following year a sheriff's deputy pulled over a van in Orangewood Estates and smelled the tang of marijuana. The driver and Jared were arrested, and Jared admitted to having a glass pipe caked with residue in his front pocket. He was charged with possession of drug paraphernalia. He began vandalizing street signs and pulling away from his old group of friends, those with whom he had set up bicycle jumps and played video games for hours.

Loughner acquired his degree from Aztec Middle College, an alternative high school connected to a community college, and then blundered from one entry-level restaurant job to another—a Peter Piper Pizza and then a Quiznos at the corner of Ina and Thornydale near his home, where three out of four sides of the corner are anchored with grocery store strip malls. He then found work as a busboy at Red Robin in the Tucson Mall, where he argued with his boss and walked out abruptly after he grew fed up with the people who worked there. "Terrible situation," he wrote to the world in an online gaming forum. "Mental breakdown!"

He began to tell his remaining friends about his new hobby of "conscious dreaming"—a state in which a person is supposed to program his own dreams by thinking hard about a certain subject before going to sleep. Part of the technique for achieving a state of conscious dreaming is to imagine that the reality of the waking world is itself a dream. He told people he preferred the world of sleep above material existence. Loughner's dreams provided him a release that he found nowhere else. Late mornings were the best to him, the period when REM activity is at its highest and the ethereal images are most vivid.

"I'm so into it because I can create things and fly," he reportedly told his friend Bryce Tierney. "I'm everything I'm not in this world."

A pertinent question emerged almost immediately after the shooting: What did the actions of such an obviously deranged person have to do with the state of Arizona?

At first look, the geography of the shooting seemed to be only a street address and a dateline. This could have happened anywhere in the country, went the local refrain. This was about a mentally disturbed young man. Nothing more, nothing less.

Pima County sheriff Clarence Dupnik had been attending a sheriffs' convention in Palm Springs, California, and heard about the shootings on the radio as he drove back via Interstate 10 across the Mojave Desert. He grew angrier and angrier as he listened to the bulletins. Giffords was a family friend and political ally of many years, and hearing the news about the shooting was, he told a reporter, "like getting hit in the stomach with a sledgehammer." Dupnik, a Democrat who had been in office three decades, remembered the gun-out-of-the-pants incident at the Douglas Safeway, and also another disquieting event: After the vote on the health-care bill, somebody had smashed out the front windows to Gabrielle's local congressional office in the middle of the night.

He arrived at his headquarters on Benson Highway at about four in the afternoon, and, shortly thereafter, told the team of FBI agents they might not wish to stand with him on the podium on which he was about to give the first law enforcement press conference about the event, which would be carried live on every television station in the country with a news department. He acknowledged the jungle of cameras, briefly described the gunman in custody, and then started to talk about Gabrielle, how she worked hard and cared about her country and was not especially concerned with partisan politics.

> And I think it's time as a country that we need to do a little soul-searching, because I think the vitriolic rhetoric that we hear day in and day out from people in the radio business and some people in the TV business and what we see on TV and how our youngsters are being raised, that this has not become the nice United States of America that most of us grew up in. And I think it's time we do the soul-searching. . . . But again, I'd like to say that when you look at unbalanced people, how they respond to the vitriol that comes out of certain mouths, about tearing down the government, the anger, the hatred, the bigotry that goes on in this country is getting to be outrageous, and unfortunately Arizona, I think, has become sort of the capital. We have become the mecca for prejudice and bigotry.

Dupnik's interpretation unleashed an avalanche of criticism, much of it from the same quarter that he was criticizing. Sharron Angle, who in a losing Senate race in Nevada had suggested that people might employ "Second Amendment remedies" against an overreaching government, sent out a press release that said: "The despicable act in Tucson is a horrifying and senseless tragedy and should be condemned as a single act of violence by a single unstable individual." Sarah Palin drew immediate attention for a map of the country she had posted on her Facebook page during the 2010 midterm elections that showed what seemed to be rifle sighting symbols on the districts of "targeted" Democrats. Gabrielle's district was one of them, and the presence of the crosshairs now looked ominous, as though the map was suggesting that the incumbent not just be removed from office but metaphorically gunned down. Palin's supporters indignantly replied that the marks were "survey marks" instead of gun sights, and Palin gave a videotaped speech in front of an Alaska fireplace expressing sadness for the victims but also lashing back at what she called the "blood libel" of journalists seeking to find fault with political speech. The shootings could not be blamed on fiery words, she said, but were instead the "incomprehensible act of a single, evil man." She added, "Acts of monstrous criminality stand on their own. They begin and end with the criminals who commit them, not collectively with all the citizens of a state."

Tucson's most voluble conservative talk show host, Jon Justice, of KQTH (a station that bills itself as 104.1, THE TRUTH), weighed in with an e-mail that said:

> I feel incredibly bad for our brave Pima County Sheriff's Officers who have to serve under Clarence Dupnik. Within hours of the horrific shooting that took place at the congresswoman's event Dupnik was telling local media that talk radio and the media was partly to blame, only to repeat his statements again during the press conference that was receiving national attention. We have no idea at this point the motivation of this murderer's act. Yet Dupnik took his moment in the spotlight to drive a political wedge into the event. They were reckless and dangerous statements made by someone who should have known better. He should have been using his time to help bring the community together. Instead his statements made Tucson appear to be a city full of hate, bigotry and vitriol.

Was Arizona's peculiar oxygen in some way responsible for the decision of a twenty-two-year-old man to go down to the grocery to assassinate his congresswoman? And was it "incomprehensible" that such a thing could have happened in Arizona at a time of social and economic unease? The question cut to the bone of what the state believed about itself as it prepared to celebrate its one hundredth birthday, and at a particularly delicate moment.

In the months after the assassination of President John F. Kennedy, a public-relations executive from the Neiman Marcus department chain named Warren Leslie published a book called *Dallas Public and Private: Aspects of an American City*, which concluded that the uniquely angry climate of his city in the fall of 1963 had probably been a contributing factor to the shooting of the president. The corporate elite of Dallas did little to rein in the extremist political groups making inflammatory statements in the months leading up to the event. Leslie wrote that Dallas was "not the inevitable site for a Presidential murder, but it *was* a logical place for something unpleasant and embarrassing to happen."

The resentments against Kennedy and his smooth establishment ways had been building for years. Congressman Bruce Alger of Dallas had organized a protest in 1960 against Lyndon Johnson, who was then campaigning for the vice presidency. The milling crowds outside the Adolphus Hotel waved placards calling Johnson a "traitor," and spit flew in the direction of Johnson and his wife. A vocal anticommunist army major general named Edwin Walker chose Dallas as a base for his operations and made calls for the invasion of Cuba, as well as for the dissolution of the United Nations. He was largely written off as a crank. On the night of April 10, 1963, Lee Harvey Oswald shot at him through a dining room window and missed. Oswald later told his wife that killing Walker would have been a heroic act similar to killing Hitler before he acquired power.

Less than a month before Kennedy made his trip to Texas to mend fences among divided Democrats, Adlai Stevenson came to make a speech for UN Day and was booed off the stage by hecklers who had been brought there by Walker. "Kennedy will get his reward in hell!" one of them screamed. Another of them spat on Stevenson as he was being hustled to his car. These audience members were not ruffians or thugs in an everyday context; they were prosperous middle-class citizens, many of them housewives, whose collective unease had been ratcheted up.

"They feel their worst enemies are other Americans who disagree with them," wrote Leslie of Walker's followers and those many others who were influenced by the spirit of paranoia. "They are not equipped to deal with contradictory evidence; when it appears, they boo it and hiss it to make it go away."

The day before Kennedy's visit, handbills were stuffed under windshields all over town bearing two mug-shot-style photos of the president under the heading WANTED FOR TREASON. "This man is wanted for treasonous activities against the United States," said the flyer, which accused JFK of betraying the Constitution by being "lax in enforcing Communist Regulation laws" and encouraging race riots among blacks in the South. The day of the president's assassination, an ad from a fictitious "fact finding committee" denouncing the president had run in the *Dallas Morning News*.

The climate had been getting so bad, in fact, that a small group of civic leaders, including department store head Stanley Marcus, had gathered privately a month before the visit and wondered if JFK might be persuaded not to insert himself into such a minefield. They ultimately did not act, reasoning that it would be embarrassing to disinvite a sitting president, who probably would not have listened anyway. The mayor felt it necessary to remind citizens to give Kennedy a civilized welcome.

"Later, the guilt we felt for Kennedy's death would have less to do with his assassination by a man only slightly associated with our city than it would have to do with our own feelings of anticipation," remembered the writer Lawrence Wright. "Something would happen—*something*. We expected to be disgraced."

It is likely that the last words JFK ever heard were in reference to the embittered atmosphere. Brightly remarking on the crowds of people lining up to cheer the motorcade, Nellie Connally, the first lady of Texas, said to him, "Well, you certainly can't say that Dallas don't love you today." The first shot struck him in the throat several seconds later, fired from the same Italian mail-order rifle that Oswald had used in his failed assassination attempt on Walker.

A report on the social context of Dallas in 1963 prepared by Southern Methodist University shortly after the assassination concluded that a pervasive culture of condoning violence as a way of settling disputes, as well as a competition to make outrageous political statements without shame or challenge, provided a logical arena for the sudden murder of a politician. The lead author, Dr. Robert E. Stoltz, also took aim at the civic milieu in which Lee Harvey Oswald operated.

"Dallas has tended to define 'goodness' in physical terms, such as the size and number of churches, length, breadth and height of buildings and expressways and the low frequency of corruption and vice," he wrote. "It ignores other statistics of 'goodness' which are available but less flattering—homicide rates, vehicular deaths, poverty, medical care for some types of patients, quality of education, evidences of real culture, etc." Dallas, in short, tended to value the splashy rather than the substantial.

Oswald's exact motivations for aiming his rifle at the president are lost to history and are still a part of the enigma of the Kennedy assassination. But events—especially violent ones—never happen in a vacuum; there are always contributing factors to any action, and human beings are far more influenced by the collective psychology of their immediate surroundings than they ever suspect. Oswald was a frustrated idealist and a pseudo-intellectual looking for a cause to which to devote himself, and the fractious climate all around him gave him a focus for his restless energy. As we will see, Jared Loughner was also in dialogue with his surroundings before he took a taxi to the Safeway.

The city of Dallas did not "kill" President Kennedy any more than the state of Arizona killed six citizens and injured thirteen. But contexts must always be taken into account, because events are otherwise meaningless.

TWO

REINVENTION

Arizona depends on reinvention. The narrative of a fresh start in a warm place is at the root of the economy, and the unsustainable nature of that dream over the long run is the largest part of what ails the state today.

The economy had fed on a mix of copper mining, cotton farming, and cattle ranching in the first part of the twentieth century, but the formula changed in the fifties to semiconductor wafers, industrial-scale tourism, missile factories, golf resorts, and seemingly limitless vistas of new starter homes and grocery-anchored malls, a desert previously considered worthless now rendered pleasant with air-conditioning, and all of it made possible by the flexibility and liberty of the automobile and the inexpensive gasoline it consumed, of which Arizona produced not a drop.

Illusions of a perfected life, free of nature and history, have been a part of the Arizona narrative for generations. In 1979, a group of state leaders commissioned a progress report from the Hudson Institute, a think tank founded by military strategist and futurist thinker Herman Kahn, famous for his view that a limited nuclear war might be winnable and the later satiric portrayal of him, by Peter Sellers, as the title character of *Dr. Strangelove.* Kahn ended up writing the report by himself, and the conclusions are true to some of the most basic assumptions about the state's economy. *Arizona Tomorrow* offered a view of the state as a technological marvel and a victory over the basic realities of nature. The desert was no longer a harsh and dry horizon but "an appealing landscape, an attractive place to live, and a new kind of adult playground," and he foresaw daily life resembling living in a moon colony, aided by the miracle of long-distance hydrology.

"Desert living with air-conditioning, water fountains, swimming pools—getting back to nature with a motorized houseboat on Lake Powell (itself a man-made lake) and going for an ocean swim in a man-made ocean* are all contemporary examples of the marriage between lifestyle and technology," concluded Kahn.

Jared Loughner's neighborhood, Orangewood Estates, is an example of the basic residential vocabulary of Arizona, which found its root in the decades after World War II. The state's economy boomed around the real-estate and construction businesses, and banks promiscuously gave credit to home buyers coming in from all parts of the country in pursuit of a Southwestern lifestyle.

A vice president of Phoenix's Valley National Bank, Herbert Leggett, explained in 1944 how cheap home lending would have an almost magical stimulating effect on the state, growing an instant empire in the sun. "The more homes, the more people," he said. "The more people, the more business. The more jobs, the more business, the more business, the more people."

The basis for Arizona's economy was an ever-ascending Escher staircase, dependent only upon the continuing willingness of other Americans seeking reinvention. Leggett called this "as near perpetual motion as we are likely to achieve." Carpenters, masons, plumbers, lawyers, res-

---

* This is a reference to Big Surf, an ocean-themed park in Tempe that has an artificial wave machine.

taurant managers, grocers, mechanics, real-estate agents: all of them fed upon the sunshine and the instant crops of people. Economies always require consumption, and Arizona offered up the mere pleasure of living as its number-one salable item. "The building of a house," said Leggett, "sets in motion more forces than almost any other type of human activity."

The introduction of cheaper materials, like particle and gypsum board, as well as the growing use of the power saw and nail gun for on-site carpentry, made it possible to erect and sell homes at an astonishing clip. The granddaddy of all Tucson homebuilders was the M.R.F. company, which introduced the "Perfect Arizona Type" home—a detached ranch-style dwelling of pumice stone shaped like an L, with a carport under the main roof and a sliding glass door that opens to a backyard that has an orange tree or the blue bean of a swimming pool rimmed with a Kool Deck. A breezy back porch with green mosquito netting nailed up became the Arizona Room for afternoon card games and pitchers of iced tea. Front yards and porches became fusty anachronisms as the heart of family life shifted into the privacy of the backyard and the comfort of the air-conditioned TV room.

Even the front door—the very symbol of a house's connection with the rest of the world—became as useless and as ornamental as a balustrade, and some of their knobs grew rusty with disuse. Families entered their own houses through the side door that fronted the carport. If the house had a garage, the master of a house could come home and be swallowed up into his home without ever bothering to interact with a public space—or the people who shared the same air. "The outside world has become an abstraction," wrote James Howard Kunstler, "filtered through television, just as the weather is an abstraction filtered through air-conditioning." Carports and garages fronted the street and defined the essentially mechanical character of the blocks.

The landscape of Tucson was ordered by wide and straight giga-avenues like Campbell and Fort Lowell and Golf Links forming squares in all diametrical directions, each square a mile on each side and containing a mosaic of tract homes, some in grids, others on curvy streets with wistful names. Their meandering was meant, dimly, to evoke eighteenth-century Spanish mission roads and also to discourage through traffic so they might be safer for children to play in, though that happened much less often than intended. Opaque pumice-stone walls about six feet high separated backyards from one another.

John F. Long, the developer of Phoenix's massive Maryvale neighborhood of ranch homes, looked back with some rue on this effect in an interview with a public television station late in his life. "The family living was transferred to the backyard," he said. "Homes used to have a front porch, and people sat on the front porch and watched other people and cars go by, and that sort of thing. Then it was the fifties, with the patio and the barbecue and so forth went into the backyard, and you very seldom see anybody in the front yard." State historian Marshall Trimble put it even more succinctly: "We closed ourselves off. We built a wall around ourselves."

These physical settings were matched by a consequent decline in the old American notions of community.

The Center for the Future of Arizona commissioned a study, including a wide-ranging Gallup poll, in 2009 to gauge the attitudes of state residents on a number of topics, including the level of connection they felt with each other and the amount of trust they had of their politicians. The results revealed a snapshot of generally isolated people who happen to love their Arizona home for its natural beauty—but not because they necessarily feel at home.

Just 12 percent of those surveyed said they strongly agreed "that people in our communities care about each other," and yet nearly half gave the state excellent marks for the geographic setting and the availability of outdoor parks and trails.

"This data was shocking, even to Gallup," said Lattie Coor, the former president of Arizona State University who heads the institute.

Even in the smallest activities that create social glue, the state looks dismal. "Arizona ranks 48th in the nation for people who say they trade favors with neighbors at least a few times a week—watching one another's children, lending tools or kitchen supplies, house-sitting and other acts of kindness," said the center's report. Regularly eating dinner with the family, a fundamental act of the most basic human unit, is notably low in Arizona, ranking forty-fifth among the states. Voter registration numbers were also feeble; only six other states showed less interest in the 2008 presidential election, even though a hometown senator, John McCain, was the Republican nominee.

"You might compare it to a ski community," said Coor, "a place where people might own a condominium and feel no real connection to the town. They come to play and enjoy themselves. They come to have a swimming pool with a yard around it. Maybe not having to put up with all that organizational stuff back home, maybe that's what drives it. But it is clear that you can exist in Arizona without having any human interaction at all."

The growth of starter communities has eaten away at traditional American ideas of mutual cooperation and what sociologists call the vital factor of "social capital." This is the sense of togetherness that creates healthy places to live, where people feel like they know their neighbors and can depend on them for the occasional good turn. Robert D. Putnam, the author of *Bowling Alone*, identified a distancing trend in American society caused by a combination of television, suburban sprawl, and a decline in civic life that was so slow as to be unnoticed. "For the first two thirds of the twentieth century," he writes, "a powerful tide bore Americans into even deeper engagement into the life of their communities, but a few decades ago—silently, without warning—that tide reversed and we were overtaken by a treacherous rip current. Without at first noticing, we have been pulled apart from one another and from our communities over the last third of a century."

I sat in the shade of a backyard patio for an hour with Jim Kolbe, a probusiness Republican who represented Tucson's northern and eastern sides in Congress for two decades, until he retired in 2006, leaving it open for Gabrielle. He is as gregarious a person as you could hope to meet, always affable and funny and with smart commentary. He spent part of his childhood on a working ranch five miles from the Mexican border. When a magazine called *The Advocate* outed him as gay in 1996, Kolbe acknowledged it and moved on, and Tucson kept right on reelecting him.

He told me that he has lived in his ranch-style home for thirty-six years and does not know a single person who lives on his block anymore. This was very different from the Capitol Hill neighborhood where he lived when he served in Congress; everyone on the block seemed to know each other. But not in Tucson. Part of it is his own fault for traveling so much, he acknowledged. But larger forces are in play, too. "It's a change in society—and I don't know if it's just in the West," Kolbe told me. "It's a breakdown in social bonds."

A big reason for that, says David Taylor, former city planner for Tucson, is the level of transience that has always characterized the state's economy. One durable rule for local demographers has been that for every three people who are moving into the state in a given year, another two will be moving out. "Places like Arizona are always reinventing the wheel because of this," he told me. "People aren't attached. They don't bond well. They think Company X is going to move them to California, so why get involved? Why bother? Sort of like mining camps when the ore runs out. The model from New England doesn't work here. We don't have the depth of experience or tradition. Pick the next ten people you meet and ask how many went to kindergarten in Tucson."

The fragile notion of shared purpose has been put under extraordinary stress by recent economic events in Arizona. The state's financial health—and its vision of itself—had been tied for decades to the mythology that the demand for personal reinvention would never slacken and that there would always be an incoming river of young families eager to sign mortgages in terra-cotta Levittowns. The easy Arizona lifestyle was especially generous to young families, who could afford an undistinguished but comfortable three-bedroom home for eighty thousand dollars and very little down. But in 2008, after a chain of Wall Street bankruptcies, bad housing loans started coming due and Arizona suffered particularly hard. The rate of home foreclosures across the nation went up 81 percent, but Arizona's rate climbed 203 percent, making it nearly the worst hit among the states behind only Nevada and California.

Construction slowed to a crawl and other businesses panicked. A dependable local rule had been that the home-building trade—with all its assorted carpentry, plumbing, draftsmanship, selling, and lawyering—could reliably provide up to 20 percent of the employment base. But then the buyers dried up, the bulldozers stopped, and the layoffs commenced, affecting not just those with regular wage jobs but also those laborers and work gangs on the fringes, many of whom were in the country illegally. U-Haul reported that the number of rental moving trucks leaving the state exceeded those coming in by a small but noteworthy factor of 1 percent.

A plunge in tax collections had aggravated a set of long-standing social diseases that had never really been dealt with in the opulent years. "Low taxes/low service" had been the intellectual cornerstone of government since the end of World War II, and it had worked well attracting semiconductor factories and the housing wave. But the cash squeeze soon got so bad that Arizona was forced to sell its own capitol building. On January 14, 2010, the Department of Administration announced that it had raised $735 million through an arrangement called "sale-leaseback," in which a bank trustee takes charge of state facilities for twenty years while the state essentially pays rent to a new landlord. These properties now in hock include most of the iconic public edifices, including both the House and Senate chambers, the ugly nine-story tower where the governor's office is located, the state prison in Florence, and the headquarters of the state police. Selling off the crown jewels brought fast cash but did not substantially fix a budget problem of epic proportions. Each year the state of Arizona spends about $10.4 billion to lock up its prisoners, patrol its highways, run its schools, keep the lights on in its museums, settle its lawsuits, pay its university professors, monitor its drinking

water, and all the other essential functions of government, but the combined sales, corporate, and income tax revenue was coming in at only
slightly more than $6 billion. The gap was the worst of the budget short-
falls among all the states. The growth machine was temporarily ceas-
ing to work. The generally mediocre public schools received further cuts
to their budgets, and an abysmally high school dropout rate became
worse. The most recent census revealed, among other things, that Arizona had become the second poorest state in the nation, behind only the
miserable doormat of Mississippi. More than 21 percent of residents were
earning less per year than the level the federal government defines as
"poverty"—$21,954 for a family of four.

Poverty in Arizona has a strong racial dimension, and some of the
hardest-hit people were also becoming the targets of anger in the legislature and on the radio talk shows. A general drop in material well-being
is almost always accompanied by fear, and then a transfer of that fear into
anger directed at a human enemy. In Arizona, the scapegoat became the
state's mushrooming population of Latinos, personified by the "illegal
immigrant" who has been an integral part of the building of Arizona's
pleasant labyrinth of landscaped neighborhoods yet remains largely out
of sight, a ghostly presence. The overwhelming energy at the state legislature in recent years has been directed toward punitive measures against
illegal immigrants.

The most prominent of these is called the Support Our Law Enforcement and Safe Neighborhoods Act, but it's one whose colloquial name
is simply a legislative routing number: Senate Bill (SB) 1070. Passed and
signed into law by Governor Jan Brewer on April 23, 2010, it makes it
a state matter—in addition to a federal offense—to be in Arizona as a
migrant without papers, and it obligates all police agencies to ask for
the registration papers of a suspected illegal migrant during any "lawful
stop, detention or arrest." Playing on fears of Mexican child molesters,
drug dealers, and carjackers became rhetorical sport in the legislature,
and a bumper sticker got wide circulation: WHAT PART OF "ILLEGAL"
DON'T YOU UNDERSTAND? The law contravened decades of a common

Arizona policing practice: avoiding this subject in interactions with Latinos for fear of creating mistrust with possible informants and witnesses
to bigger crimes. Arizona's local cops also historically lacked the time or
the manpower to go after migration as a crime in itself, having more
important things to do. But the new law would allow an ordinary citizen
to sue a police department it felt was letting migrants squirm through
their grip. The law earned a condemnation from President Obama, who
said it would "undermine basic notions of fairness that we cherish as
Americans, as well as the trust between police and our communities that
is so crucial to keeping us safe." His Justice Department filed suit to keep
portions of the law from being enacted. Arizona quickly earned a place
as the SHOW ME YOUR PAPERS state in the national consciousness, and
it became briefly fashionable for companies and the governments of
other Western cities to declare that they would no longer hold or attend
conventions in Tucson or Phoenix.

The paranoia has ticked upward as a fundamental shift in demographics promises to make Arizona a majority Latino state within the
next ten years. The white population's dominance has begun to be
eclipsed in numbers and to grow collectively older even as the Latino
population has sprung upward in both number of households and the
number of youth. No city in the country embodies this more than the
Phoenix metro area, where just 44 percent of the people under eighteen
are white, compared with 85 percent among senior citizens. This makes
it the number-one city in the nation to show what demographers call a
"cultural generation gap"—divided not just by race but by age. Arizonans, in short, are not really acquainted with one another—within their
own neighborhoods, and especially not among broader categories of
race, income, or generation. The narrative of the state has never put
particular emphasis on that idea, preferring individual liberties and
lifestyle choices over shared destinies.

"There are certain parts of the country, and Arizona is one of
those, where you don't necessarily see a strong social network," said Dan

Ranieri, the executive director of the mental health network La Frontera. "We are a stark version of what is going on everywhere."

✤

In order to understand how Arizona grew up as it did it helps to examine more deeply how it has been packaged and sold to the rest of the United States.

The European influence on Tucson began in 1692, when Jesuit missionaries followed the Santa Cruz River northward into a lonely northern frontier they called Pimeria Alta. They found a small prehistoric volcano that a local clan told them was called Cuk Son, for "black base."

They bastardized the name into Tucson, erected a fort and a convent, and built a whitewashed church several miles south. They suppressed some minor insurrections among the Pima Indians but mainly helped them run punitive campaigns against their new enemies to the east, the Apache, who attacked under a full moon to steal cows and weapons. The Spanish found themselves drawn into *la guerra de fuego y sangria*, "a war of fire and blood," that flailed in varied iterations for more than two centuries.

The Indian raids were only aggravated by the discovery of new wealth. In 1736, when a Yaqui Indian found big chunks of silver near a natural water hole about sixty miles to the south in present-day Mexico, it set off a prospectors' rush to the area, which became known as Arizonac, for the Pima Indian phrase *ali shonak*, which means "small spring." The silver turned out to be largely a mirage, not much more than a shallow reef. The boom quickly dried up and the settlement fell apart, but the legend of the buried treasure hidden in the spring became a regional myth among the Spanish settlers—a local El Dorado—and the name Arizonac became synonymous with fast riches, in the same way that Klondike would become a byword for a gold strike in the 1890s.

The capital of the scruffy region was Tucson, at the base of that black hill, and it might have remained part of the republic of Mexico to this day, a multiethnic soup of Spanish, Pima, and citified Apache, but it became a part of the United States because of two driving factors—technology and race.

The railroad came into widespread use in the United States during the 1840s, and it brought a whole new understanding of time and space. The rough places in the continent, like the future territory of Arizona, suddenly became important links in what would be the welded joints that would soon bolt the country together. When Congress sent out surveying parties to scout out the easiest iron road to link ocean to ocean, the thirty-second parallel—which passed through what is now southern Arizona—was favored by the future Confederate president Jefferson Davis, who was then the U.S. secretary of war. A slave-colony promoter named James Gadsden went to Mexico City with a congressional mandate to buy a vast chunk of land south of the Gila River for $10 million, a deal known as the Gadsden Purchase.

Tucson thus became a slave-state prize within an awkward wedge of new American territory, its borders marked by piles of white rocks that were just as quickly knocked over and scattered by resentful Tucsonenses. The "government" was a thin brace of U.S. Army soldiers hated by the locals for their rude bearing and their drinking binges. An Irish-American mining engineer named J. Ross Browne passed through Tucson around this time and was not happy with what he saw:

> A city of mud boxes, dingy and dilapidated, cracked and baked into a composite of dust and filth; littered about with broken corrals, sheds, bake-ovens, carcasses of dead animals, and broken pottery; barren of verdure, parched, naked, and grimly desolate in the glare of a southern sun, adobe walls without whitewash inside or out, hard earth-floors, baked and dried Mexicans, sore-backed burros, coyote dogs, and terra-cotta children.

But if Tucson was a ragamuffin burg, Phoenix was a cockeyed real-estate scheme. The Hohokam Indians had built a sophisticated culture in the valley of the Salt River approximately between the years 650 and

1450. The secret to their success was canals, which diverted the precious water away from the bitter-tasting Salt and into fields where they grew corn and squash. They put as much as sixty thousand acres under cultivation and left a chain of forts atop the knobby peaks; one could pass a message to another by waggling a shiny object in the sun. Then the Hohokam disappeared—nobody is sure why. One theory has it that a flood destroyed the canals, another blames tribal warfare. The canals filled with silt and sand, almost erased from the land.

After the U.S. Civil War, when swarms of ex-soldiers went looking for silver on the Hassayampa River fifty miles outside present-day Phoenix,* a beady-eyed Georgian named Jack Swilling organized a shovel crew to dig out a section of the old Indian canal system to irrigate vegetables for the silver miners. The farming community settled on its name after an English resident named Darrell Duppa, who had a taste for whiskey and high oratory, made a rambling speech about a new civilization rising from the ashes of an ancient one, like the mythic twice-born Greek bird. The street layout was a proper midwestern grid: The north-south streets were numbered, the east-wests named for American presidents. And newcomers flooded in, most of them trying to get away from the dead hand of the East.

"This is a place where you would come to reinvent yourself," said Marshall Trimble. "If you were successful where you were from, why would you come out to this godforsaken, inhospitable place? Broken health, broken wealth, broken lives. They were, quite frankly, losers."

Swilling later died in the territorial prison at Yuma, addicted to laudanum and serving a sentence for a stagecoach robbery he didn't commit. The supply town he helped found grew phenomenally, even without a transcontinental railroad link or a heritage of Spanish settlement. Phoenix's founders believed their pure Anglo culture was a crowning virtue. An 1891 chamber of commerce publication would brag about "a valley of wonderful fertility" in which there were "none of

---

* Then called Pumpkinville.

the sleepy, semi-Mexican features of the more ancient towns of the Southwest."

Phoenix would fancy itself, as Los Angeles eventually would, as a "white spot," a paradise of midwestern Protestant values in the midst of spectacular rugged promontories where a man and his family might reinvent their lives in the cleansing air of the West. The Mexican or indigenous peoples were relegated to the far margins of daily life and their cultures sanitized and bleached almost beyond recognition, and therefore no longer frightening; yet those same cultures, through home design, cuisine, and charming street names, became a Southwestern form of imperial nostalgia. This differed somewhat from the way things were done in Tucson, which came as much from economic self-interest—and plain lust—as it did from notions of tolerance. It was common practice for the bachelor American men to take young Mexican women, often teenagers, as their brides.

Though the local attitude toward Mexicans was more easygoing in Tucson, a different kind of racial paranoia was in the air. Apache raiders had run cattle off ranches in night raids and, in 1871, killed a settler from Connecticut and his Mexican mistress, whose cheap breast pin later was later rumored to have been found in the possession of an Apache woman. Many of Arizona's penny newspapers from this era read like bills of indictment against the Apache menace—"make no truce and show no mercy to adult males," counseled the *Weekly Arizonan*—and shooting them on sight had become standard procedure for many settlers. "We have a horror of them that you feel for a ghost," recalled one. "We never see them, but when on the road are always looking over our shoulders in anticipation." The lust for extermination was mounting.

The new mayor made things worse. William Oury was a humorless Virginian who had seen a lot of blood, and therefore had credibility. Why didn't he write history?, someone once wanted to know, and he snapped: "Because I'm too damn busy making it!" He had traveled west as a young man to join the Texas War of Independence and was posted to the Alamo shortly before it was surrounded by General Antonio López de Santa

Anna's army. Commander William Travis sent him out as a courier to plead for reinforcements shortly before all inside were slaughtered; it made him one of the last Anglos to leave the fortified chapel alive. He later joined the hell-raising vigilantes known as the Texas Rangers and fought in northern Mexico for the U.S. Army; there he found a war bride: a nineteen-year-old Mexican named Inez Garcia. By the time he arrived in Tucson to run a dairy farm in 1856 he had a rich stock of yarns as well as fluent Spanish learned from his wife. The two street duels he survived in Tucson did little to injure his reputation. People started calling him "Uncle Billy," and he got himself appointed the first mayor in 1864, and then became the head of the less savory Committee of Public Safety, which dedicated itself to solving the Apache problem—bluntly and thoroughly. The federal government was doing nothing to send troops or security to this border free-for-all, and Arizona citizens decided to go it alone. The hysteria was reminiscent of the present-day feelings about immigrants from Mexico.

Oury and his friends planned to make their point at a miserable place called Camp Grant near the flats of the San Pedro River, where the walls of the canyon close in. A soft-hearted captain named Royal Whitman, a Quaker, had allowed about five hundred Pinal and Aravaipa Apaches to squat nearby at a place they named Big Sycamore Stands Alone, where they received government handouts of flour and dried beef. For Oury it must have seemed like a replay of his Texas rangering days, as he and his friend Juan Elias gathered up forty-eight Mexicans and ninety-four revenge-minded Tohono O'odham Indians into a brigade to teach a lesson to "the most bloodthirsty devils that ever disgraced mother earth."

They marched for two days over Redington Pass toward Aravaipa Creek, and when the sun came up on April 30, the six Anglo commanders, including Oury, watched from high ground as their O'odham and Mexican subalterns charged into the valley and opened up a killing zone. Heads were dashed open on rocks, women were raped, and children were kidnapped for later sale in Mexico. One hundred were dead within half an hour. The wickiups were burned into ashes and the corpses left to draw flies in the rising sun.

The committee thundered back into Tucson in a cloud of triumph and ambiguity, all of them sworn to an oath of secrecy that was quickly broken as the stories leaked out in taverns. Eastern journalists called the massacre a disgrace and ran stories exposing a "Tucson ring" of wagon freighters who had been deliberately antagonizing the Indians in order to keep doing business with the army and reaping profit from war, which was, complained one exhausted general, the "economic foundation" of the whole territory. President Ulysses S. Grant threatened to bring down martial law if there was no trial for the perpetrators—and there would be, a hollow one, in which the one hundred defendants were acquitted by a jury within minutes; sidewalk opinion in Tucson held that the action had been distasteful but necessary, though few were aware of just how gruesome and one-sided the slaughter at Aravaipa had been. The Apaches lost their historic claim on lands to the east of Tucson and accepted resettlement to the San Carlos reservation, where they live today. After one last spectacular breakout by Geronimo in 1885, the Indian wars in Arizona came to an end. "The survival of the fittest holds here as everywhere and the dominant race has asserted itself," boasted a promotional pamphlet called *The Resources of Arizona.*

The Camp Grant massacre went down the memory hole. Few of the participants wanted to talk about what happened. The pillars of the community remained pillars. When the tracks of the Southern Pacific Railroad reached Tucson on March 20, 1880, Oury himself gave a florid welcoming address in front of the locomotives. Five years later he made an end-justifies-the-means speech at Pioneer Hall. "Behold now the happy result immediately following that episode," he told the audience. "On the Sonoita, Santa Cruz, and all other settlements of southern Arizona, new life springs up, confidences restored and industry bounds forward with an impetus that has known no check in the whole fourteen years since that occurrence."

The railroad did far more to change Tucson than the forgotten slaughter. The freighting firm of Tully and Ochoa was soon out of business. Tucson's population rocketed to nine thousand within a year. The oligarchic Latino character of the town, and the romances between old men and teenage brides, began to diminish. The main drag—Calle de la Alegria (Spanish for "Happiness Street")—had been renamed Congress Street. The new immigrants from Texas and Ohio built homes in the style of British manors: a square box plopped in the middle of the lot to suggest verdant fields. Many of these homes were shipped out on the Southern Pacific Railroad as prefabricated kits. Tucson had little native vegetation that could be considered "verdant," so the newcomers imported citrus fruit trees, chinaberry trees, shrubs, and rose bushes—as well as carpets of tough, all-weather Bermuda grass—to disguise the ragged character of the desert that surrounded them on all sides, shielding the houses from relentless sunshine and affording privacy from neighbor eyes.

Big Water arrived in Arizona courtesy of the federal government. In 1902 Congress passed the Reclamation Act authorizing the construction of dams, and dusty Phoenix was one of the top beneficiaries. The largest masonry dam in the world was built in a canyon at the confluence of the Salt River and Tonto Creek, creating a massive artificial lake. The dam itself was a kind of stone sandwich, a design called "broken range cyclopean rubble," that amounted to limestone walls on either side filled up in the middle with concrete and boulders. Theodore Roosevelt came out in 1911 to dedicate the dam named in his honor and predicted that Phoenix would be "one of the richest agricultural areas of the world." The Salt River promptly stopped flowing and became an empty indentation, its contents now sluiced onto succulent green fields of alfalfa and cotton. A rifle club designed a self-consciously "Western" flag for Arizona in anticipation of statehood: It depicted a copper-colored star beaming red and gold rays, in imitation of a setting sun.*

---

* It was not made the official flag until 1917; the governor hated it, and others felt it looked too much like the "rising sun" design adopted by imperial Japan.

But Arizona's petition for statehood was vetoed by President William Howard Taft because its constitution permitted the recall of judges, who were then mostly the defenders of industrial giants such as the copper industry. Explaining himself, Taft wrote: "No honest, clear-headed man, however great a lover of popular government, can deny that the unbridled expression of the majority of a community converted hastily into law or action would sometimes make a government tyrannical and cruel."

Arizona caved in to the president's demands. It removed the offending provision, broke out the bunting, and held a statehood ceremony on Valentine's Day in 1912, making it the last and youngest state among the lower contiguous states. And the new legislature immediately put a ballot before the voters to change the constitution back to the way it was before Taft started meddling. This passed decisively, and thus the jigsaw puzzle of the continent was closed in a gesture of defiance to the federal government.

Complaining about interference from Washington—while at the same time demanding that it do more to kill the Apache, secure the border, and rearrange vast quantities of water—had been a consistent practice throughout the history of Arizona up through and beyond statehood.

THREE

THE COUNTRYSIDE

My parents moved us to the edge of Tucson when I was eleven years old, into a new subdivision called Shadow Hills. We were one of the first families to live there, and our house was a lone adobe-colored box in the midst of desert.

In the heady days of the late seventies, when borrowing was still cheap, the Fort Worth, Texas, megacorporation U.S. Home purchased two untouched square miles of native desert, slapped on an arbitrary tag sufficient for Anywhere, USA, and tricked it out with sewer extensions and a rosacea of twisting streets bladed into the rocky soil—streets with modern-colonial names like Camino Alberca (Swimming Pool Street), Camino Arturo (Arthur Street), and a fishhook-shaped artery, Camino Padre Isidoro (Father Isidoro Street). To this day I have no idea who Father Isidoro was or what kind of church he might have pastored, or if he even existed. Or was a developer's gag name.

These rock-asphalt ribbons did not follow the contours of the washes. Square concrete culverts were poured wherever they had to cross one. I spent a lot of time hiding out in a nameless box just to the west of our house, alone, as though it was a private treehouse. Only once, after a vicious flash flood, did any water flow through it.

Most of my time was spent in solitude. Ours was one of the first houses in Shadow Hills, and virtually nobody my age lived within a mile. My parents built a trapezoidal pool with a dark brown bottom, but there was nobody to swim with. On the side of the house was a limbless saguaro that was slowly dying. One of the men who had helped build the house had shot it repeatedly with a pneumatic nail gun and its side was full of rusting metal; its ribs were rotting from the wounds. I rode my bicycle, a motocross assembly-required job from Sears, in endless circuits through Shadow Hills.

I acquired a map of all the lots from one of the air-conditioned model homes with fake fruit bowls on the table, and—for lack of anything better to do—started to make my own map of the tangle of culs-de-sac and the lots that were sprouting with 3-BR houses like teeth in baby gums. Even those houses that were finished were locked chests. Their big garages fronted roads with no sidewalks. I knew no one in those chests that lived near us, and barely even saw them, except when they were sealed in their cars.

Shadow Hills had been carved out of a leftover tract of land next door to an older neighborhood called Catalina Foothills Estates, the life's work of a 1920s developer named John Murphey who had been entranced with the new Spanish revival architecture he saw in the Hollywood Hills and Pasadena. At a State Land Department auction he bought seventeen hundred acres of land where the hardpan of the Tucson basin begins to tilt upward at the north into a rippled series of hills. He targeted the posh winter visitors with visions of dream haciendas in the desert and put advertisements in the *Arizona Daily Star* touting the "virgin forests" of saguaro and calling it the unspoiled "Beverly Hills of Tucson." The city had been spreading outward like spilled liquid in the dawn of the automobile era and was desperately trying to shed its image as an asylum for poor Mexicans and sufferers of tuberculosis—known as "lungers"—who had come out for the dry air and clustered in a slum neighborhood called Tentville.

Murphey had also taken inspiration from the magnificent improbability of the El Conquistador hotel, a faux Spanish resort built at the urging of a booster group called the Tucson Sunshine Climate Club, which made heroic efforts to advertise the warm weather to a better class of visitor than the pathetic lungers. The El Con, as it was known, had a main building topped with a domed bell tower sixty-five feet tall. There was a palm-lined driveway, a rose garden with 350 varieties, a curio shop stuffed with Mexican geegaws, and, of course, a swimming pool. This succulent design was a reflection of a larger urge in Arizona to deny its own environment. Up in Phoenix, the Valley Beautiful Committee had started a LET'S DO AWAY WITH THE DESERT civic campaign, telling participants to shun cactus and other native growth in favor of rosebushes and shrubs. In the Foothills, however, the giant saguaros were protected by deed restrictions, and a homeowner enjoyed spectacular privacy: The night sky filled with moony mountains and an extravagant carpet of stars.

Nothing felt right to me in Shadow Hills, or human, not even like the early sixties neighborhood bordering a golf course that we had come from in northern Phoenix. My skateboard was no good on those new asphalt streets; it would grind to a terrifying halt at the slightest pebble, and I was thrown enough times to create an ugly arm rash. I set up divisions of green plastic army soldiers against one another in a battlefield of modified earthworks outside the house, under a palo verde tree, until my mother found it and told me to clean it up. I learned the role-playing game D&D, but there was no one to play it with. Back in those impossibly ancient days when we lived in Phoenix, a fellow Cub Scout named Scott Hudson and I had been fond of a board game called *Superstar Baseball*, which was a statistical matchup between some of the greatest baseball players of the twentieth century, a forerunner to fantasy leagues. In Scott's absence I laid out the game by myself and played our two old teams against one another. But that soon grew boring and wistful. My star pitcher was a historical character from the Philadelphia Athletics named Lefty Grove, and I was fascinated by that name—a "grove" of trees sounded exotic, and "lefty" sounded friendly. I stole a plank of plywood from a U.S. Home construction site and a bottle of metallic blue spray paint from my father's garage shelf and painted the words "Lefty Grove Field" onto it, and then leaned it up next to a saguaro cactus at the bulbous knob of an empty cul-de-sac. I imagined where the bases would be and where the ghost runners would stand. I imagined myself the first baseman. It absurdly excited me that my new junior high school was called Orange Grove, though there were no groves of orange trees anywhere in sight, just cactus. The school was a cluster of pumice-block pyramid classrooms with a long oval track tucked behind it.

This place should never have excited me in the slightest, as I came into it unprepared for real work and thoroughly choked by the aphasia of preadolescence. As the new kid for the first time I found that I had none of the native charisma that tends to attract fresh friends. Given my obsession with long-dead baseball players and lack of physical grace, I didn't have much to say that commanded interest. I ate lunch alone each day, shivering in the PE cage in my windbreaker, which was blue with white piping. My spindly frame made me a target, and I got picked into stupid fights, without a shred of courage or heroism inspiring them. Junior high–level schools in every society are merciless ponds of social Darwinism, and at Orange Grove I was plankton. The more popular boys taunted and tripped and wedgied; the girls only laughed or ignored.

I learned to be on my guard constantly, stiff as a wire. I failed multiple quizzes and stopped doing my homework in favor of watching television—bad television—without any pleasure: *Three's Company, Diff'rent Strokes, Bosom Buddies*. I spent even more of my time making bicycle loops around the nascent U.S. Homes, a roving gang of one. My father kept a gun in the house, a .22 caliber pistol wrapped in a cloudy plastic bag, and I found myself wondering what it would be like to shoot myself with it. There were cheap white panels on the grip and a neat stack of oily bullets in the magazine. I never did fire it, but I knew where it was hidden: in a closet. After I read *The Monkey Wrench Gang*, Edward Abbey's rollicking novel about a group of ecoraiders in the Southwest, I took it upon myself to start pulling up the wooden survey stakes on the empty lots and tossing them in the desert washes, in some fatuous mini-protest against "development." I would sometimes steal into an unfinished house in the late afternoons to smash out the windows with rocks. From these same concrete pads of the housing frames, which were scented with sawdust and fresh caulking, I stole short lengths of rebar steel and flung them like ninja knives at the sides of saguaro cactus, where they made a satisfying, fleshy *thunk*, and the trees bled green juice like tears. The combat effect was even better from the seat of a moving bicycle, a bit like shooting a Comanche from a horse.

The counselors at Orange Grove noticed my scholastic ineptitude and social deracination and sent me to a psychologist with a brittle smile who made me take a bunch of learning disability tests without explaining why. Then came the news that I had officially failed seventh grade and would have to do the year all over again, in full view of everyone. The news was delivered in an hour-long "retention conference," attended by my parents, in which all of my teachers explained, one-by-one, why I was not fit to go on to the eighth grade. This was a public execution. *Flunked*—the word seemed as harsh and clumsy as my whole being, which in the spring of 1981 felt like a rounding error of the universe.

Things did get better, eventually, though in slow increments and with no magical transformations, except perhaps for the dull magic of time that slowly grinds by. No orchestral codas swelled. I grew older and a little more out of my own walls. I started forcing myself to do homework. I stopped trying to interest anyone else in Lefty Grove or antique baseball statistics and started running miles for the track team, performances that were still inept—dead last was my customary finish, and I sometimes vomited with the effort of the last sprint, green puke caking my jersey—but I also managed to make a few friends and won a portion of acceptance just for the trying. One evening after a meet, near the drinking fountain outside the library, an extraordinarily pretty girl named Christy gave me a full-on hug, the first real one I had ever received from a nonrelative, and said softly, "You did very good today, Z-man." My body felt exhausted and electrified. Here was a real nickname at last, not a mean one. I grew taller, though not less skinny, and the harassment faded. My high school, Canyon del Oro, was an eight-mile drive up Oracle Road, and I made some real friends there in my second year. Hesitantly, I threw myself at the school's newspaper. I began to love everything about it: the way the page crystallized reality into neat columns; the hard rationality of deadlines; the chemical smell of the ink from the printers; the sense of subversive power that came from being able to lob stink-bomb stories against some administrative outrage or another.

Most of all, I loved that the newspaper gave me a way to feel like I belonged, but *without actually belonging.* The identity of "press" allowed me to float among a raft of different activities, watching and summarizing but not participating. Taking on the role of reporter forced me out of my fundamental shyness, because talking to people was an absolute necessity, but I did not need to contribute anything to the exchange other than a series of pleasant questions. Most people were happy to talk about themselves anyway, and I learned an invaluable social survival skill.

I also shrank even deeper into myself, though in a more imperceptible way than the simple avoidance of pain. The posture of official impartiality was never difficult for me; it wrapped around me like a warming jacket. I dodged commitment to any cause; in a way, to do so would have been a tacit confession that *yes, I belong here. This is my place.* My more ethereal duty was to "seek the truth," or whatever that phrase meant when it came to writing down what somebody said and setting it up in conventional words that felt honest. Participation without touch. All those words, the rational string of words, could make everything manageable. The peculiar ethic of newspapers became my organizing principle for the world: a compulsion that required bone-rending work and a priestly denial of self.

My guy friends didn't get it at all, and that was okay. There were other things to do. Our hobbies were common teenage vice. We faked IDs for beer—an easy stroke of an X-ACTO knife in those days—and drank it in the desert. Marijuana was sometimes there, sometimes not. The greatest entertainment was to take our parents' cars out after school into the cul-de-sac neighborhoods and look for curbside garbage cans to run over and flatten into the dust, scattering trash in the xeriscaped yards like a minicyclone. Sheriff Clarence Dupnik's deputies arrested us a time or two for petty vandalism and misdeeds. It was in one of these tract neighborhoods in the floodplain of the Canada del Oro wash (Valley of Gold) that my girlfriend and I awkwardly but sweetly lost our virginities to one another on the carpeted floor of her bedroom, playing scripted roles for one another that still felt entirely ours.

Down where Ina and Thornydale cross, massive shopping strips were going up on all corners and I took a job as a burger chef at a Carl's Jr. fast-food restaurant for minimum wage. The spattering machine-processed beef and bacon turned the brown uniform greasy after a few days. I stayed on for a year, addicted to the money that bought gasoline.

The best times of all were in the car, making lone roundabouts of Tucson in the same outwardly concentric patterns as I had ridden my motocross bicycle around Shadow Hills, listening to pop music on KRQ and dreaming of other places. I told my girlfriend that the name of that wash, Valley of Gold, always seemed ridiculously ironic to me. *Gold:* What a joke. Bruce Springsteen had made a comeback in the mid-1980s, and I had the older songs "Born to Run" and "Thunder Road" loaded onto a small battery-operated cassette player; I played them until the tapes stretched. I knew what Springsteen was talking about, or imagined that I did in my eighteen-year-old longing—fate, despair, hope, and eventual victory through the act of escape. My driving circuits were long and compulsive and without direction. I drove at night as an antidepressant and tranquilizer: Camino Miraval to Skyline Drive to Sunrise to Sabino Canyon to Tanque Verde to Old Spanish Trail, a random crescent in front of the dark granite walls of the Santa Catalinas and through all these anonymous errata of lit-up houses that seemed so untouchable and closed, and me an interplanetary satellite zooming past on some obscure mission. I was in search of a horizon I couldn't name. To be more precise, I wanted out. After a meandering first year at the University of Arizona, I accomplished just that.

My grades hadn't been all that stellar, but they were enough to get me into a liberal arts college in Wisconsin, which seemed like a far-off enough place and more qualitatively "real" than where I'd come from. In my twenties I chased newspaper jobs, which is where I always felt most humming with purpose—safe within the walls of indisputable fact, one of the good guys who could be counted on not to take a side or be stained with bias. Knowing without being known. I made it a point to change newspapers and cities every two or so years, to see America from the ground up: the city council squabbles; the crime-scene tape; the camps for the homeless; the floods; the elections; the helicopter crashes; the veterans' parades. On Christmas visits to see my parents in Tucson I was struck by the muscular show of mountain against sky that made the physical setting so distinct, and which I hadn't really appreciated while growing up. There were times when I scrutinized Arizona for clues about where I had come from and what kind of man it had made of me, this prickly urge for independence mingled with a contradictory yearning to be liked by everyone: an occasionally flammable mixture, surely a souvenir from those difficult extended years at Orange Grove. These inquisitive homecomings dulled over time, though, and it eventually became another plain-Jane metropolis in the Sunbelt, albeit a familiar and vaguely comfortable one where I had been fated to spend vital years, and for which I would probably always have hopelessly tangled feelings.

I came to know it much better in my thirties. After trying to write a novel and becoming engaged—and then disengaged—to a woman I loved in San Francisco, I was offered a job in Phoenix at *The Arizona Republic*, the biggest paper in the state and a generally respected one. I rented a loft apartment downtown with high windows and a view of palm trees and an Episcopal cathedral and walked to work every morning on shabby and cracked sidewalks, across the same routes where my grandmother had walked to her elementary school in the 1920s. I was introduced to the lawyer-lobbyists who helped run things at the Capitol. I had lunch with some of them at Mexican restaurants that had misters spraying fine fogs of water to keep the patio temperatures cool. The possibilities to become superficially "known" were quick and easy. The city had been drunk with growth and buzzing with new arrivals since the end of World War II, and the quest for the good, leisured life hadn't ceased at all. The suburb of Scottsdale—once a honky-tonk strip of art galleries that called itself "The West's Most Western Town"—had become a nightclubbing haven and sexualized playground. Gated communities and condominiums bowled out north of the Loop 101 freeway toward a horizon of stucco and hardy squares of Bermuda grass that looked like they had been spray-blasted onto the dry desert ground. The weird green fragrance of flooded lawns and golf fairways hung like fetid perfume. I remembered childhood sounds: cicadas buzzing; mourning doves calling for mates in a low arpeggio of six notes. It was an easy place to take a psychic snooze for a while, amid familiar smells and streets.

I remembered reading a line from Walker Percy's novel *The Moviegoer* in which the hero, Binx Bolling, has quit his search for any larger purpose in his life and, in an existential surrender, started seeing a lot of movies. At one point he took his secretary out for a drive along the Mississippi Gulf Coast in his convertible and realized he does not love her like the day before. "But life goes on and on we go, spinning along the coast in a violet light, past Howard Johnson's and the motels and the children's carnival. We pull into the bay and have a drink under the stars. It is not a bad thing to settle for the Little Way, not the big search for the big happiness but the sad little happinesses of drinks and kisses, a good little car and a warm deep thigh." My own life was starting to feel like that, pleasurable in the moment but the heart of it set aside in some essential way, mountains not climbed, books not written, the stories I put in the paper dull and drained of purpose, the rational words that I had loved becoming floating black particles in a throwaway broadsheet where only the names changed each day, an ink-and-paper version of a sporting event.

Twice every year, a nonpartisan policy group in Phoenix put on an event called Arizona Town Hall, where 150 randomly chosen participants in the governing class sequestered themselves in a resort hotel somewhere for two days, debated a big question, and made a report that the legislature could either notice or ignore at its pleasure. The *Republic* had dutifully covered these confabulations for almost half a century. My number came up, and I was told to go up to El Tovar, the outsize railroad hunting lodge at the South Rim of the Grand Canyon, and write up a couple of eight-inchers. The assignment was a dull one, but it was a chance to go easy for two days, file something quick and unchallenging in the evenings, and then drink on the company tab. There was a party the second night, where I met Jim McNulty, the white-haired Irish prosecutor from Bisbee who had represented southern Arizona in Congress as a Democrat for a brief spell in the early eighties, before a Republican kicked him out. I had always gotten a thrill out of meeting those people who were in the news when I was a kid—I had read the *Arizona Daily Star* religiously every day with some amount of fascination—and told him it was a pleasure, which it was.

Sitting next to him was a woman about my age, attractive, wearing a white blouse open at the neck and a small gold chain necklace. Her hair was whiskey-colored and her voice was of a mildly squeaky register—girlish but not unserious. When she laughed at something McNulty said she pressed her eyes closed, showing a flat wall of teeth, and her cheekbones went even higher. She pushed him on the arm with mock disdain. Her hands were small, slightly fleshy at the palms, and had short unbitten fingernails, though her fingers were slender. She introduced herself as Gabrielle Giffords, a friend of the McNulty family. Then it came out that she was a newly elected member of the Arizona House of Representatives. Mortality check: I was getting to be an age where people in my peer group were already starting to run the show. But Gabrielle did not come across as haughty. There was nothing about her that broadcast anything but bright interest in who I was and a touch of bemusement with her surroundings. I can't remember what we talked about in the ballroom, but the conversation moved to the bar with one of the editorial writers from the *Republic*, and we all talked about the sport of politics.

We drank beer in the light of an electronic dartboard and walked around the mule corrals outside El Tovar. We talked and talked. She had come from a different side of Tucson from me, far out on the east side, in a rambling old house off North Soldier Trail, which I knew chiefly from my aimless drives. I must have passed her property a dozen times without a glance. Her family had owned El Campo Tire & Service, a local chain that advertised heavily on TV with a four-note guitar riff that everyone who lived in Tucson was primed to recognize.

It has long been one of my faults that I am slightly surprised when people take an instant liking to me—*O thanks be to ye storied halls of Orange Grove*—and it was a minor marvel to me that we started a friendship after the town hall. I was far from unique in this regard; Gabrielle made new friends like she breathed. She once told me that the best part of running for office was having a built-in excuse to approach a stranger she wanted to talk with.

She took me to her family's house one night early on, out on North Soldier Trail toward the escarpment of the Catalinas. It was a drafty estate brimming with Southwestern art that seemed at once the germ of the Tucson it adjoined and yet wholly separate. Her mother, Gloria, cooked us steaks roughly the shape of a baseball, wrapped with bacon, a classy but seemingly effortless production. Her father, Spencer, came rumbling in barefoot, wearing a T-shirt and shorts, and they started in without a pause on what Gabrielle called "the Spencer and Gloria Show," making me feel totally at home, like I had known them for thirty years instead of being taken in that very night.

Nobody ever born in this world has a dull family. Some just require a closer inspection. Gabby's family requires no such search. Their energy hits with the force of a summer monsoon. Gloria is a bespectacled art conservator who had grown up in the high plains town of Colby, Kansas, and came to the University of Arizona in the sixties to study Mexican art. Altar screens in Catholic churches became her specialty. Her nickname is Jinx, and chatting with her is less of a conversation than an experience, more cloud than line. She loves to show off her extensive collection of Southwestern art and oils that she had done herself. It was from Gloria that I learned one of the best pieces of writing advice anyone ever gave me, and it was in the context of oil painting. Take a few bold initial strokes in the space of a few seconds and don't intellectualize too much. Your original impulse is probably correct. This was drawing from the subconscious, and she did it fast and well. She showed me around her new studio at the base of the Rincon Mountains one afternoon, and after I admired a canvas portrait of a long-haired woman in a sitting position, it was promptly handed to me. My protests were futile. It is an effortlessly elegant piece of art, and Gloria probably did it in half an hour.

Gabrielle's father, Spencer, is a balding, ursine, open-faced man with a room-filling guffaw, occasionally ribald, always hilarious. He had taken over the tire business from his father, Gif Giffords, who was the son of a rabbi who had emigrated from Lithuania in the 1910s. His given name was Akiba Hornstein, and he changed his surname to Giffords to avoid anti-Semitism. The choice of neologism seems to have been as random as leafing through the phone book; how and why he picked it is still a family mystery. Eventually he ditched his first name, too, and became the euphonious "Gif Giffords." He moved out to Arizona from New York City, obtained a franchise license to sell Dunlop tires, and started El Campo Tire & Service Center as a single gas station in 1949 at the corner of Twenty-second and Country Club Road. His trade soon mushroomed into multiple locations and grew up with the fantastic auto-driven growth of the Sunbelt. The town's sizable Latino population was a prime customer base, and the company sold a lot of wholesale tires to the shops in Mexico called *llanteras*. Gabrielle laughed about her last name. It sounded friendly and breezy, the result of some lost whimsy on the part of her grandfather, her own marker of the American capacity for reinvention, improvisation, and hope.

Gif Giffords had devoted a large portion of the annual budget to radio and TV ads and starred in them himself in the fifties, wearing thick Coke-bottle glasses and delivering minihomilies and fables along with the folksy tire pitches. His standard opening was "It's a good, good evening." These commercials were Gif's own way, his son always thought, of being the rabbi/teacher he had once wanted to be. El Campo branded itself "The Buck-Stretcher," which was also the name Gabrielle had given her horse when she was growing up.

In Spanish, the name "El Campo" means "The Countryside," and Gif Giffords had a knack for spotting well-trafficked street corners in his growing city, on which he built service bays with brick arches framing the windows in a style reminiscent of Taco Bell. Inside they smelled of oil and new rubber, and were filled with the clank of wrenches.

FOUR

SELLING THE VILLAGE

One of the better El Campo locations was on North Oracle Road, the biggest collector road in the city, which had also functioned as the main highway to Phoenix back before the interstates were built. It wound through ranch country and empty desert north of the dry bed of the Rillito River before curving around the west flank of the Santa Catalina range.

There wasn't much up here in the forties except for a few cotton farms in the valleys and an isolated grove of orange trees, date palms, and bougainvilleas. The last ranch road of significance up here was Ina Road, for a homesteader named Ina Gittings,* who had a day job as the head of the physical education department at the University of Arizona. The crossing of Oracle and Ina would soon become a hot corner to buy land, and the man who had seen its potential first was an immigrant named Silvio Nanini, who was born on a flower farm in Ponte Buggianese, Italy, in 1885. His immense fortune, like that of Gif Giffords, would be founded on the growth of American highway culture.

---

* The street is pronounced EYE-nah, but after it became a major thoroughfare, Gittings wrote several irritated letters to the newspapers explaining that her name was EE-nah. .

Nanini left Italy on a steamer when he was fifteen, changed his name to Sam, and drifted to Chicago in 1911, eager to make money. One of his ideas was to start a candy store, and when he would make taffy, he aimed a portable electric fan to blow the fragrance of it out onto the street, the sweetness its own best advertising. He bought a Diamond T truck with some friends and started an asphalt-hauling business called Rock Road Construction, which soon grew big from all the municipal highway contracts being doled out in northern Illinois. They later built a string of concrete plants and paved the runways at what would become O'Hare airport.

In 1936, Sam started vacationing in Tucson, telling everyone that his wife, Giaconda, suffered from asthma and the dust-free thermal belt of the Southwest was good for her lungs. A bit of family legend has it that Sam went out on horseback with a real-estate dealer, and they came over a rise that afforded a lengthy view of empty Sonoran desert stretching out to the base of Sombrero Peak, of a horizon of mesquite and ocotillo crisscrossed with a few lonely dirt roads. Many years later Jared Lee Loughner would grow up, go to school, work at fast-food restaurants, and attempt to go to community college on the same horizon that Sam Nanini viewed that day. "I want all of it," Sam was supposed to have said. "But the condition is, the deal has to close tomorrow." He would eventually buy thirty thousand acres for an average of about twenty-five dollars per acre. At the eastern edge of his new estate was the corner of Oracle and Ina, where the Safeway at La Toscana would stand one day.

Lots of cars heading to Phoenix, but zero foot traffic. You would not walk up there unless you were crazy.

Nanini built a tawny rectangle of shops there he called Casas Adobes Plaza—literally, "mud houses"—a fifties strip mall of the sort popping up in suburbs all over the place but done with a little Mediterranean class. The storefronts were lined with Roman columns and the sidewalks were shaded with olive trees; marble frescoes were shoehorned into the walls; a fountain was shipped over from the Italian quarry town of Carrara. A Food Giant took the biggest anchor space—what a later generation of real-estate cowboys would call a "pull store"—and a quirky hardware emporium called Bullards took up the second-biggest. Defender Drug had a lunch counter, which was the only thing resembling a restaurant for miles. Surplus palm trees were planted in the median of Oracle Road.

One design element had symbolic power above all others: ten acres of parking was out in front. Shopping was becoming a ritual you did with a car once or twice a week instead of going to the market on foot every day, as refrigerators and freezers were becoming as easy to buy on credit as the car. Casas Adobes therefore featured parking spaces *out front* to advertise. The automobile and the shopping center would attract the development just as surely as taffy scent blown down the street.

This was not the Main Street of the sidewalk and the pedestrian. Here in Tucson, and all over the nation, common spaces were being set back from the street level and surrounded with lakes of black asphalt, the same way that homes had shrunk into their lots in imitation of English manors, with sidewalks discouraged and rare. The outdoor passageways between Sam's specialty shops were some of the only pedestrian spaces within five miles. A person who would go there on foot looked slightly suspicious.

The land around this shopping center was divided into three instant neighborhoods with interchangeable names: Casas Adobes, Casas Adobes Heights, and Casas Adobes Country Club Estates. Each lot had to be a minimum of one acre, which guaranteed a more affluent class of home buyer and meant that it would also be exclusively white. There would be no press-stamped homes in Casas Adobes. This was custom-builders territory. Nanini broke with the Tucson developer's tradition of making up phony Spanish names for his streets, Camino Fill-in-the-Blank, and instead used names reminiscent of his native Italy: Via Assisi, Siena Drive, Leonardo da Vinci Way. Giaconda Drive was for his wife. He told the newspapers that he wanted to build "the best community anyone has ever seen," and he was rewarded with fawning coverage. His silver cowboy belt buckle was a giant S, and he wore it when trotting around on his favorite horse.

Sam didn't talk much in Tucson about where all of his money had come from. But as was inevitable for a Chicago construction boss in the thirties, he had had dealings with the underworld. According to his grandson Steve Nanini, one day in 1931, as Sam went to city hall to pick up a check, a black Cadillac limousine pulled up to the curb and a hulking figure emerged, grabbed him by the arm, and told him to climb in. Sitting there in the backseat was Al Capone, who said, "You know, Nanini, you're doing pretty good, and we need your help. . . . I have some business I want to talk to you about." Capone asked him to repave the driveway in front of his westside house and replace the Olympic-size swimming pool. The crews were there the next morning and Capone was pleased with the work when it was finished. "You did a great job," he told Nanini. "We won't forget you." Rock Road soon had a number of lucrative city contracts that seemingly came from nowhere. Nanini also wrote a letter to the Federal Bureau of Prisons in support of clemency for mob figure Louis Campagna, though he himself was never convicted of a crime.

Tucson was also the retirement home of Joseph "Joe Bananas" Bonanno, who had overseen a network for shakedowns and heroin-running in New York in the fifties. A funeral home he owned was supposed to have been a primary dumping ground for corpses; they were simply stuffed into the coffins of other customers and buried in eternal embrace with a stranger. Bonanno went into hiding in 1968, and then bought a home at 1847 East Elm Street, telling people he was retired because the Sicilian "traditions" of respect and obedience were no longer valued among the younger mob muscle. He bought lots of land around town, including thirty acres in Sam Nanini's Catalina Citrus Estates, and went out to strip-mall Italian restaurants. A place called Conti's across the street from what would eventually be La Toscana Village was a favorite, and he went there with crowds of sycophants. The *Arizona Daily Star* gave him softhearted treatment and covered his ninetieth birthday party like a Chamber of Commerce banquet. "He's been a wonderful, intelligent, loving godfather to us all," said a Pima Community College professor, charitably looking past his many suborned homicides. Senator John McCain sent a congratulatory note by telegram.

But Tucson was never a mafia base of operations. The city only provided for its geriatrics and outcasts the same type of quiet pleasures that it was offering to tens of thousands of other intra-America migrants—an unobtrusive government, low property taxes, an orgiastic display of cheap land, and machine-cooled interiors that fronted a heroic wilderness. One Chamber of Commerce brochure from 1958 promised a playtime milieu of swimming pools amid a dotting of postcard-perfect saguaros: "Ranch living has become almost standard with Tucson executives who are still within easy driving distance of all the city's commercial and industrial areas." Why would you want to live in Des Plaines or Worcester when this was an option? The segregation was tidy and nearly complete, even though immigrant Mexican labor had quietly helped to build a huge number of the homes in the Foothills.

The city had rocketed to prosperity on the same factors that had driven the Gadsden Purchase in 1854: race and technology. Then the race question had been one of American slaves and not cheap Mexican labor, and the technology had been that of the railroad instead of the automobile. But the base factors were the same.

None of this invented landscape would have been possible without artificial cooling. Summers were close to unbearable, and one common night practice was to hang wet bedsheets from the eaves of a porch and drag a cot nearby, where the evaporation created a cooling effect. This trick of nature was aided with the advent of a device called a "swamp cooler"—a large box lined with wet excelsior pads and a large fan that blew out moisturized air. Chemical air-conditioning was more expensive, but in the twenties the Carrier Engineering Corporation of Newark, New Jersey, introduced the Weathermaker unit, which could hang mounted in a window. Phoenix soon led the nation in unit sales, which were up to one million per year by 1953.

The era of the wet bedsheet was over. Adobe walls became decorative instead of practical, as the A/C unit became like a family hearth without the conviviality of a central gathering spot. It also enticed big defense companies to relocate there. "Motorola management feels that refrigeration cooling is the complete solution to the Phoenix summer heat problem," said Dan Noble, the executive vice president of the transistor company, which moved a plant to Phoenix in 1949. Howard Hughes built a missile factory in Tucson two years later, and his company made an appeal for new managers based on cowboy grit and a swimming pool lifestyle. "Arizona was settled by men who dared to be different . . . and carved out a new life in their own frontier," said one of their promotional brochures. "If you are interested in not only a new way of personal life but a different concept of professional life, we would like to talk about specific opportunities for you at Hughes-Tucson."

Though the selling of Tucson almost always involved promoting the cowboy image that had become a staple of American culture through dime novels and Western television dramas, there was actually a dearth of activity associated with ranches. As the historian Lydia Otero has pointed out, the city was importing almost all of its chilled beef from Los Angeles or Phoenix packinghouses by the time of the automobile era, and U.S. Census data at the time of World War II listed almost nobody who was employed in any sort of trade that involved cattle "with the possible exception of specialty souvenir and western apparel retailers." The prototypical Tucsonan was no grizzled cowpuncher but rather a wealthy retiree who wasn't interested in paying high taxes. The graying gentry were Tucson's future, said one city official in 1966, because they "require no schools and few services."

Abundant rounds of golf and tennis kept things lively on the weekends, and few lures turned out to be better for attracting bank lending than a big golf resort, which functioned as security in late-twentieth-century Arizona, much like fields of good clay loam had in nineteenth-century Iowa. Town building always requires a core commodity, and here the tangible product was leisure and lifestyle. Jumbo-sized tract homes lined up around the fairways like bungalows at a boardwalk. One of the first of these, Skyline Country Club, was envisioned by its founders as a second-tier Palm Springs for bored Californians. Their estate was among the best, a plateau in the northernmost part of the foothills hard up against the saguaro-speckled wall of the Catalinas, with a gorgeous view of the nighttime lights of the city below. Any hoi polloi from that city would face scrutiny from the twenty-four-hour guard at the entrance road if they came up for a look. Those without an explicit invitation were barred. An official club summary of its history says with no irony: "John Bender and Leonard Savage were so enamored with the pristine site in 1959, they dreamed of a way to preserve and privatize it, making it permanently accessible to privileged residents, members and guests."

That noble word—"dreaming"—invariably shows up in the origin stories of the mega–golf resorts, as though importing nonnative grass and erecting casitas for high-income visitors, and keeping out the riffraff, elevates a successful business plan into a deed of valor. A floor-covering distributor named Lou Landon had come out from Chicago the previous year and found a ranch for sale in the bottomlands of the Canada del Oro—"Valley of Gold"—a dirt drainage which flowed only in pounding rains. He hired the Maddox Construction Company to come out and make what he called the Oro Valley Country Club. Sam Nanini founded his own cotton and alfalfa farm down the wash. He seeded the flatlands with Bermuda grass, bulldozed in some artificial topography, and hired Robert Bruce Harris to draw the new meadows of what would become Tucson National Golf Club, an island of emerald ringed with million-dollar homes. "Golf," said Nanini, "will become one of America's most popular participating sports, because deep within everyone there's a desire to excel in some way, and golf provides that opportunity." A publicity photograph showed Harris in the midst of bulldozed land, holding a roll of blueprints and pointing off in the distance. Sam Nanini stands awkwardly next to him in a porkpie hat, his face utterly blank, his eyes as flat as glass.

The northwest side of Tucson mushroomed up like this along the spine of Oracle Road—an archipelago of leisure communities, golf resorts, and family starter homes and second homes on the choicest hill-tops for the absentee wealthy; sandwiched between them were the fake-arched retail plazas with their chain supermarket anchors, gas stations with flanks of pump islands, and occasional mobile-home warrens with false escutcheons and lattice-board and flowerpots covering up the sun-cracked wheels. "It's been crazy," recalled Sam Nanini's barber, Tom Blakeman. "When the country clubs were built out here, it was destined to grow." The seat of government was fifteen miles away at the Pima County Courthouse, where a three-man bloc of supervisors empathetic to the homebuilders guaranteed that the planning codes were weak sauce, commercial rezonings would always go smoothly, and anything that looked like annexation would be stomped like a tarantula. Property taxes were rock-bottom. So were services. The sheriff did patrols, the fire trucks would come if you called, but that was about it. Water was dispensed from private companies. The schools, housed in modernist huts, were reliably mediocre. The nearest library or park was down in Tucson, whose downtown was steadily becoming a shabby husk of half-emptied office plinths. The big department stores—Jacomes, Steinfelds, and the rest—had left for the air-conditioned indoor suburban malls, the first of which, El Con, had been built on the chipped remains of the vanquished El Conquistador resort, a victim of bankruptcy. Only its water tower remained. Its garish turquoise dome was trucked up to Nick Gemematas's new shopping strip mall off Oracle Road, Casa Blanca Plaza, where it was hoisted atop the new retail village as a kind of trophy wrenched from an older Tucson that had been just as caught up in an architectural fantasy.

One of the only forces that attempted to stitch northwest Tucson into a coherent village, or at least the pantomime of one, was a weekly newspaper called the *Territorial*, which took its name from a television program. "We had picked out all kinds of names for our paper and had just about settled on the *Times*," said the founding publisher, Ed Jewett.

"But this old printer was nuts about a weekly television western called *Tombstone Territory* and suggested that we ought to use the word 'territory' somewhere in our title. I thought, well, this used to be a territory, so why not call it the *Arizona Territorial*?" To the side of its stylized Old West serif nameplate, the paper billed itself as "Servicing the Catalina Foothills, Casas Adobes, and Country Club areas," a motto that revealed perhaps more than the publisher intended. He had come out to Tucson as an air force public relations man in the early 1960s to ease the city's jitters about being at the center of a ring of Titan II nuclear missile silos, and thusly an attractive target for the Soviets' first launching. The newspaper came with a lot of photos of new houses, profiles of residents at play, and coverage of rezonings.

Ed Jewett's son, Jack, sold most of the ads for the *Territorial*, and he went on to get a law degree, serve three terms in the state legislature, and is now president of the Flinn Foundation, which supports biotechnical research. When I met him in his office recently I asked him what effect the *Territorial* may have had on making northwest Tucson a more interconnected place.

"Well, it wasn't a true community," he said flatly. "It was a place designed by developers. There was no real glue that held it together, no central character, and we tried to force it. For me, what was real about the place were just a few traditions. There was an annual pancake breakfast, for example. A Kiwanis Club. There was one center—the Casas Adobes center—where there was a flower shop, the Coat of Arms restaurant, the local Food Giant. That was kind of the glue."

The northwest side of Tucson was an expression of the old American yearning for liberty, but it did not at all reflect the American tradition of an interdependent community. As James Howard Kunstler has observed, community *is* the economy—one never happens without the other. And in a geography where the economy was footed almost entirely on the values of privacy and the leisurely enjoyment of wealth, one could hardly expect an interconnected mass of people who cared about each other to spring up as if by magic. The deep structures that would have encouraged it simply weren't there. Genuine moments of shared purpose happened on rare occasions, and usually by accident and chance. For the unmotivated, it rarely gelled. For those who sought it, there was more effort than usual required, given the lack of physical commons. The national virtue of togetherness was never drawn into the design. There was a distinct divide in between the Foothills, with its curving empty streets, and the grid of straight angles in the valley euphemistically called "the inner city."

Empty land had been a blessing to Nanini, and it made attractive bait for those who themselves wanted to make a monument to their own work and leisure, yet the acreage also functioned as a curse, because it encouraged people to follow the impulse of personal retreat rather than engagement. Developers had negotiated settlements with the county to occasionally provide some land for an elementary school, or pay an "impact fee," but there was no thought given to the interconnectivity of all the neighborhoods that had been bladed overnight out of the desert scrub. The open spaces that the newcomers had sought pulled them apart, catering to and giving physical shape to their worst impulses of solitude even as the northern reaches of Tucson functioned as a perfect dealer's showcase of individualism: one's own lot; one's own building envelope and property perimeters; one's own interpretation of a carefree Arizona life. The shared public spaces were not parks or sidewalks but the roads where people were boxed in their vehicles.

In this comfortable remove from the reality of the valley, it would have been difficult to formulate a more certain prescription for systematic loneliness. People with nothing but time on their hands began to make trips to the ABCO and the Food Giant just to see other people. "Now American supermarkets are not designed to function like Parisian cafes," wrote James Howard Kunstler. "There is no seating, no table service. They do not encourage customers to linger. Yet some shoppers will spend as much time as their dignity affords haunting the supermarket aisles because it is practically the only place where they can be in the public realm and engage in some purposeful activity around other live human beings."

❖

What is the true essence of a friendship? What draws us to certain selected people on a level that goes beyond the fact that they merely amuse us? I have never found a satisfying answer to this question in a general sense, but I can say without a doubt that what I most respected about Gabrielle was the way that she was able to turn herself into the kind of rooted person that I had wanted to be. My inner strategy had always been one of escape, a silent self-declaration to the lasting failure at Orange Grove and every other disappointment, *Well, hey, I don't really belong here anyway, and never have.* Gabrielle chose instead to dig a foxhole and fight. I was not at all her only friend, of course; she had multiple confidants and collected people in her life like treasured artwork, but this, too, was a trait I admired, and maybe because the way she did it was similar to my own way, which was to keep archipelagos of friends from different eras that didn't necessarily intersect.

I know part of the reason why I liked her is that she saw Arizona in a way that I hadn't really considered. From disparate spots within both her parents—Spencer's tire trade across the border and Gloria's pursuit of colonial art—Gabrielle had inherited a deep appreciation for its attachment to Mexico, and they had taken her there often, especially to a vacation house in the seaside town of Guaymas. There was a small scar on her lower cheek that she'd received from fainting on Mexican asphalt. They had gotten out of the car to switch seats when she passed out in the heat and went down. Mexico never was the alien forest to her that it tends to be in the imagination of many Arizonans, who see only the grimy border cities and dart across only as an afternoon ceramic-buying adventure. Gabrielle understood it as fundamentally attached to the United States, with its own respirations that demanded curiosity instead of fear. She spoke fluent Spanish, which had been polished during a year she spent on a Fulbright scholarship in Chihuahua, living with a colony of old Mennonites who had settled there in the twenties. It was intimidating to listen to her talk at what seemed to me to be light-speed Spanish with people in her neighborhood south of downtown, which was one of Tucson's oldest, and one with a faint echo of Europe.

In Barrio Viejo, the narrow town houses are packed tight on the blocks, and the lot lines go up to the sidewalks, per the guidelines of the 1573 Law of the Indies. These homes were standing when William Oury was plotting the Camp Grant massacre. Gabrielle's house was a detached adobe flat concealed behind a high metal gate. Parked in the yard was her Toyota 4Runner and parked inside the house on the polished poured-concrete floor (she disliked carpet) was a Vespa motorbike painted with Southwestern designs.

We took meandering walks around Barrio Viejo when I would come down to Tucson. Her gait was a liquid slide, as though there was a slow boogie-woogie playing in the background of her thoughts. One summer night she took me to a crumbling brick crib full of flickering glass candles, just south of the parking lot near the convention center. This was a spot she cherished, and I felt embarrassed to have grown up in Tucson and not even heard of it until she showed it to me. Walking around with Gabrielle was like that; her mind encompassed the horizons of the place where she lived. El Tiradito is a shrine dating to the 1870s that is not officially recognized by the Catholic Church because it commemorates the death of a sinner, a nameless traveling gambler and seducer who was supposedly killed by a jealous husband. Another version of the story involves an illegal border crossing. A son came up from a Mexican village to find his lost father, who had come to Tucson for work. He shows up at the house and is invited in by his father's new wife, who explains that her husband was out chopping wood. When he came home he failed to recognize his own son, assumed the young man was there to cuckold him, and then chopped him to death there in the kitchen with the ax he was holding.

El Tiradito means "the castaway" or "the outcast." People scrawl down wishes and prayers on scraps of paper and stick them into cracks between the bricks, like a Southwestern version of the Wailing Wall. A lot of them involve hopeless love and lost causes. In 1971, Tucson's shrine to the loner was put on the National Register of Historic Places as a political maneuver: It blocked the path of an expressway connector that would have plowed more asphalt and exhaust through the barrio. Gabrielle knew all about this semihidden history, knew where the really good hole-in-the-wall taquerias were on South Sixth, knew whom to call on the city council about a problem with the lights at Santa Rita Park, things that I could not have figured out.

Another time we went out walking at night and wound up at a hipster bar on Congress Street, which had been a post-Eisenhower ghost drag when I was a kid but had made an impressive rebound in the nineties with art galleries and a few beery nightclubs with live music. We sat outside in plastic chairs on the sidewalk patio and she took birdie sips of a Negra Modelo, as was her custom. Beer bottles were like hourglasses to her. They had been grilling steaks on this patio and, as a gag, she filched the meat thermometer and stuck it under her bare armpit to see if the mercury would rise. It did by just a hair, and she laughed in that Gabby way, with her head cocked back comically, eyes squinted shut.

A happy drunk in a Hawaiian shirt wandered out to the patio and joined us. He either worked at this bar or knew someone who did, because he was gleefully mixing up mojitos, the Cuban rum drink with crushed mint. He drew the word out with each new round—*mojiiiito*. I sipped mine and wished the guy would buzz off. Gabrielle ignored the drinks and drew the guy out a bit, which shut him up about the mojtios. He had been fired from his computer job and didn't have a lot of hope for finding a new one. The story got melancholy and took a detour through his woman trouble. But she did not interrupt. She never interrupted people.

This seemed a revealing habit to me, a small crack that gave you a peep of what lay inside the walls. If you started to talk at the same moment with her, she always stopped and ceded the floor to you, even when you tried to give it back. I took it as either a mark of exceptionally good manners or that perhaps she just really preferred to listen. She had the gift of drawing a translucent bubble around whomever she was chatting with, clueing them with nonverbal energy into the small conspiracy she had immediately developed with them against the rest of the world—a private cahoots. I have noticed that this is a spellcasting talent of truly successful players: university presidents, CEOs, and diplomats. In Gabby's case it felt completely artless and unconscious. Her heart seemed guided by an affinity for others. Her pointed curiosity could make them feel either special or a little intimidated by her close attention. Her way of showing disapproval was to be light-hearted about it, in a giggly way that defused awkwardness but telegraphed disappointment under the laugh. "Charisma" is a word I've often heard in association with Gabrielle, but it was of the sort that played best not over the rostrum but in a one-on-one conversation, and not with the slightly manipulative edge that the word sometimes implies. I never once heard her tell a lie, in public or private.

As she listened to the drunk ramble on, I could see her brow get wrinkly and her eyes turn a highly efficient color. She had told the guy of a lead he ought to chase—one of her many friends around town who owned businesses—and as we were walking away west on Congress, she started making an out-loud list of other ideas she could e-mail to him.

Once she showed me a stack of her old homework from Tanque Verde Elementary School, stored up lovingly in a cardboard box by her mother. Amid the colorful construction paper and drawings was a short essay on lined paper, written with the kind of thick pencils that can fit into a child's fist. The question from the teacher had been what she wanted to be when she grew up, and she hadn't answered with an occupation like firefighter, dancer, or politician. She wrote instead that the point of life was to try to be a good person "and not think about death too much." That last part I can quote directly. Perhaps this essay had come immediately after that awful moment in childhood when the intellectual reality of dying finally hits home—not just for Grandpa but for *us*, that beyond this experience of light, sound, and color there might be nothing waiting on the other side but silence and darkness with no end.

Gabrielle's first coping strategy for this inconceivable possibility wasn't a bad one, and, in fact, it would later shape her adult life.

She didn't grow up with much talk about religion in the house—"I was raised to respect all religions," she once said, in a debate about a symbolic church-state issue—but she decided to embrace the Judaism on her father's side after a junket to Israel sponsored by the American Jewish Committee in 2001. Feeling the tactile sensations of the land of the Bible, talking with Israeli politicians, and seeing the tense environment up close had impressed her. She called it "a land of contradiction, of complexity and simplicity." In a political context, too, voters like to know what kind of spiritual filter their representative is presumably passing the issues through. On the biographical questionnaires that elected officials are constantly filling out, she began to write "Jewish" on the religion line, and spoke up more in her speeches about how she was beginning to think of herself, without mincing words, as a Jewish woman. This hurt her not a bit in Tucson, where the casual anti-Semitism that had been floating about in Gif Giffords's day had almost totally evaporated. She became an attendee of the Congregation Chaverim, a synagogue on the northwest side with an open doctrinal attitude. Even there her beliefs were more about the collective good than her private concerns, rooted primarily, as her rabbi, Stephanie Aaron, would say, in the Hebrew concept of *tikkun olam*, which means "healing the world," or bringing justice into broken places.

Yeah, but was there any such thing as a benevolent God or a life after this? I asked her this in the back corner of a Fourth Avenue bar called Che's Lounge. Were we really going anywhere? This was a question that has haunted me ever since my own awareness of my inevitable death, which had been prompted at age nine after I read a *Peanuts* Sunday strip in which Snoopy tells Woodstock that he has decided to stop worrying, because most of what he was worrying about wasn't going to happen anyway. A little voice then sounded up from the murk of my subconscious: *Well, except for death*. That always gets you. No compromise or negotiation. The sudden thought of a silent forever not too many years away, nonsight, nonhearing, nonexistence, *non*, *non*, *non*, so terrified me that I cried all evening long, head in my arms at the kitchen table. There was a distinct possibility that all the churches and their soothing words were just a bunch of socially constructed nonsense covering up a howling nothingness. Ever since, and into adulthood, it has been one of my primary frustrations (I believe I speak for many here) that positive empirical data about this question is denied us, lying beyond the furthest edges of sensual perception. Whether that's by clever design or by the intrinsic meaninglessness of the universe is yet another maddening riddle. Though I believe the evidence favors God, the best we can do, beyond having faith, is to surmise.

So what happens, I asked her, when we come to the end?

She shook her head over her untouched beer and smiled, almost playfully.

"Game over," she said.

Her belief at that time in her life—in her early thirties—resembled an idea that dates to the ancient Greeks: that death is the thing that gives life its essence. Without an opposite, a thing has no meaning. There is no wet without dry, no warm without cold. The purpose and texture of life was highly charged because it had to come to an end. Beauty is only beauty because it cannot last forever. Everyone had to decide at some point what their life is supposed to mean in this extremely valuable context, and she had made the existential decision after getting out of the tire business that her purpose for being born was public service and helping other people. That was the unified field theory of her life. All of her waking actions were going to be guided by it henceforth. And she meant it.

Gabrielle hated the idea of a wasted day. She rose early and quickly got restless if no activities had been planned—even a two-hour filler like a desert hike or a bike ride or a museum visit. For Saturday morning entertainment she went to community board meetings. She wrote cursive thank-you notes as a compulsion. I never saw her desk clean. Energy poured out from inner kilowatts that she seemed to possess like few others I've met. She was burningly *alive* in an essential way. Once in an e-mail, trying to persuade me to do something, she quoted me a lengthy passage from the Paul Bowles novel *The Sheltering Sky*, which is about a married couple adrift on a bad holiday in the Moroccan side of the Sahara Desert. "Because we don't know when we will die, we get to think of life as an inexhaustible well. Yet everything happens only a certain number of times, and a very small number really. How many more times will you remember a certain afternoon of your childhood, some afternoon that is so deeply part of your being that you can't even conceive of your life without it? Perhaps four or five times more, perhaps not even that. How many more times will you watch the full moon rise? Perhaps twenty. And yet it all seems limitless."

Embracing vanishing life meant, for her, embracing the place where she was from. She had left it behind once, much as I did. She chose to go not to the University of Arizona but to Scripps College in Pomona, California, an all-women's school where she majored in Latin American studies and sociology, and then for a graduate degree in urban planning at Cornell University in Ithaca, New York, where she played up her Arizona cowgirl heritage for effect, wearing vests and cowboy boots to class. She was drawn to urban planning because of the negative example of some of Tucson's worst mistakes—the six-lane avenues, the leap-frogging subdivisions, the lack of human interconnectedness of the end result.

She cut short a job as a consultant with Pricewaterhouse in Manhattan to come back when her father called her and said he was too sick to run El Campo anymore. She came out and took over as CEO, resolving to make the best of it. "I really think I can change this industry," she told *Inside Tucson Business*. "The tire world is hard to relate to—it's not very glamorous. . . . I really think there's a great potential for independent tire dealers." She religiously watched the competitors' advertisements and had her salespeople call them for prices to make sure nobody was offering better deals.

So we were both early-midlife homecomers, but one of the critical differences between us was that Gabrielle *wanted* to be there, whereas I viewed it as a distraction, a kind of airport layover. I knew I would probably squeak out again, à la "Thunder Road," and while I was stopped there I could get to know a few people and maybe tell a few good stories, and moon about how Arizona was a beautiful but messed-up place, a dirge about the inherent sinfulness of the earth that a Calvinist might have recognized. Gabrielle chose to make this flawed burg her home, to be present in the present time and simply accept it, and to throw herself into the cause of making things in Arizona just slightly better for her having been there, without any psychological reserve. Her attitude was similar to the existentialism of Albert Camus, who had said that the work you do on earth may never have any transcendent value, and may in fact be meaningless and one day swallowed up by the white-dwarfing sun, but that it was through the work itself that meaning is ultimately created and where the personal rebellion against dark death and the ridiculous fate of the universe takes place.

Tucson kept pushing out, reaching around and in back of Pusch Peak like a tentacle, going farther and farther up Oracle Road into what had been virgin desert. Golf-and-casita mazes more capacious than anything Sam Nanini could have imagined sprang up as Rancho Vistoso and Dove Mountain and Saddlebrooke, selling mostly to the middle-aged and the elderly.

The game of golf—pastoral in appearance—was the major pilot fish for the spreading urbanization of Arizona. One economic study claimed it was responsible for at least six thousand full-time jobs in the state, with annual cash revenues higher than that of milk, cotton, or farm-grown vegetables. High-toned spa resorts also catered to the vacationing wealthy and gave Tucson some international panache. In 1979, Mel Zuckerman founded the Canyon Ranch Health Resort on the site of an old dude ranch on the northeast side of town, and it quickly became a favorite of visiting celebrities and Condé Nast magazine writers. "We have wonderful scenery and climate, a stable and able corps of well-educated professionals, and a commitment to assuring guests an excellent vacation experience," Zuckerman told a journalist.

At the corner of Oracle and Ina, where most of the auto-centered growth had begun, the trust that controlled the old Nanini inheritance announced that it was demolishing an outdated financial center, sweeping the footprint clean, and erecting a new supermarket plaza anchored by a Safeway.

The corner seemed vaguely cursed, though the car-traffic numbers were golden. The Tahiti Restaurant had burned down because of a grease fire in 1976. The glass atrium at the Nanini financial center was too large and weird looking. Tenants had mostly stayed away, and the occupancy rate was bad. The second-growth plaza would be called "La Toscana Village," in celebration of Sam Nanini's Italian background and in homage to the Mediterranean theme across the street at Casas Adobes Plaza. The county paved the parking lot in exchange for the rerouting of a wash underneath the lot, so there was, in effect, an unseen subterranean river flowing right by the Safeway. But grandson Steve Nanini wasn't pleased with the first blueprints of the facade. The squat towers of the new grocery were too garish, "a Disneyland front," he thought. "I was going to do the deal," he told me, "but got disenchanted with doing a strip center of that nature."

Ownership soon passed to CSY Investments of Roseville, California, which was owned by a thirty-year-old Hong Kong multimillionaire named Chee S. Yaw whose fortune had come from clear-cut lumber harvesting all over Malaysia. The Chinese takeover of the British outpost of Hong Kong was looming, and the wealthy feared the new government was going to seize their assets. They dumped liquidity into whatever Canadian or American real estate looked promising, and Tucson offered up a land banquet.

One of these properties was La Toscana Village, in front of which at least sixty thousand cars were passing each day. Yaw hired a Tucson developer named Andy Kelly to head the project, and Kelly didn't disappoint. Nanini had already sold building pads for a Safeway and a Walgreens that were—unfortunately—next to each other, which minimized the foot-traffic potential between the two. But Kelly was determined to do a total project instead of a bastardized one, and he leased out a nail salon, a video store, and a Chinese restaurant to fill out the appendage. "It was an easy shopping center," he concluded. "I was proud of it."

The firm of Gromtazky Dupree and Associates from Dallas, Texas, was hired to design the architecture, including the gray cast arches, mansard roof tiles, and patio spaces with outdoor tables that gave the plaza a Tuscan dressing, though it was indisputably a grocery with a lakelike parking lot. The archways were designed to provide a lot of shade from the sun, keeping it directly off the plate glass of the front windows, and as a capturing space for breezes.

"The geometry in the arches and the buildings is proud in its character," the original architect, Kevin Morrow, told me when I called him up. "The mission was to develop a sense of place. I think it matured pretty nicely." The shopping plaza officially opened for business in 1992.

People who lived nearby in Sam Nanini's original neighborhood were mostly pleased with the results, even those who were inclined to be cranky about the noise and traffic. Pete Vucoc, an activist with a house nearby who had successfully led an effort to keep a big Home Depot store away from another location, said La Toscana conformed with the philosophy of putting shopping plazas at major intersections rather than in the middle of long streets. That way at least a remnant of node development might be preserved. "It was very impressive and [there was] a lot of friendly support for it," he said. "I never heard any criticism, and there was [sic] plenty of chances for that."

The Tuscany theme might have been an accident of Steve Nanini's ancestral nostalgia, but it also happened to tap into a wildly popular design motif in the urban Arizona of the twenty-first century. That section of north-central Italy—with its dewy associations of Lombardy poplars, crisp wines, and rich royal patrons and their pet artists—is second only to Spanish mission in the volume of its architectural quotation. Scottsdale features more than twenty different businesses with some version of Tuscan in their name, including restaurants, apartment complexes, subdivisions, a golf course, a nail salon, and a day spa called Villa

Toscana. There is a Tuscan Estate Homes and various Tuscan-style custom-built McMansions dotted here and there in the desert, with wrought-iron balconies and spider cracks deliberately chipped into the exterior walls for added *palazzo di pirro* credibility. The madness for the Tuscan vocabulary is closely linked with the image of "sun, hills, good food, warmth, friendliness, wine," a branding expert told Jaimee Rose of *The Arizona Republic*. All the usual menu items, in other words, sought by internal American migrants in a mildly exotic place like Arizona, where they could reconstruct a fresher, grander, and more relaxed version of themselves in midlife yet where the dollar is legal tender, the television programs are in English, horseradish is offered upon request, and the traffic laws are unthreatening.

R. Brooks Jeffrey is the head of the Drachman Institute of the College of Architecture and Landscape Architecture at the University of Arizona. He told me that La Toscana Village is in sync with the local habit of what he calls "putting a dress on it," that is, a conscious rejection of the native values and landscapes of Arizona in favor of an evocation of a disconnected place. "It really bothers me [that] we have this inferiority complex about what we are. Do we need to associate ourselves with civilizations that are long gone? Our built environments should reflect the desert. This says that the way we naturally respond to this place is somehow inappropriate. This year it's Tuscan. Next year, it'll be something else."

This simulacrum of a "village," then, a bad photocopy of an older America, was the true patrimony of the northwest side. Having lost a memory of the actual past, and in the liberty-seeking desire to escape one's own confusing past, we had created a terra-cotta horizon of an invented past, one with the most tenuous and wandering sense of what Tucson was actually supposed to be. "We had a pioneering spirit," reflected Jack Jewett. "But how much of that community was real and how much did we try to force?"

Shops came and went from La Toscana Village and the traffic thickened on Oracle Road. The Blockbuster video store went under and a

Beyond Bread sandwich shop took its place. Casas Adobes Flowers moved in from across the street. Geppetto's failed and its shell went up for lease. The red bricks on the ersatz arches faded a bit in two decades of sunlight. Commerce was transacted, box wine was drunk, hasty salad meals were digested, receipts were banked, managers quit and were replaced, old customers died in their sleep and went unseen without further explanation, and life went on as it always had. In January of 2007, Gabrielle Giffords, newly elected to the U.S. House of Representatives, picked Sam Nanini's Casas Adobes shopping center, across the street from La Toscana Village, for the very first event where she set out to meet her constituents in a casual place, an event called Congress on Your Corner.

I had to be careful about my friendship with Gabrielle in one small way: There was probably no scenario in which I could have written about her at length in the news columns with any objectivity. I therefore could not cover the legislature for *The Arizona Republic*, which would have been ridiculous good fun. When an offer to temporarily fill in at the capitol bureau came along, I had to turn it down. Though she was in the minority (the Democrats being a more or less permanent minority), she would have shown up in the daily mishmash of events, and it would have been tricky. Gabrielle was, in the words of another reporter, "the belle of the ball" down there in any case.

Unlike many other politicians of both parties, for whom whining about reporters is a cherished pastime, Gabrielle genuinely seemed to like the people assigned to cover her and went out of her way to get to know them. Perhaps it was her respect for the intrinsic value of hard data, or the openness of American government, or maybe she just liked to read good material. I think she also understood the pragmatic valuation that so many elected officials forget—that reporters tend to respond to rejection on the level of a whacked puppy, and that whether consciously or not, too many unreturned phone calls and refusals to dole out necessary information results in suspicion and, in advanced cases, hostile or bitchy coverage. The worst criticism of the press I ever heard Gabrielle make was one that I actually agreed with: The majority of reporters are just plain lazy and don't work hard enough to get the real inside story of why events play out the way they do. Her problem with reporters, such as it is, is that they are not aggressive enough.

I was beginning to question my own taste for the fight. The *Republic* had gone through a sea change of management, and stories were getting shorter and airier. The Virginia corporation that owned the paper was asking for eye-aching page designs that included a swirl of colored graphics, charts, and tidbits, plus lots of space devoted to microneighborhood news in a city where neighborhoods were probably some of the most synthetic creations in America. The job was getting less fun by the day. I was reassigned to cover the government of the city of Phoenix from a rehabilitated broom closet on the eleventh floor of city hall. It was a prestigious beat, and there was ample opportunity to make at least a tiny bit of positive difference and write about some of the issues that had always bothered me about Arizona—lax zoning, unsustainable growth patterns, free passes for fast-nickel builders—but the new format of the paper wasn't built for that sort of thing, and it was easier on most days to just roll with the flow.

Being a reporter had been a means of self-protection. Now it seemed less like a holy mission and more like a rote chore. I felt different thoughts flopping around inside, looking for a way to get out. I wanted to write longer and harder stories, to be some hazy version of a "real" writer and say necessary things that would have no logical estate in a newspaper. As my thirty-fifth birthday approached, the point that the Bible says is the midpoint of a man's life span of "threescore years and ten," I knew I had to make a change, and it probably involved an act that was becoming a *Groundhog Day* recurrence over the long haul, which was, once again, packing up the car and leaving Arizona. That also meant leaving behind nearness to Mom and Dad, time spent with an aging grandmother, a steady paycheck, dependable health care, familiar landscapes, and the friends I'd made.

One of them, in particular, gave me a hard shove toward what eventually turned into an extremely good decision.

In the late spring of 2003 I went down to Tucson to see my parents, and Gabrielle was free that weekend, too. I really wanted her final opinion on this before taking action. We had a coffee at the Epic Café and then went walking south on Fourth Avenue, the closest thing to a bohemian quarter that Tucson has yet pulled off. It grew up in the twenties as a strip of businesses catering to the nearby student ghettoes at the U of A and became funky and a little druggy in the seventies, with used-clothing stores and bookshops and an old journalists' hangout called The Shanty, which had an outer façade with a silhouette of a Gay Nineties character doffing a bowler cap. There was a smattering of blonde-girl college bars where the ID checking wasn't always rigorous and the sticky standby of Che's Lounge where Gabrielle had delivered her pronouncement on mortality.

I can't remember exactly how the conversation unfolded, though I'm sure it involved a certain amount of out-loud agonizing on my part on whether ditching my job was truly a wise or dumb decision, and whether I was condemning myself to poverty, failure, etc. She listened for a bit, and then started in on me.

I had become a journalist for a deeper reason, she said, and the only true failure would be the one that would settle in like a vulture on a branch if I did not pursue this possibly foolish ambition flailing around inside. It was important to follow that calling and not look back. Everything would work out; the material things would take care of themselves; the important thing was creating the words and following the dream.

By this point, and as she was reaching a kind of peroration, we were sitting on a wooden bench outside a clothing store some storeowner had put there as a hospitable gesture to passersby, and I rested my elbows on my knees and hunched forward a bit in the sun, a confessional posture. Then came the fragment from that afternoon that I can repeat directly. It still ranks as one of the best, most well-timed bits of encouragement anyone has ever given to me. "I believe in you," she said.

I remember clearly that wooden bench and I remember her saying those words. They didn't have a magical effect at that moment, and I probably offered some kind of embarrassed thanks and moved the conversation on to another place, but it was exactly what I needed to hear in that moment, and I never forgot it. It settled like a drop of food coloring in a glass that eventually turns the whole water red.

There are throwaway lines in everybody's life that end up having a time-release impact: a muttered comment from a coach, a parent's hasty evaluation, a teacher's observation scribbled in the margins of an essay, a friend's advice at a critical hour. Those casual words can draw blood and hurt grievously, but they also have tremendous power to uplift and embolden. What errata we latch on to from the roaring river of words that passes through our ears isn't always plainly logical, and this certainly wasn't the first time she had said a really nice thing to me, but her summary analysis on a shop bench at the side of Fourth Avenue on a May afternoon marked the apogee of that particular choice to leave my career as a newspaper reporter and step out into unmapped territory. I reminded Gabrielle of that exchange on the bench years later, and she had no memory of having spoken that phrase to me, but it didn't matter at all. The encouraging words that friends toss at each other are like that. Most of the words don't really stick; they are pleasant rain wash that evaporates quickly and is forgotten, but some do burrow their way into the heart word-for-word, and the listener remembers them with diamond clarity, even if the speaker does not.

From that point on, it was a relative breeze. I ended my lease the following week and walked into the editor's office and quit with cordiality and thanks. And on the night of July 4, after my last full day at the paper, on what turned out to be my last-ever day as a newspaper reporter, with my Jeep loaded to the roof and ready to roll north to I wasn't sure where, I stood on the roof of a midtown Phoenix parking garage and watched the popping of municipal fireworks with Gabrielle, and we promised to stay in touch, of course. Friends drift like migratory birds through different phases in a life, and there are always pledges to "stay in touch," but she turned out to be of the sort that really meant it.

After a month of sleeping in the Jeep and bathing in roadside rivers, I ended up in Missoula, Montana, in a cheap apartment whose window looked out onto a faded advertisement painted on the side of a brick building. The apartment was also next to a division point of the Burlington Northern Santa Fe, and the crashing of the boxcars coupling at night made the walls shake to the joists. I bought a five-dollar folding card table from the thrift store across the street, and put my old Macintosh on top of it, and started writing short stories. They weren't terribly good. That didn't matter. I proved to myself that I could keep my ass steady in the folding metal chair for long stretches and tease out the words. I slept on a blow-up mattress and made soups that lasted for half a week. In the evenings I would take walks down along the Clark Fork River, rubbing my fingers, looking at the brown hills, and feeling on fire with possibilities for the first time in years.

Gabrielle wrote postcards to me, full of chatty tidbits about what she was up to in the legislature and the "zzzzz . . ." of her dating life, which frustrated her to no end, because the modern courtship waltz demanded a studied coolness to the other so as not to seem desperate; the "competition to care less," as she put it—a phrase I loved. There was no phone in my small room, so I talked to her on the pay phone down in the stinky lobby at appointed times. How was the writing going, she always wanted to know. Was I ready to do her proud? One day a postcard arrived with a picture of the South Sixth Street Bridge in Springfield, Illinois, and on the back was her cursive.

> *What if you slept? And what if, in your sleep, you went to heaven and there plucked a strange and beautiful flower? And what if, when you awoke, you had the flower in your hand? Ah, what then?*
>
> *—Coleridge*

I tacked it above my computer. Not long after, an e-mail arrived with the subject line "China Magic." She'd gone off on another international legislative junket—this one was to Beijing, sponsored by the National Committee on U.S.-China Relations—and one of her fellow attendees was a U.S. Navy pilot and NASA astronaut named Mark Kelly, with whom she had had some conversational sparks. He was at the end of a marriage and she was in a so-so relationship, but it was worthy of extraordinary comment. When he flew a jet on a mileage mission into Davis-Monthan Air Force Base near Tucson, he paid a call on her, and then told her to look into the sky at a certain time. He dipped a Warthog wing in tribute to her as he flew out. This was heady stuff. Fast cars and other such nifty motor machines had always been like catnip to her. A military jet was setting a higher bar.

I moved away from Montana after a few months of nonstop typing, crashed on the floor of a friend's New York City apartment, and then got a small deal to write a book about the seamy side of the diamond business, with which I had had a lasting obsession after being given back the engagement ring from my lost fiancée from San Francisco. I made two do-or-die research trips to Africa and loaded up on credit-card debt, still living on vegetable soup. Kelly got divorced, and he and Gabrielle started dating seriously that year. No "competition to care less" was present with them. For their first date she took him on a working trip—an official tour of the Arizona State Penitentiary, which she thought he would like because his dad was a cop. She switched from the House to the Senate. Mental Health America of Arizona named her legislator of the year, partly for her work on a failed bill to prohibit insurers from imposing limitations on the treatment of the mentally ill. The state's broken mental health system had been a crusade from her first run for office.

A phone call came from her in the winter of 2005. The local congressman, Jim Kolbe, was calling it quits after twenty years in office. He was a Republican, but a moderate one, and Tucson had a lengthy heritage of supporting Democrats that went back more than a century. The Eighth District was drawn in a way that congressional districts really ought to be drawn—that is, not gerrymandered all to hell, and with a relatively even mix of Rs and Ds. This was a once-in-a-generation event. Perhaps once in a lifetime. Gabrielle had done some hasty soul-searching and thought she might have racetrack odds. Of course it would not be a safe seat. She would probably have to ask, if not plead, for her job every two years. But her temperate record in the Arizona legislature, combined with a pragmatic nonpartisan style that had won her a lot of allies and donors, would make her an automatic giant in the Democratic primary. People found her extremely hard to dislike, even though she could be a ball cutter behind the scenes, when necessary. "I think I'm going to do it," she told me.

Now came a question. Could I help?

Here was a dilemma. Though I was no longer a newspaper reporter, I was still clinging to the code of ethics that forbids overt political activity. My own convictions were fuzzy and without solid labels, but I did have a basic sympathy for benign government programs that attempted to make life better for those who were born without material advantages. I believed the reason America was a great nation was the way it tried (though not perfectly) to give common people a chance at the good life: a free public education, a scholarship to a land-grant college, unemployment insurance, equal protection from criminals by cops who didn't treat them as subhuman, banking laws that would let them have a checkbook instead of having to go to payday lenders. And the furniture of a society that was open to everyone: parks, museums, libraries, and trains. I usually voted the Democratic ticket for these philosophical reasons, but I didn't go around talking about it. To give money to Gabrielle would make my convictions a matter of federal record. And to go assist her with a political event, or even wear so much as a button in public, would be violating a principle of a trade where I was no longer in the guild but still felt spiritually connected. For the very first time, I would be displaying a *bias*. Taking a side.

We were by then deep in the Iraq war, which I privately considered a boondoggle, and I had a problem with the force and simplicity by which the bad intelligence was sold to the electorate. I had felt in my bones from the start that the weapons-of-mass-destruction rationale was a stupendous falsehood. The low standard of proof never would have held water in another realm. And I was taken by surprise by the scorn heaped on those who questioned it—how doubting the wisdom of a foreign military adventure could somehow be twisted into a lack of love for one's country. This is an ancient trick of statist rhetoric, and I got to witness it in my generation. I began getting jingoistic e-mails from a friend from high school, one of those with whom I had giggled the hardest at seventeen while we egged houses and flattened garbage cans. He now lived in a stucco tract home on the edge of Tucson and worked in the home-building industry. These e-mails were strident toward anybody who questioned our need to invade, occupy, and dominate, if not destroy, Iraq. I made the mistake of getting baited, responded with some sarcastic retort, and the e-mails got progressively nastier and without room for compromise. Muslims were "animals" and "filthy ragheads" who deserved racial profiling in airports. People who opposed war were "hippies." Liberal voters "hated America." And so forth. "You know, someday," he wrote me, "there will be another internal conflict here in America . . . a conflict that will result in an uprising. . . . I know exactly who will win (Hint: the Libs will lose.)"

In its apocalyptic hostility, if not the exact language, it mirrored what I was hearing from local hosts on drive-time talk radio. Ugliness seemed to have been unleashed by 9/11, as well as by the uncertainties of an economy that had to keep growing or die. Without a palpable uniformed enemy, Americans were tearing at each other's throats. Did it need to be this way?

I thought of the way that Gabrielle refused to demonize or dismiss people, even the obstructionists in the Arizona legislature with whom she had to deal on a regular basis. Her attitude was less about temporary victories and more about getting things accomplished in the public interest: incremental change that came through sweat and compromise and hard work and not grand superhero gestures for the cheap seats. I didn't agree with her about everything, but a 100 percent overlay of belief is never going to happen with anyone. *Wouldn't the nation be much better off,* I thought, *with more thoughtful people like her in a high position?*

Helping Gabrielle would be inserting myself into the dirty game—a commitment made, a bias declared. My relationship with Arizona had been long and complicated and profoundly mixed. But I was an Arizonan and always would be, by nature as well as by history. It seemed like it was long past time to stop bitching from a distance about all the flaws of my home place and start trying to do something good and positive for it, even in a small way.

There was another powerful element at work, if I am honest with myself. Love has always been a cautious word for me. An expensive one. The feral loneliness of my childhood had made me wary of deep associations and taught me to treasure those who did take root in the heart. I have loved—really truly loved—maybe twenty people in my life. Gabrielle had quietly come to be one of them. There was no romantic element to this, no trace of Eros. It wasn't about that. There is an invisible boundary where the respect and admiration within a friendship do cross over into love, and love has its costs. I called Gabrielle and told her I would move back to southern Arizona that summer to help her.

FIVE

CITIZENSHIP

The town of Bisbee is a leftover from a younger Arizona. Draped in a saddle of the Mule Mountains, the old copper camp looks more Italian than American, with Victorian shacks clinging to scrubby hillsides and a Main Street walled with brick commercial buildings that winds up the drainage of a valley called Tombstone Canyon. The city is a jumble of neighborhoods crammed between the hills at odd angles. At the approximate center is a giant bean-shaped hole that's bigger than three NFL stadiums, surrounded with a rusty chain-link fence, and bordered precariously on one side by Arizona Highway 80. This is the Lavender Pit, the heart of the old Phelps Dodge mining properties, which ceased all operations in 1975 yet has never been officially "closed," mainly for tax purposes. When the mine petered out, the seventies counterculture discovered the funky miners' cottages and the ruined Gilded Age vibe and the dirt-cheap living. An overlord no longer, the Phelps Dodge company sold its luxurious Copper Queen Hotel to an amateur developer for one dollar. Bisbee became a regional haven of art galleries, a Bolinas without the beach but within six miles of the Mexican border and the attendant bazaar of dope. The slopes around town were pitched so crazily that the old high school had ground-level entrances on all four of its floors, which sounds like a tall tale and isn't. In front of the art deco

Cochise County courthouse is a socialist realist statue of a copper miner. He has punched-out chest muscles, and underneath him on a plinth are the words DEDICATED TO THOSE VIRILE MEN THE COPPER MINERS WHOSE CONTRIBUTION TO THE DEVELOPMENT OF THE WEALTH AND LORE OF THE STATE OF ARIZONA HAS BEEN MAGNIFICENT.

This would be my home base for the summer primary season. Cochise County was the massive mountainous balloon on the east side of the congressional district, impressive in size but light in population, which consisted mainly of cattle ranchers, active-duty military stationed at Fort Huachuca, a lot of military retirees who liked the sunshine, aging hippie burnouts in Bisbee, a few rich émigrés living out a cowboy fantasy in custom haciendas, and a big bloc of Latino families near the border in Douglas whose voting habits were strongly Democratic but unreliable in turnout. I was the unpaid volunteer coordinator for the county, which meant it was my job to coax enough volunteers to knock on every known Democrat's door to get them excited about a possible Congresswoman Gabby.

Five hopefuls had already crowded in beside her, and the strongest of them by far was Patty Weiss, a former 6:00 P.M. newscaster from KVOA, who had been pushed out of her job by station management in her middle age. "I have always thought that I would like to serve in Congress," she told the *Star*. "I am a fan of democracy." She couldn't match Gabrielle on facts or experience, but she argued compellingly from the heart, and her name recognition had been soaking into people's dinner hours via television for thirty years. "It's like having Walter Cronkite run for office," exulted the head of the county Democrats. The perception of her populism made her a front runner, and she lined up a raft of endorsements from local pols and donors that ordinarily would have gone to Gabrielle, who was a default establishment pick because of her time in the legislature.

I first went down to Bisbee to meet some people and find a place to crash in the company of Gabe Zimmerman, a young guy who had just finished his degree in social work from Arizona State University and had taken a campaign job for a pittance. The money didn't matter nearly as much as the chance to get a Democrat elected to the U.S. House. He would be my de facto boss in the Tucson campaign office. I liked him instantly. He had dark hair that was a bit on the shaggy Beatles side and his compact car was a mess, with food wrappers, empty Big Gulp cups that had held Diet Dr Pepper, and disordered stacks of glossy campaign flyers scattered all around. When he listened to you he did so with a thoughtful look and his mouth hanging open just a shade. Getting thrown off a porch or having a phone slammed down on him—hazards for any political canvasser—didn't ruffle him a bit. He advised me to keep a sense of humor and not worry too much about holding volunteers accountable. The important thing was to get most of the doors knocked on at least once.

Gabe had old-fashioned ideas about civil service and the responsibility of government to spread justice around. He seemed like a time-traveler. A guy like Gabe could have easily been born in London during the time of the Reform Act of 1832, or been a National Recovery Administration caseworker in West Virginia during the New Deal, or been beaten up on the bridge at Selma. We drove out to Bisbee in separate vehicles—he'd be leaving, but I'd be staying—and a big violent thunderstorm swept through the desert as we climbed up the road that went into the Mule Mountains. Water cascaded off the cactus-covered slopes, and we watched as a mudslide crept toward the road. The squall passed after fifteen minutes, and the skies cleared, following the Arizona weather statutes to the letter. Gabe introduced me to the impressive nucleus of friends he'd already made in the county: a veterinarian, a school principal, a bartender, an electronics salesman, a clinic manager, a county prosecutor, a crusty "Rosie the riveter" woman whose history of political hell-raising went back to her time on the industrial lines in World War II. A sociologist might have called this the network of weak social ties that are so important for establishing a healthy community. Gabe had dug it up within days.

Bisbee was the locus of our efforts. The copper-mining heritage, with all its union activism, and the more recent influx of art lovers, gays and lesbians, and assorted free spirits had made it a virtual dendochronology of Democrats who we could afford to leave alone in the general election. But for the primary, it was key persuasion territory. And from there we could also talk to a lot of ranchers elsewhere in Cochise County. I spent a lot of my days driving from town to town in a white Dodge pickup with a computerized list of voters, a stack of Giffords signs, and a post-pounder hammer in the bed. I erected as many of those red-and-blue signs as I could in places where thickets of them were growing on the side of the road and—when I could get away with it—on strips of land that were probably in the legal right-of-way of the Arizona Department of Transportation. Some of them stayed up longer than they should have.

The western entrance to town was the Mule Pass Tunnel, which was finished in 1957, and it functioned as a metaphor for the looking-glass nature of Bisbee. Here was a trick: On the west side of it, if you kept the radio tuned to 96.1 on the FM dial, you got KLPX, a station of my youth that spewed out a timeless stream of Rush and Ozzy Osbourne. The signal went fuzzy in the tunnel, and on the other side you emerged to KBRP, the little community station downtown that broadcast a stew of strange little talk shows at the approximate wattage of a hair dryer. It wasn't even powerful enough to reach beyond the Lavender Pit. But it completely swallowed up the sound of KLPX's corporate-programmed music at the edge of the tunnel and signaled that you had arrived at a few oddball square miles where time had been frozen during the Spanish-American War, only to be quickly defrosted and refrozen during a year of Vietnam.

One night, after downing a few cocktails in the company of Fred Miller, the bartender at Café Roka, I got in the Dodge and drove up the winding road to the top of Mule Pass, directly above the tunnel's mouth. I tossed a few metal stakes, the post-pounder, and a giant Giffords sign down the fifty-foot precipice and then carefully inched my way down. I made it to the top of the tunnel's lip without injury, took a reckoning of the angle, and then, when no car headlights could be seen coming up the hill, I quickly pounded in a few stakes and mounted up a Giffords sign that was in full and unavoidable view of oncoming traffic. This was ADOT territory, but it stayed up there for several weeks, I think because nobody from the highway crews wanted to scramble down that slope from the top of Mule Pass to rip it down.

Most other evenings I crawled around Bisbee with a clipboard, searching for addresses to check off my list. Affixed to my shirt was a sticker labeled GIFFORDS FOR CONGRESS, a bold patriotic sandwich of red-and-blue made a tiny bit feminine with a line of cursive script for the name Gabrielle. Putting one on for the first time was like the sigh of air going out of a dead balloon. I was accepting the brand. I mounted a lot of concrete staircases put there on the slopes by the Civilian Conservation Corps as a make-work project in the thirties, the homesites having been blasted out of the hills by miners' dynamite. Some of the bungalows were hiding in the brambles of wildly overgrown shrubs. I would knock on the door and go brightly into my spiel about Gabrielle. These doorjamb conversations were usually affable, and often wandered into nonpolitical territory, which was a treat. Part of what I had always loved about being a reporter was the way it drew me out of my observational fortress. The job forces you to go talk to strangers, which can be a wonderful thing.

It brought me a little bit closer in some ways to my father, whose own personality formation also tends toward the introverted, and whose greatest pleasure at his job as a midlevel banker had been the excuse to shoot the digressive bull with one client or another. His employer, the state icon Valley National Bank, had also been swallowed by an out-of-state cost-chopper, as my newspaper had, leading both of us to take early retirements wondering what the hell happened to the professions that had made us feel a little less lonely. Even a butterfly like Gabrielle had once told me that holding office, or running for office, was an excellent pretext to go meet random people who might otherwise be sealed in their solitudes. This was a better citizenship than I'd ever had before: a deeper version of citizenship; an attempt to take ownership of our problems and make our flawed state just a hairsbreadth better.

Canvassing for Gabrielle was a reminder of how variegated the world

really is behind front doors. I talked to old Latino miners, bored housewives, U.S. Border Patrol agents, hot-dog-stand owners, rich architects,
and meth addicts. I met a few guys who'd been in prison, mostly for dope
smuggling. Over in the Lowell neighborhood was a woman who wanted
to know about Gabrielle's personal feelings on firearms. The subtext was,
as it often is, *Will this politician want to take away my gun?* I wanted to
make sure I gave the correct answer, so I called field director Daniel
Graver at headquarters for clarification and then went back to her door.
"Well, she owns a Glock," I told the woman, and that seemed to satisfy
the question enough. I made it a personal mission to knock on every door
in San Jose, a glut of *Brady Bunch* tract homes built in the sixties and
now going to seed. Gabrielle had printed up glossy pieces of literature
about herself, in sepia tones with hokey Old West typography and photos
of herself riding a horse. An Arizona Original, they read. On Satur-
days I armed myself with pocketfuls of Gabrielle propaganda and cheer-
fully bothered the passersby at the weekly farmers' market in the Warren
section of town.

There had been an ugly mob incident at the nearby baseball diamond early in the past century. Bisbee had grown extraordinarily rich
and busy during World War I. Copper was an excellent tool for mecha-
nized combat: It went into bullet jackets, artillery shells, and electrical
wire. The price rocketed from thirteen to twenty-six cents a pound in
two years, and work shifts went on twenty-four hours a day in the subterranean honeycombs under the town, where there was already 150 miles
of mine-car track. The occasional strikes called by the International
Union of Mine, Mill, and Smelter Workers looked more sinister in this
patriotic climate, and people began to whisper that seditious forces
were at work, especially the violent but inept agitators called "Wobblies"
(the nickname for members of the Industrial Workers of the World) who
had become like cutout Halloween goblins for a frightened nation. On
July 11, 1917, Phelps Dodge president Walter Douglas made a speech in
the copper town of Globe in which he warned of a "German influence"
behind the strikes. The next morning in Bisbee two thousand vigilantes

from the Bisbee Citizens' Protective League, all wearing white kerchiefs, went to the doors of suspected union workers and took them out of their homes at gunpoint. Cochise County sheriff Harry Wheeler watched from an open-topped car mounted with a machine gun as the men were herded down to the baseball diamond and told to swear an oath against the unions. Those who refused—1,186 in all, mainly immigrants from Mexico, Britain, and various European nations—were packed into boxcars from the El Paso & Southwestern Railroad and taken for a ride to the east. At 3:00 A.M. the train shuddered to a stop and the men were ordered to step out into the New Mexico desert. The train pulled away, abandoning them there with no water. Nobody was ever convicted of a crime in the Bisbee Deportation. "Just like the Camp Grant Massacre, Arizonans supported 'frontier justice' even when the frontier was a company town," wrote historian Thomas Sheridan.

Immigration was supposed to have been the burning issue of this season, but I found very few people in Cochise County who were going to cast their congressional votes because of it. Of much more concern was foreign policy. What did Gabrielle want to do about Iraq, and also the fighting in Gaza that had recently erupted? Her position on Mexican immigration was a relatively tough one, but it was moderate by Arizona standards. People who came here should be required to learn English and be given a legal path to citizenship. And the Border Patrol needed more cash and tools. "We need enforcement-plus," she told a voter. "We need money for high-tech solutions, not low-tech Vietnam-era solutions."

I made a kind of peace with Arizona that summer. For the first time it seemed like a place that was attached to a distinct history, not an invented one, and where a person could cultivate not just a plausible life but one rich with purpose and friendship. At nights I stayed up late talking with Bob Etter, in whose house I was staying for free. Bob was tall and bald and said gently sarcastic things out of the corners of his mouth. He had worked as an account executive for Whirlpool and then for the Detroit automakers for thirty years, lived in a rambling house on a lake, and had gone through a series of marriages before deciding that he no longer owned his stuff, his stuff owned him. Bob quit writing praise for new Fords, sold the house, and went on a cross-country road trip. On the roundabout way back through the Southwest, he detoured though Bisbee because of a travel article that he'd once read, took a look around, and realized within ten minutes that he "was home." He didn't bother to go back to Detroit, just called a mover to have his stuff shipped out, rented a small room on O.K. Street, and started working as a waiter in a bed-and-breakfast to stay afloat. Eventually he started teaching business classes at the community college and bought and fixed up an old cliffhanger of a pillared house that had been a "hospitality center" maintained by the Phelps Dodge Corporation for visiting salesmen during the thirties. Liquor and party girls were of course an element of the hospitality. Bob was a preternaturally amiable guy and quickly got known by most people in town. "Just Bob," they called him, to distinguish him from the other Bobs in town with nicknames. He was as comfortable in his own skin as anyone I've ever met. We drank bottles of Electric Dave's beer on his porch and watched the summer monsoons and talked late into the night about books, cars, women, politics, and why a life can take such strange twists.

Gabrielle, meanwhile, was pulling even with Patty Weiss. The debates between them were held in small rooms to small crowds, but they got lots of press coverage. Gabrielle landed a few strong punches after Weiss criticized a few committee votes she had made in the Arizona legislature. "You know, Patty, you've been lecturing all week about ethics and about clean elections and special interests," she said, "but we've all seen this game before. You don't have a strong record to run on and so you turn around and you go negative. We don't do that here." She also lambasted her newscaster opponent, saying she sounded like "a reporter for Fox News." As Election Day approached, Gabrielle's numbers got even stronger, and it became apparent that her years of building friendships were paying off. She had a bigger network of people willing to rap on doors in the get-out-the-vote phase—the last four days before the election on September 12—when cajoling citizens out to the fire stations and libraries to do their optional duty can swing the balance. She ended up winning the district by a wide margin and Cochise County by a handful of votes.

I watched from the back of the ballroom at the Viscount Suite Hotel in Tucson as Gabrielle walked up to the stage to make a speech. Her pace seemed slow and deliberate, as if she was in a trance. There was a strange new energy around her. She looked as calm as Joan of Arc. "People were crowding close. They just wanted to touch her," Gabe told me later. Patty Weiss showed up and made a display of removing her own campaign sticker and replacing it with Gabrielle's—a classy gesture.

This night, for me, represented a victory of substance over style in southern Arizona. Gabrielle had done the hard studying, had shown up to picayune neighborhood meetings at inconvenient hours, and had listened to people until she was glassy-eyed with fatigue. She had done this year after year. And the resulting organization and discipline were enough to beat away a news personality who enjoyed far broader fame.

Other, equally good news came that night. The victor in the Republican primary was Randy Graf, a professional golf instructor from Wisconsin who lived in the retirement city of Green Valley. He had gray temples, a boyish smile, not much political savvy, and a single wedge issue about which he was an absolute fanatic: illegal immigration. He was locally famous in GOP circles for having hung a portrait of George W. Bush upside down in his office because the president had called for a guest-worker program to give at least a few migrants some legitimacy. He had so thoroughly alienated the Republican incumbent, Jim Kolbe, that Kolbe refused to endorse him, effectively pointing voters to Gabrielle, whom he liked personally. Graf seemed happily oblivious to his own unelectability, perhaps because of the loud cheering he always got from the hard-core immigrant bashers in his base. "Gabby wanted me," he told them on election night. "Now she's got me."

She did indeed. Her victory against him was virtually assured. He ran a few attack ads against her that didn't work. President Bush was wildly unpopular. Mainstream Republicans felt squeamish about Graf and either voted for Gabrielle or stayed home. I felt comfortable enough to leave Arizona until the last few days before the election. And then, stunningly, my old friend was a member of Congress.

I had to go to D.C. on some errand a few months after she had been sworn in, and went up to the fourth floor of the Longworth Office Building to see her bronze nameplate in the hallway. Daniel Graver, with whom I had worked on the campaign, had been hired for her Washington staff, and he took me walking out on the narrow ledge outside the office windows, where there was a view of the setting sun. It seemed giddy and impossible that Gabrielle had attained such a position: a place where she could, with luck and study, make a tiny incremental nudge in the national destiny. She was a backbencher, to be sure, a single vote among 535 considerably titanic egos, and a minority freshman with a long road toward seniority. But she had been gifted by House minority leader Nancy Pelosi with seats on a few powerful committees—Foreign Affairs and Armed Services—as well as the more wonky Science Committee, which oversees NASA and, with it, the fate of her future husband's space shuttle program. She would have to spend a ridiculous amount of her time raising cash for the next cycle, as District 8 would always be a dog-fight in its current shape, but if she could hang tough and keep making the Republicans waste their resources on her term after term, she could pound her flag even deeper and, down the foggy tunnel of the next twenty years, be present as a vote against another hubristic disaster like Iraq, or a table-pounder on a committee that tips the balance toward a Manhattan Project for solar energy, or one more vote for a sane immigration reform that would stop people from dying in the desert, or just the unshowy work of making sure that federal college scholarships didn't get zeroed. In a world of infinite and fundamentally unpredictable moving parts, she at least was a few degrees closer to the center.

It seemed to me then that history is not a solid block of marble but is made up of ten billion buzzing human particles all acting in unconscious relation to one another. And that with enough patient, steady, ponderous work among a dedicated group of those buzzing particles, the fate of the whole world might be marginally altered for the better.

I stayed in Gabrielle's small apartment just off Capitol Hill that night and left her a few housewarming gifts: a nonfiction book called *The Political Brain* that I thought she would probably like, as well as a six-pack of Negra Modelo. "For Emergencies Only" I wrote on a blue index card taped to the side. Three years later I was again going through town when she was away on business, and I borrowed the keys to her apartment again. Inside the refrigerator was that same pack of beer, untouched, with the note still attached.

Our friendship attenuated in the months after she was elected. This was entirely necessary. Her already jammed calendar was rapidly quintupling, and I had already made up my mind that I was not going to be among the line of people seeking a slice of her day unless I had a compelling reason. She would instead be the one to call me, which she did from time to time, volunteering less about herself and always inquiring about how I was doing and what I was working on and what girl had been stomping my heart. She poked at me in her playful but serious way to resume going to church, a habit from which I had retreated in disappointment and doubt several years before. Yeah, maybe, I told her. We'll see. I almost never asked her about congressional process; I figured she got enough of that elsewhere. "Awww," she would say at the end of each conversation. "I miss you. When do I get to see you again?"

She was still Gabby from down the block, of course, but she no longer inhabited the city of Tucson. Instead, Tucson inhabited her. Gabrielle had become a "United States Representative," and as such she was the bodily distillation of eight hundred thousand people. There is a *blue* quality to the federal government—an untrifling shade of deep cobalt that permeates the offices and the suits and the personalities of those who are part of its reach. This blue is the weight of more than two centuries of continental dominion, the united strength of an occupying empire existing everywhere and nowhere, both maddeningly inefficient and thunderously capable and detail-obsessed. This national hammer was what broke the Confederacy, the kaiser, and the Nazis, invented the atomic bomb, desegregated the schools, flew to the moon, and brought us into Iraq and Afghanistan and ran up trillions in debt. FBI agents are rarely mistaken for local cops. Their tailoring is sharper, their lips tighter, their eyes without laughter. They are *bluer*.

Gabrielle had just become blue. Lobbyists would be hanging off her forearm like never before; the third-floor antechamber of the Arizona Senate, with its worn-out carpet, was going to seem like a bake sale, not to mention the wildly divergent demands of a constituent base who would now be asking her not about barking dogs or the cracked basketball courts at Himmel Park but about their sons in Afghanistan and the wisdom of a federal handout to General Motors and a galaxy of other problems on which she was expected to be an overnight expert. She would have to channel this bumptious, groaning mess in a way that was hopefully pleasing to her constituents and didn't cause too much damage to the world.

The term "politician" has become a dirty word in our vocabulary, perhaps because politicians so often disappoint us for their seeming lack of integrity and their willingness to make compromises that look like sell-out deals. Knowing Gabrielle made me wish the word could be rehabilitated. I think it takes enormous talent—a talent I will never possess—to screen out the white noise and reconcile the conflicting interests of a thousand shouting voices trying to tell and sell you at every hour, and do so in a way that doesn't embarrass you or make it hard to feel good about yourself each morning. "It's not glamorous," she told me. She had said virtually the same thing about the tire business ten years before. One secret of congressional offices is that they run mostly on autopilot, and members do not suddenly become polymaths on every item of importance regarding the U.S. government. Staff briefings and party advisories are like training wheels for the hassled member. Almost every bit of her time was spent in the company of one or two eager staff members, or raising money over the phone.

A few years into her tenure she took me to the phone bank at the Democratic Congressional Campaign Committee, and it was a depressing sight: rows of cubicles with padded push-board walls and bare white desks with telephones. Members were supposed to come in here and dial for dollars in their free time, with a finance director at their side who held a computerized list of CEOs, philanthropists, and assorted other fat cats. Donors are as vulnerable as anyone else to the most basic of human opiates—feeling important—and they tend to be flattered when a member of Congress rings them up for a personal ask. Gabrielle didn't enjoy this (nobody did), but it was the brutal reality of governance in twenty-first-century America, and she was in no position to do anything different. Keeping office required raising money. In the age of television, it always would.

Another factor was at work—a much more conventional one. She got married, which always changes any friendship. But she married well. I had always liked Mark Kelly, and he made her deliriously happy. It cheered her up immensely during low moments on the 2006 campaign when he was able to fly a military plane into Tucson for a visit. "He's her natural Prozac" was how a campaign staffer put it. Mark and his twin brother, Scott, were sons of an Irish Catholic cop from West Orange, New Jersey, and Mark had a pleasing residue of Joisey in his vowels, though he had lived in Houston for many years.

Gabrielle told me that one of the many small traits she loved about him was the generous way he talked to people who wanted to shake the hand of an astronaut at parties. They tended to ask him the same (understandable) questions—number one was "What does the Earth look like from orbit?"—and he would answer with a thoughtful response that was as excited and detailed as if he were describing it for the very first time. He was deadpan funny in conversation, modest about his unbelievably cool job, and never made you feel intimidated to be in his presence.

Mark proposed to her on the campus of the National Maritime Academy at Kings Point, New York, where he had gotten his undergraduate degree, and she pulled me into the dark granite bathroom of an East Midtown skyscraper the next day to show me the diamond ring he'd given her. This was at a cocktail fundraiser she was throwing at some rich

Democrat's apartment, and she was as giddy and nervous as I'd ever seen her, though her speech to the crowd several minutes later was as measured as if she were describing a cookie recipe.

Their wedding was on November 10, 2008, at an organic vegetable garden near the small town of Amado in the Santa Cruz valley, near where Apaches used to swoop out of the Santa Ritas to harass settlers before the railroad arrived. She wore a gown of recycled material, and he had a line of Navy officers in dress whites give a salute with drawn swords. Steaks and chili peppers sizzled on the grill.

She would be entering into an unusual cohabitation. Mark had two teenage daughters from his prior marriage and so moving away from southeast Texas was not an option for him. And she, of course, was caroming back and forth every weekend between her apartments in Arizona and Washington. That traveling line would become a triangulation over the North American continent, and she would be racking up frequent-flier miles into the sixth digit. She would later say that they tried to see each other every two weeks, but it turned out to be more like every three. But the love between them was palpable. Her wedding ring had an inscription engraved inside, alluding to his job, that said: *You're the closest to heaven I've ever been.*

As they were exchanging promises before her rabbi under the *chuppah* canopy, a brief evening rain shower passed overhead, scenting the desert with a clear metallic tang, and they smiled at each other, embarrassed and electric, like two children with a secret. Watching her under the canopy was a bit like watching her walk up to the stage that night of her primary victory at the Viscount Suites, robed in the invisible ermine of a greater office. I can't really explain this feeling any further, except to say that she was beautiful that evening, incredibly beautiful, and my heart swelled up with gratitude for her, and for having seen her made so unabashedly happy.

❊

On January 7, 2011, the night before he went on his mission to shoot Gabrielle in the head, Jared Lee Loughner checked into a Motel 6 out by the freeway, on the far end of West Ina Road. A dust-covered banner advertises Low Weekly Rates. Rooms here cost about forty-five dollars a night and come with the blatting of compression brakes from trucks on the freeway and blasts from the horns of passing locomotives on the Union Pacific track. But Loughner wasn't there to sleep. A recorded robocall had been made automatically to the Loughner house the day before. "Hi, this is Gabby Giffords. Come to Safeway tomorrow and tell me how we can make government work better for you." Investigators believe this is how he became aware of the imminent Congress on Your Corner.

Staying in motels near his parents' house had become an occasional indulgence for Loughner. It was like running away from home, except within easy reach of the house, in a familiar place. He paid for one night in room 411. He then called up one of his oldest friends, Bryce Tierney, with whom he once got arrested for smoking marijuana. On voice mail he left a cryptic message. "Hey, it's Jared. We had some good times. Peace out."

At some point he got onto the Internet, researching the biographies of famous American assassins, as well as the federal death penalty.

At 2:34 A.M., he went to the Walgreens at Ina and Thornydale—the strip-mall crossroads where he had been taken by his mother to go shopping since he was a boy—and picked up a roll of 35 millimeter film that he had developed. The pictures showed him posing in a red G-string pair of underwear. He was holding his Glock pistol against his bare butt and near his crotch in a way that suggested erotic playfulness with the weapon.

He then made a final post on the wall of his Myspace page: "Goodbye, friends . . . please don't be mad at me."

At 7:04 A.M., he walked into the Walmart store near the Foothills Mall, a two-anchor shell from the mideighties that had seen better days. He attempted to purchase some 9 millimeter ammunition, but apparently got nervous and left before the sales clerk brought it out. He then went to another Walmart—they aren't hard to find on the northwest side. He successfully purchased three clips' worth of ammunition at the Cortaro Road power center and a black bag designed to carry diapers that fit him like a backpack.

He drove his Chevy Nova back to the house on North Soledad and took the black bag out of the car. His father, Randy, saw him and asked what was in the bag. An argument ensued. Loughner ran off down the wash next to the house, the same one where he used to play as a child. Randy got in his own car and cruised the neighborhood looking for him but could see no trace of his son.

Loughner apparently ran and walked a little over a mile to the Circle K on Cortaro Farms Road. The Chevy Nova that his father had restored for him was in the driveway and out of reach. Apparently worried he would miss a critical window, Loughner made a call from the pay phone outside the convenience store. A taxicab arrived within a few minutes, and he told the driver, John Marino, to take him to the Safeway at Oracle and Ina.

"Is Giffords here?" he asked the intern at the front of the line.

SIX

THE INFLUENCING
MACHINE

Schizophrenia is a disease best described as diabolical. Its cause is still a mystery, and its various emanations through the mind are so difficult to track that there is a serious debate about what part of the brain is the center of the pathology. Scientists can only work off shadows and traces on MRI scanners. But the surest signs of it are the symptoms, which are a peacock's tail of misery: catatonia, delusions, hallucinations, and bursts of inexplicable violence, all without any obvious physiological linkage. It can last for years, in many cases a lifetime. There are about 2.4 million who suffer from it in the United States.

Mental health professionals define the disease as "a mental disorder that makes it difficult to tell the difference between real and unreal experiences, to think logically, to have normal emotional responses and to behave normally in social situations." Schizophrenia, in short, is to have a fundamentally altered sense of what it means to be human. Crushing loneliness is almost always a natural side effect, and an aggravator.

The best evidence indicates that the disease originates in the limbic system, the primitive and little understood core portion of the brain near the spinal cord through which most external stimuli are received and processed. Diseases that affect this area, such as epilepsy and encephalitis, have been known to provoke symptoms that look very much like schizophrenia, and electric activity in the limbic system has been shown to be abnormal in schizophrenic patients. Studies of the MRI images of patients with schizophrenia show that the cerebral ventricles have swollen in size to be about 15 percent larger than those with unaffected brains. But whether this is a cause or an effect is still a matter of conjecture. Some studies of pregnant women done in the nineties have suggested that catching the flu, or even using painkillers, in the second trimester could be a risk factor for the child, who might develop the disease two decades into the future.

For centuries it was defined with catchall terms such as "lunacy" or "madness," thought to be the result of a curse from God or an upsetting event that someone witnessed. Physicians in the late Middle Ages called it "dementia praecox," and a few of the worst cases were confined to hospitals such as London's Bethlehem, the origin of what was then a slang word, "bedlam." The Maryland psychiatrist E. Fuller Torrey, an expert in the field, has found the influence of it on artistic creations as diverse as the paintings of Hieronymus Bosch and certain short stories of Edgar Allan Poe, especially "The Tell-Tale Heart," in which the tortured narrator imagines he can still hear the beating heart of a man he has murdered. The Swiss psychiatrist Eugen Bleuler coined the term "schizophrenia" in 1911, which, in German, literally means a split in the functioning of the mind. This does not mean the patient has twin or multiple personalities, a common misunderstanding promulgated by the use of the word to describe an institution or a policy that seems to have dual identities and the syrupy and exaggerated movie *Sybil*, which is about a heroine with fourteen different personalities she constructed as a defense against child abuse.

In young men, the disease often starts showing itself between the ages of sixteen and twenty-two, which can make it a stealth disease masked in the general drama of leaving late childhood forever and going into a bold but uncertain future. This is a period of life when youthful ventures into beer and drugs are typically at a high point, relationships with girls are fraught with hormones and bad poetry, and, for the bookish, influential reading can create some thrusts of intellectual derring-do that are later repudiated sheepishly. The very worst aspect of schizophrenia is that those who suffer from it are generally not aware of their own sickness and are frustrated that others cannot comprehend the brilliance of what are actually delusions.

They also tend to resist treatment, not just because they don't believe they're sick—it's *everyone else* who is crazy—but because the soothing doctors with their charts and lab coats and their drugs are usually seen as just another element of the omnivorous conspiracy.

Torrey compares the cognitive machinery of the brain to an old-time telephone switchboard operator who plugged various wires into the appropriate circuits. Schizophrenia frustrates that sorting process, connecting visual stimuli to the wrong emotional response. "It is as if the switchboard operator not only gets bored and stops sorting and interpreting, but becomes actively malicious and begins hooking the incoming stimuli up to random, usually inappropriate, responses." Normal conversations become difficult—the empathetic connections just aren't there for them—and the general unpleasantness of being around a schizophrenic person tends to drive away all but the most stalwart or patient friends.

Schizophrenia has nothing to do with lack of intelligence or empathy. Many patients can be extremely articulate in their fantasies and tenacious in their search for hidden meanings, pursuing them with the rigor of a Ph.D. candidate. The voices they hear are subjectively quite real, not moans from the funhouse, and what they do in response makes perfect sense. The Princeton University mathematician John Nash, about whom the book *A Beautiful Mind* was written, suffered from debilitating, though not violent, schizophrenia that made him wander around the campus helplessly. When asked how someone with an intellect as powerful as his could be so easily conned by hallucinations, he answered matter-of-factly, "Because the ideas I had about supernatural beings came to me the same way that my mathematical ideas did. So I took them seriously."

The visions are rarely pleasant. The effect is described as a world constantly on autoshuffle, with disconnected images coming fast and furious with no cohesive logic. One patient told Torrey of a visit to the principal's office: "Profound dread overwhelmed me, and as though lost, I looked around desperately for help. I heard people talking, but I did not grasp the meaning of the words. The voices were metallic, without warmth or color. From time to time, a word detached itself from the rest. It repeated itself over and over in my head, absurd, as though cut off by a knife." The normal functions of the mind that a healthy person takes for granted are broken in schizophrenics.

Violent behavior is sometimes associated with schizophrenia, and it can be especially terrifying because it is so random. One peculiarity of New York City is the very rare person on a subway platform who suddenly moves forward and tries to shove a fellow commuter in the path of an oncoming train; a study of twenty of these incidents found that fifteen of the suspects, roughly three quarters of the pushers, had a case of diagnosed schizophrenia. Another NIMH study, cited by Torrey, indicates that people suffering from schizophrenia who get into a fight are twenty times more likely to have deployed a weapon—such as a knife or club—than people with no illness. For those schizophrenics who kill there may not be any moral filter because the violence makes perfect sense in their brains.

"They aren't killing someone—they are purifying," said Dan Ranieri, of La Frontera. "The idea that they are taking a life is not a concept they understand."

There is a body of thought among a few renegade psychiatrists that schizophrenia has been exaggerated and may not even exist—a phony disease. The British psychoanalyst Ronald Laing postulated in the 1960s that those who heard voices and saw visions were only trying to have an expression of individuality inside a corrupt society. Another one who advances an antipsychiatric view is Dr. Thomas Szasz, who has called schizophrenia an invention of the hospital industry, which needs illness in order to justify its big budgets. He complains that schizophrenia fails the test of "being approached, measured or tested in a scientific fashion"—many MRI studies to the contrary. His denialism was in the spirit of French philosopher Michel Foucault, whose landmark *History of Sexuality* suggested that clinical definitions of insanity were only a "discourse" of the science power-elite, who needed labels to create meanings for their profession.

The expression of schizophrenia that receives the most popular attention—probably because of the spectacularly ugly behavior that it causes—is paranoid schizophrenia, the form suffered by Jared Lee Loughner, who saw an insidious plot on the part of government to control its citizens by making them speak words in a certain way and use ersatz money not guaranteed with gold. Paranoid schizophrenia usually sketches a world in which the sufferer is the only one who can perceive the fantastic web of people out to control him or her, or take advantage in some way. Even so, there is a multiplicity of forms listed in the *Diagnostic and Statistical Manual of Mental Disorders*, including schizoid personality disorder, paranoid personality disorder, and schizoaffective disorder (which represents the classic form of the disease mingled with a lacing of manic depression). The differences between all of these are blurred and subject to a vast amount of technical dispute over who is suffering from what.

There is evidence, though, that those people prone to schizophrenia who live in urban areas—especially those low on social capital—are more at risk of developing the disease, by an estimated factor of two. The English psychiatrist E. H. Hare wrote in 1956 of discovering high rates of schizophrenia in Bristol and concluded that the "social isolation" and human disconnectedness of the city had been important contributing factors. The lack of friendships in an indifferent environment is a multiplier on a basic physiological problem.

Even more critically, the cultural context helps determine the types of delusions that patients such as Jared Loughner experience.

In 1933, the psychoanalyst Viktor Tausk published an article in *Psychoanalytic Quarterly* called "On the Origin of the 'Influencing Machine'" in Schizophrenia" in which he described a common delusion among patients, mainly men, who described a powerful gadget somewhere in the cosmos that was controlling their thoughts. "The patients are able to give only vague hints of its construction," wrote Tausk. "It consists of boxes, cranks, levers, wheels, buttons, wires, batteries, and the like." This omnipotent machine forces the patient to "see pictures" and feel odd feelings by means of invisible rays. It was this diabolical machine, they insisted, and not them that ought to be blamed for whatever outbursts and violent behavior had been channeled through their unwilling bodies.

Tausk's observations reveal a very important element of schizophrenia germane to what happened in Tucson that remains poorly understood by scientists: the way in which the schizophrenic's thoughts are a patchwork of reality cherry-picked from the environment that surrounds him. His journal article was written not in the age of television but in one of radio, when a box that beams voices was becoming a feature of every middle-class home. Though gripped by worldwide depression, a century of industrializing society had conditioned people to believe in the power of steam engines and electricity. Machines had entered most every corner of Western existence—a tyranny of steel and wires—and it was only natural that a schizophrenic would grab on to and use that image.

The surrounding environment most definitely plays a part in crafting schizophrenic delusions. In 2001, South Korean scientists compared the cases of schizophrenic patients admitted to National Seoul Mental Hospital and Hanyang University Hospital with those of two hospitals in Shanghai, China. The frequency of hallucinations was similar in patients of both nations, but the content was markedly different. In South Korea, the patients gravitated toward religious or superstitious visions, and several expressed fear of secret agents from North Korea. Guilt about perceived transgressions was also a dominant theme. But in patients living in China, the delusional content was more of an explicitly political nature, with the subjects often believing they were a relative of a powerful Communist official or had emperors as ancestors. Personal guilt was far less present. A study of a third group—in Taiwan—showed a notable percentage expressed a great fear of street gangs, reflecting an unpleasant reality of life in urban Taipei. Such manifestations were not nearly as present in patients from Seoul, where gangs are not a predominant feature of urban living.

These findings replicated the results of an earlier, 1993 study of schizophrenics that included a population of Chinese immigrants to Korea who collectively had lived through more unstable times than their counterparts in either nation. "The Korean-Chinese patients in our study have lived through more political crises than the Korean and Chinese patients," wrote lead researcher Kwangiel Kim. "Delusions regarding political themes were thus highly sensitive to the local political situation."

In other words: same disease, same symptoms, but different *content*, which appears to be dependent on the cultural environment.

"These studies reconfirmed that delusional and hallucinatory themes or content are sensitively influenced by a patient's cultural or political experiences at the time," concluded Kim. "Likewise, their symptomatic manifestations may be influenced by the state of acculturation in each country."

Even in the midst of their delusions, schizophrenics still perceive what is happening around them. Their walls are porous. Their minds are still pliable. The machine is broken, but it is not deaf or blind.

"If you can learn math, can you unlearn it?"

The question came from the intense young man in cargo pants, barely thirty minutes after the first class of summer semester had begun. This was Elementary Algebra, Pima Community College, a five-week class that met three times a week. About thirty students had enrolled, Pima's usual motley assortment of recent high school graduates and middle-aged people. It was May 31, 2010. The teacher, Ben McGahee, had been doing some basic review, discussing how to calculate the area of a triangle, and he tried his best to elide the question and get back to hypotenuses. But the young man, named Jared Lee Loughner, was insistent. He held forth that the number eighteen was actually pronounced "six," and the teacher started to work out problems on the board in such a way that his back was never fully turned on the classroom's most talkative member.

The northwest campus of Pima Community College was built on a slope of scrubland once owned by Sam Nanini; the godfather of real estate in this part of town also happened to have once owned the land that the Safeway and the rest of La Toscana Village was built upon. His grandson Steve Nanini donated it to the county for use as a botanical gardens, but the hill was oriented to the west and the sun and airflow would have been all wrong for the healthy growth of plants. It was simply too cold and shady in the mornings. So the county leased it to the college district for a new regional campus and an irate Steve Nanini filed a lawsuit seeking it back. Courts ruled for the county and the campus opened up in 2003. "With more than 84,000 square feet of space," said the college on its Web site, "the Northwest Campus's modern facilities offer students the very best in 21st-century advancements for their educational experience." There are five superblock cubes, lettered A through E, and the heart is a high-ceilinged library and "computer commons." The outside walls are painted a warm brown; the effect is like that of a blend between sixties modernist junk and an ancestral Pueblo cliff dwelling.

In 2010, unemployed fast-food worker Jared Loughner was here for a chance at redeeming himself, and not getting far. The only people who got to know him were the counselors and the police. He had enrolled in a poetry class and turned in strange work. When a student read a poem about abortion, he wondered out loud why "we don't just strap bombs to babies?" and offered other unrelated comments about war and death. One student told the dean she feared Loughner was carrying a knife. A Pilates instructor who gave him a B said she felt intimidated by him and called a police officer after he threw down his work and yelled that his grade was "unacceptable." The cop didn't confront Loughner but hung around until class was over to make sure there were no eruptions of violence.

There was at least one student in his Elementary Algebra class who had seen schizophrenia before and knew something was dreadfully wrong. Lynda Sorenson is a pleasant woman in her fifties who had moved to Tucson in 1981 to work in a beauty salon called Gadabout. She had grown up near Hyde Park, New York, and one of her jobs as a young woman was as an observer at the Hudson River Psychiatric Center, a giant, spooky-looking institution perched on a hill. This was not the most glamorous health-care job ever created; Sorenson's role was basically to watch deeply sick people in their cells overnight to make sure they did not hang themselves with their bedsheets or slash their veins with a sharpened spoon. Many of those patients were schizophrenic and carried on in a world only they could understand. One insisted she was the Virgin Mary and was indignant at her confinement, as the mother of God would be. On one bad day she managed to smash her way through a second-story window and jump to the ground below, breaking her hip in two places. She got up and kept running away, oblivious to her injuries. What Jared was saying now about six and eighteen sounded a lot like the nonsense that had come from behind the walls at the Hudson River Psychiatric Center. So, too, did his grin and giggle.

After that memorable first day of class, Sorenson sent an e-mail to a friend of hers about it.

> I was afraid that he would be teaching way over our heads, but I have to say, so far, as good as it could be. One day down and nineteen to go. We do have one student in the class who was disruptive today, I'm not certain yet if he was on drugs (as one person surmised) or disturbed. He scares me a bit. The teacher tried to throw him out and he refused to go, so I talked to the teacher afterward. Hopefully he will be out of class very soon, and not come back with an automatic weapon.

Sorenson also unloaded about this obviously mentally ill young man to her husband, Graham, a bearded and outgoing man from a small town in Wales. They had met in an unlikely way: After years spent working in the beauty business, she began to have trouble breathing, and her doctor told her she would soon have permanent lung damage if she didn't get away from the chemicals used in the hair treatments. Looking for a new line of work, she became fascinated with the science of aromatherapy and started making posts on a Web site called theguidetoaromatherapy.com. It was there that she started e-mailing back and forth with Graham, and the relationship moved to the telephone. This turned to a transatlantic visit and they married on September 15, 2001, and got an apartment together at Catalina Foothills Lodge, a now-faded guest ranch built in the fifties. She and Graham pooled their cash and opened up their own aromatherapy shop in Tucson, called Luna, which they had to shortly close down for, among other reasons, Sorenson's newly acquired allergy to lavender, which was a career-ending injury in the aromatherapy business.

Sorenson had enrolled at Pima the year before in a burst of resolve to pick up some credits and earn the degree she had abandoned a long time ago. It was a difficult time for her all around: She had recently survived a pulmonary embolism that blocked the flow of blood to her lungs and almost killed her. Just as she was recovering, her mother experienced a stroke and died several months later of pneumonia and dehydration. Sorenson thought about withdrawing from Pima in the summer but decided the best course was to press onward with her life and hope that school would provide a distraction. The math credit she needed led her to Elementary Algebra and Jared's loud insistence that six was actually eighteen and that the Constitution gave him the right to say so.

The snickering interjections continued through early June, and Sorenson became convinced that a severe mental illness, and not drugs, was causing the outbursts. "It wasn't just that it didn't relate to math," said Sorenson. "It made no sense. There was nothing there that made any sense at all. He was very insistent about it, even as the teacher was trying to get him to be quiet. He would say the teacher was perpetuating a scam, that the college was perpetuating a scam, and that he had First Amendment rights." She thought to Google him, looking for clues to his background, but found only a picture of him that had run in the *Arizona Daily Star* a few months before. He had been an unpaid volunteer at the Tucson Book Festival and was holding up a large flatboard crossword puzzle display, smiling innocuously into the camera. One of her classmates, a younger, pregnant woman with blond hair, told her that the managers had to throw Jared out of the In-N-Out Burger on Oracle Road where she worked. His food had come out to the counter in a way that displeased him and he started hollering about the Constitution.

On June 10, Sorenson wrote in another e-mail to her family:

> As for me, Thursday means the end to week two of algebra class. It seems to be going by quickly, but then I do have three weeks to go so we'll see how I feel by then. Class isn't dull as we have a seriously disturbed student in the class, and they are trying to figure out how to get rid of him before he does something bad, but on the other hand, until he does something bad, you can't do anything about him.

Four days later she sent an e-mail to a teacher friend in which she mentioned Jared and invoked the classic American media-opera of a gun rampage and the consequent journalistic frenzy over the man who lost all reason and pulled the trigger.

> Anyone capable of helping me to understand why I might use algebra in the next 50 years of my life when I haven't in the first 50 would be a freaking genius. Have not met the person who can do that yet, although I do ask, repeatedly. We have a mentally unstable person in the class that scares the living crap out of me. He is one of those whose picture you see on the news, after he has come into class with an automatic weapon. Everyone interviewed would say, Yeah, he was in my math class and he was really weird. I sit by the door with my purse handy. If you see it on the news one night, know that I got out fast.

On days when there was a quiz, Jared would scribble furiously and turn in papers that were decorated with equations. Some computed. Others were gibberish. One turned in came with the words "Mayhem Fest!" scrawled at the top. Some of the young men in the class would occasion-

ally yell back at Jared, telling him to shut up, but he paid them no attention. Sorenson never said a word to Jared and resolved to avoid him. She
began arriving early to choose a seat near the door, in case Jared should
come to class with a weapon and start shooting. One day she walked into
the classroom early and discovered Jared up at the front, grinning mani-
cally and drawing figures on the board that she couldn't see and didn't
want to. Sorenson went back out into the plaza and hid behind a concrete
pillar. "Jared's in there," she told McGahee in a semipanic. It was McGahee's first year as a teacher, and he wasn't exactly sure how to handle this
dicey situation. But he did agree with Sorenson that Jared had serious
problems—probably involving drugs—that needed to be dealt with at
levels higher than a classroom. He got in touch with the administration
about it and, when the next disruption happened in early June, he called
for a fifteen-minute break. When class resumed, counselor Delisa Siddall, backed up by a police officer, showed up to escort Jared from class.

He complained to her that his freedom of speech was being infringed.
"He has extreme views and frequently meanders from the point," wrote
Siddall. "He seems to have difficulty understanding how his actions
impact others, yet very attuned to his ideology that is not always homog-
enous." When Sorenson got a chance to thank Siddall for intervening
and tell her about her fear of Jared, the counselor could only give her a
pained smile and say that unless an overt threat came out of his mouth
or his pen, Jared had to be given his rights as a student.

Sorenson remembered saying to the counselor, "He is the kind of
person who would come into class with an automatic weapon, and all of
us would be saying to reporters, 'Wow, he was weird.'"

Jared was soon back in class, muttering about the Constitution and
the meaning of numbers. He had a habit of looking at every single member of the class, trying to engage them with eye contact, an expression like
"a sick Cheshire cat" on his face. The Constitution was becoming his no-
strings license to rant, and those who tried to shut him up were impinging
on his rights. In one attempt to find a new job he walked into a county
employment center with a video camera and began recording people.

Somebody at the front desk told him to quit it and he refused. Supervisor Mary Brodesky came out to see what the trouble was. "He pulled out a crumpled copy of the Constitution out of his pocket and waved it at me, saying it was his right," she wrote in a report. "I attempted to calm him down but eventually asked him to leave the building, which he did."

On September 23, a little under two weeks after his twenty-second birthday, there was yet another classroom outburst at Pima College, and Officer Dana Mattocks had to be called out to mediate what was becoming a ritual. Jared insisted that his "freedom of thought" was being threatened. He also tilted his head "with a confused look in the countenance of his face" and a "sustained bobbing of the eyes." He was upset because the Constitution was written on the wall "for all to see" and that the teacher should have been able to understand his thoughts, which he had telepathically embedded in the homework, and given him a passing grade for his efforts (as renegade as he was, Loughner showed an acute concern for his grade point average). Another counselor, Dr. Aubrey Conover, had a meeting with him four days later to discuss an incident in a biology class in which he had loudly complained about getting only half credit, for turning in an assignment late. Loughner claimed that he was "only asking a question," which was his right under the First Amendment. He also said he hadn't legally paid for his classes because "I did not pay in gold or silver."

Conover was mystified by this and pressed Jared, who only "said something about the Constitution and changed subjects." Throughout this meeting he smiled weirdly at odd times. But he agreed to sign a behavioral contract in which he would promise not to interrupt any more classes with strange comments. A meeting was scheduled for the following week for him to sign the agreement.

But before that indignity could happen, Jared took a video camera to the campus one evening, hit the record button, and wandered through the high cubic canyons of the classroom blocks, lens rolling and bobbing. Crickets can be heard in the background near the beginning, and near the end somebody is playing an acoustic guitar in a courtyard, an unexpectedly serene sound in the midst of a rant. Jared uses the mannerisms of a documentary filmmaker or an investigative journalist. His tone is one of tired condescension, as if explaining something perfectly obvious to a slightly dense viewer. He also giggles to himself throughout.

Alright, so here's what we're doing. We're examining the torture of students. We are looking at students who have been tortured, their low-income pay, and two wars. The war that we are in right now is currently illegal under the Constitution. What makes it illegal is the currency. The date is also wrong. It's impossible for it to be that date. It's mind control. [To a passerby, he shouts:] How's it going? Thanks for the B! I'm pissed off. I lost my freedom of speech to that guy! And this is, this what happens. And I'm in a terrible place. This is the school that I go to. This is my genocide school. Where I'm going to be homeless because of this school. I haven't forgotten the teacher that gave me the B for freedom of speech. That's where my sociology class was. And here's the microwave I'll be using when I'm homeless. This is the cafeteria where they make illegal transactions. This is Pima Community College. One of the biggest scams in America. The students are so illiterate that it affects their daily lives. Here's the best part, the bookstore. The bookstore, the bookstore, the bookstore. It is so illegal to sell this book under the Constitution [*sic*]. We are also censored by our freedom of speech. They're controlling the grammar. They control the grammar. This is the police station. This is where the whole shaboozie goes down with illegal activity. If the student is unable to locate the external universe, then the student is unable to locate the internal universe. Where is all my subjects? I could say something sound right now, but I don't feel like it. All the teachers that you have are being paid illegally, and have a legal authority over the Constitution of the United States under the First Amendment. This is genocide in America. Thank you. This is Jared, from Pima College.

Apparently proud of his work, he posted it on YouTube under the alias 2Ploy and with the title *Pima Community College School—Genocide/Scam—Free Education—Broken United States Constitution.* He adorned the accompanying text with the statement "i don't trust in god" and quotes from the Constitution.

YouTube had become his preferred canvas of expression. He had already created several minimalist videos there—not really videos at all, just words on a black background—in which he rambled about creating a new monetary system and seizing control of "grammar" from the people in the government who were trying to brainwash the public.

"Firstly," went one typical screed,

> the current government officials are in power for their currency, but I'm informing you for your new currency! If you're [*sic*] treasurer of a new money system then you're responsible for the distributing of a new currency. We now know—the treasurer for a new money system is the distributor of the new currency. As a result, the people approve a new money system which is promising new information that's accurate, and we truly believe in a new currency. Above all, you have your new currency, listener?

In another video lecture Loughner said he was thinking of designing his own coins and minting his own currency, which would not be subject to the control of the authorities. What wasn't backed up by gold or silver, he averred, was not "real." The categories of reality and fantasy were increasingly blurred; chronological events no longer felt rational. Sleeping and dreaming were constant themes. "All humans are in need of sleep. Jared Loughner is a human. Hence, Jared Loughner is in need of sleep." And then, "I'm a sleepwalker—who turns off the alarm clock. All conscience dreaming at this moment is asleep. Jared Loughner is conscience dreaming at this moment. Thus, Jared Loughner is asleep."

What was real, and what was imagined? These were paramount concerns for Loughner in the autumn of 2010 while the election season was going on around him. One of his last videos made reference to the congressional district Gabrielle represented. "The majority of people who reside in District 8 are illiterate—hilarious," he wrote.

There is almost no living soul in Tucson who thinks of their town as "District 8," which refers only to the jagged federal boundaries set every ten years by an independent state commission. This specific bureaucratic reference is telling. He was almost certainly keeping up with the news. Four years earlier he had gone to a forum and asked Gabrielle a question. "What is government if words have no meaning?" She sidestepped the weird inquiry, and he left angry, telling friends Gabrielle was just another "illiterate." He kept a thank-you note that her staff had sent him, which misspelled his last name as "Loughney," possibly because his signature at the event was a scrawl.

But he apparently forgot about the congressional district and the woman who represented it until the fall of 2010, when Pima College was going sour for him.

Though it earned barely a few dozen page views, somebody forwarded the link of his "genocide school" creation to Pima College police. Within the week a suspension letter had been drawn up for Jared Loughner for violating the student code of conduct. Pima College police also thought enough of this video to subpoena it and the IP address of the poster from YouTube's corporate office, perhaps as evidence with which to sue Loughner in civil court. Three Pima College officers went to his house to deliver the notice by hand, with one stationed as backup in the neighborhood in case trouble should start.

Jared's father answered the door, and after putting away the family dogs, invited the officers into the garage with Jared, who sat through the entire hour-long meeting in what Officer Mattocks described as a "constant state of trance." The police read him the letter of suspension out loud, every word, as though it were a medieval scroll being read to an illiterate, and then told him that if he wanted to come back, he needed to provide a letter from a mental health professional certifying that he would not be a threat to himself or to other people.

At the end of what must have been an awful conversation for everyone, Jared said: "I realize now this is all a scam."

Pima College had thought enough of his outbursts to throw him out, and that the denouncement happened in front of his parents might have even deepened his self-hatred and isolation. Yet there are no signs that anybody sought treatment for Loughner. Though he had not made explicit threats against anybody at Pima College, his clear signs of schizophrenia stayed only inside the files of the counselors and police. They were not forwarded to any other law enforcement agency, even though photographs of him were circulated among officers at the college in case he should show up unannounced. And a critical next step was not taken.

An Arizona law passed in 2002 says that "any responsible person"— a parent, a friend, a cop, or even a total stranger—can start a legal process to get a sick person some treatment or committed to a hospital. Arizona's law is progressive in this way. Most states require the person to be an active danger to themselves or others, and there is a long history of worried parents making up stories of suicide attempts or murderous language just to get their unwilling adult schizophrenic children into the system somehow. Arizona's provision includes a category of "persistently or acutely disabled," which means, in legal language, "a severe mental disorder which, if not treated, has a substantial probability of causing the person to suffer or continue to suffer severe and abnormal mental, emotional or physical harm that significantly impairs judgment, reason, behavior or capacity to recognize reality." Though there is still room for a lot of interpretation in this test, most people in Arizona who reach the point of being brought before a judge do get committed.

Two months after Loughner's suspension, records show, he went to a retail outlet called the Sportsman's Warehouse near his house on Thornydale, a half a block from where he had once worked as a sandwich maker at Quiznos. He produced $550 in cash, submitted to a federal background check for prior convictions or a record of mental incapacitation—he passed with no problem—and walked out with a Glock 19 semiautomatic pistol. That same month, he paid $60 for a tattoo of a bullet on his right shoulder, telling the artist that he dreamed for fourteen hours every day.

He never did get violent or directly threaten anybody in Elementary Algebra, despite Sorenson's worst fears. The class ended, she received an A, banked her necessary math credit, and thanked the professor. She let the weird young man slip away from the front of her mind and turned to other things.

On the morning of January 8 of the next year she was listening to Beethoven's Seventh Symphony on her laptop computer. The feed was from an Internet radio station in London. The Christmas tree was still up. She was posting photos to Facebook of a weaving project she was doing, and up popped a box, an instant message from a friend named Susan:

> I got an e-mail 10 minutes ago from a friend who said she was leaving the Safeway at Ina and Oracle when there was an assassination attempt on Gabby Giffords. Shots were fired and she saw people lying on the ground near Gabby's booth. Don't know if anyone was shot but we are hearing helicopters overhead. Crazy!

Sorenson put a hand to her mouth and began to cry a little. Oracle and Ina was only about two miles from her apartment at Catalina Foothills Lodge, and she knew and respected Gabrielle. Graham was down at his usual weekend haunt at the Starbucks on River Road, and she sent him a text: "Someone has just tried to assassinate Gabby Giffords up at Oracle/Ina." He came rushing home, and they hugged fiercely. The built-up static electricity from her fuzzy slippers against the carpet made a sharp pinprick pop between them. They spent the next several hours in front of the television. At one point she told her husband she had an odd feeling that the man who had done it—a hooded person in his twenties with a backpack, witnesses said on the news—was the vocal student with the cockeyed smile from her Elementary Algebra class. The leak that afternoon of the kid's name confirmed her weird hunch. Her hands started to shake and, not knowing what else to do, she called 911 with her fragmentary piece of information about the person who had done this. She made a Facebook post for her friends:

OMG. It was the crazy guy from my math class this summer. He scared the crap out of me.

The American disaster tableau she had envisioned last summer—public carnage, an army of police, and a legion of neighbors talking into microphones about how he was an oddball loner—was all happening now in front of her. Except the bloodshed had not been at Pima College but at the Safeway up Oracle Road.

Sorenson has since second-guessed herself multiple times, wondering if she did the right thing. Should she have gone further in insisting that Jared was a danger to others? "If I had to do things differently, I sure as hell would," she said to me, at the same Starbucks where Graham was the morning of the shooting. "But I told the teacher, and I thought that was enough. I assumed—and I'm not trying to shove blame anywhere else—that because of the shootings at Virginia Tech that there was some type of mechanism at schools that would recognize a mental health issue and do something about it. If anyone was in a place to know what mechanism was in place, Pima should have. They failed not only the people in class with him, but ultimately the people at the Safeway that morning. They really dropped the ball. But in some way, we all had a responsibility."

Pima College quickly went into what Graham called "clampdown mode." Administrators refused to answer any questions about Jared Loughner or why he was not referred for psychiatric treatment, even after he was thrown out of school with a letter explicitly citing his mental health as a factor in his suspension. The college sent out an e-mail to all its students and faculty asking them not to talk to the media about Loughner or the college's actions. "Their concern," complained Graham, "is with their own culpability, not with the community."

✦

What kind of parents would raise such a kid? The question was on everyone's mind in the days following the shooting. When the media encampment sprang up outside the flat-roof seventies rancher where Jared Loughner had grown up, reporters knocked on doors all around Orangewood Estates looking for anyone who might have had encounters with the mother or father. Photographers waited patiently for them to emerge so they could get shots.

Bad parenting, it was thought, must have been in some way responsible. A narrative began to emerge: Randy Loughner was a mean, eccentric man who was unpleasant to his neighbors and probably had a rough relationship with his son, too. Amy Loughner was a nice woman, but extremely quiet and retiring.

"And you look at the parents and say, 'Yeah, well the dad's really angry,'" neighbor Stephen Woods told the *Daily Mail* of London. "He has some issues, the father. I think it's trickled down on the son. And it's too bad."

Another neighbor, George Gayan, told the Associated Press that he and the Loughners used to be friends but had a falling out. "As time went on, they indicated they wanted privacy," he said. Yet another man told the *Daily Mail* that Loughner was like a ghost, slipping out at odd hours. "On the other hand," he went on, "he's probably the best neighbor I ever had. He doesn't talk to you and doesn't borrow." That statement could have applied to half of Tucson.

James Beran, who knew Jared growing up, told *The Arizona Republic* that Randy and Amy were "very, very different from most parents," not putting pressure on Jared in matters of schoolwork or his jobs. Randy was a bit closed-off but could be decent if you talked to him when he was in a good mood.

The house itself looked like a bunker. There was a big, malformed prickly pear cactus out front with leaves the size of dinner plates. Randy Loughner erected a wooden slat shield in front of the door so nobody could see him or his wife coming or going. He plugged the diamond-shaped holes in the pumice walls that surrounded the backyard and chased away a photographer who had leaped inside. Amy Loughner was said to have spent most of her waking hours crying in the bedroom. A friend of the family's, Bub Hebert, spoke briefly on the telephone with Randy, who was nearly incoherent and kept breaking down in tears. "Thanks for thinking of us," he reportedly said. "I'm going to have to call you back when I'm able to talk." Hebert never heard back from him.

When he saw the house on television, sixty-one-year-old Roger Salzberger looked with disbelief. He had been one of the two men at the Safeway who had tackled Jared Loughner and one of the only people at that event who had volunteered on Gabrielle's last campaign in 2010. He had tirelessly canvassed the northwest side for her and recalled knocking on the door of the Loughner house with a handful of Giffords literature in the intense hours right before the November 3 election. The distinctive cactus was the giveaway. Salzberger had owned a nursery for nearly a quarter of a century, and he often used the plants in people's front yards as a conversation starter.

He had spoken with Amy Loughner for about five minutes, and "it was about as normal a conversation as you can expect to have with anyone when someone rings your doorbell at six o'clock in the evening." He could recall nothing in particular she said, or anything about Amy, other than that she seemed like a friendly enough woman. A little more than two months later he would be pinning her son down amid the dead bodies on a bloodied sidewalk.

The parents "broke their silence," as the newscasters put it, six days after the shooting. A representative of the federal public defender, who wouldn't give his name, stood in front of the swept dirt outside their home on Soledad Drive in Orangewood Estates and handed out photocopies of an eight-line statement. It said:

> This is a very difficult time for us. We ask the media to respect our privacy. There are no words that can possibly express how we feel. We wish that there were so we could make you feel better. We

don't understand why this happened. It may not make any differ-
ence, but we wish that we could change the heinous events of
Saturday. We care very deeply about the victims and their families.
We are so very sorry for their loss.

These words had the feeling of being passed through a lawyer or two,
but they seemed to fulfill a collective need, a thirst for public sorrow. That
the Loughners were giving no soul-baring interviews made the shootings feel all the more pointless; the public needed to see remorse. The
typed statement ameliorated the desire somewhat, though many still
concluded that a horrid childhood and a bad relationship with the father
had been a proximate cause of the massacre.

A month after the shooting I talked to someone who had spent a lot
of time in the Loughner house who had a different impression.

Wyatt Bills works as a cook and a freelance guitarist, and had known
the father for a decade. The two got to know each other after Wyatt's
band—an ensemble called Tongue Dried Sun—rented out a rehearsal
space in a sterile commercial cube on First Avenue that also housed a
bug exterminator. The band started talking with some of the friends of
the landlord, one of whom was Randy. He was about two decades their
senior, but mellow and relaxed and interested in their music. He had a
35 millimeter Canon and offered to take some photos of them playing
their gigs at bars, which he did for free. A friendship developed, and the
band would go over to the spooky-looking house on North Soledad for
weekend barbecues, where Randy made roast turkey and steaks and
what Wyatt considered to be "sweet-ass fried tacos," as he told one hilarious story after another, a cooler of beer at his side.

"These people on the news, they aren't the people I know," said Bills.
"He was natural telling us a story. He wanted to make us laugh."

Randy Loughner is a man with a bushy mustache and a mane of
salt-and-pepper hair. He grew up on Tucson's southeast side, near Avia-
tion Highway, and is reportedly the son of a onetime Davis-Monthan
Air Force Base airman originally from Jeanette, Pennsylvania, named

Alpheus Loughner, whom people called Big Al. He had been arrested six days after Randy was born in 1952 for robbing a series of grocery stores with a gang of four accomplices, according to news accounts. One of these stores had been a Safeway on East Speedway and Richey Boulevard, but Alpheus Loughner told a judge that he hadn't participated in the stickup but only waited in a car parked outside. The gang had also hit a Safeway on North Park Street as part of a string that netted them upward of twenty-two thousand dollars and fell apart only when one of them began talking to police. The *Arizona Daily Star* called Loughner "the solemn Pennsylvanian" and ran a large photograph of him walking from court on July 17, 1952. He is still alive. I called him at his home in rural north Texas and, in a brief conversation, he said he couldn't remember anything about the Safeway robberies. He also told me he did not know who his grandson was. "I left that place and divorced that woman sixty years ago, and it's all done," he said. "I have got no interest in any of it. Do you know what I'm saying to you?"

His son Randy eventually got a job erecting metal-studded walls at a drywall company but quit that for more itinerant work. Always talented with tools and conscientious about his craft, he made his living on small-time construction jobs, installing pool decks, laying carpet, and restoring old cars for cash. When situations got tight for him, he liked to say with a smile that he was "peacocking on a prayer," meaning that he would gut out the trouble until it had passed. Randy bought the house in Orangewood Estates when it was brand-new in 1977 and, shortly thereafter, met a woman named Amy Totman at a rock concert that he had attended alone. They married at the Pima County Courthouse in 1986 and had their only son, Jared, two years later.

They doted on him as he grew, and took an active interest in Jared's musical talents and taste for old-school jazz. Amy regularly drove him to saxophone lessons, and Randy bought him an electric race car track and a set of drums. Live music poured out the windows in the evenings; neighbors loved to listen to it, even if the family wasn't the outgoing sort. Randy walked his son down to Thornydale Elementary each day.

When he grew old enough to drive, Randy gave him the restored Chevy Nova.

"Randy and Amy were so proud of him," said Bills. "They weren't parents who just set up drums in the living room and said, 'Play whatever you want.' They listened to him. They're loving parents; they left him out of nothing."

When Bills and the other members of Tongue Dried Sun came over to the house for cookouts, Jared exchanged pleasantries with them but shied away from hanging out. He was about ten years younger than they were, for one thing. He also showed little interest in playing billiards with them on the patio, preferring to play video games by himself. But there was no sign of active friction between him and his father. The house was also immaculate, which Bills credited to Randy's value system.

"He's one of those people who take pride in what they own," he said. "You may as well call it American, or whatever that used to mean—not running up a mortgage but taking pride in what you owned. If you need to paint a car, or take it apart, or build a wall, he's going to know. He's a proud man, proud of what he's accomplished, proud of his home."

That pride extended to the behavior within his family. None of his longtime friends had ever heard that Randy's father—Jared's grandfather—had been accused of robbing Safeway grocery stores in the fifties. He never spoke of it. A man who has known Randy for many years called him a strict father who could silence Jared with a burning glance across the room. "I remember a shy kid that had to live by a lot of rules," he told me. "He acted like a kid that had gotten beat, but I never saw him get touched." Another onetime friend, Steve Fegan, agreed that Randy Loughner had the potential to go into impressive fits of anger when provoked. "You never knew when he was going to blow a fuse." But Fegan was also there at Tucson Medical Center the night Jared was born in 1988 and said that Randy, despite his occasional temper, appeared to be a loving and protective father toward his son.

Bub Hebert has known Randy two decades and last saw him at a swap meet at Tucson Raceway Park in October, at the height of the election season and during Jared's descent into insanity. They exchanged pleasantries, and Randy mentioned that Jared was getting out of control, but seemed to dismiss it as a youthful phase. "He said he was getting wild," recalled Hebert. "Smoking dope and drinking. But damn near every kid in Tucson does that. I'm sure they could never fathom that anything like this could happen."

The Loughner family's relationship with Tongue Dried Sun waned a bit after the band stopped its regular performances. Wyatt Bills said he would see Amy from time to time in the Albertson's supermarket where they shopped up at Ina and La Cholla, and they would exchange hellos. Nobody ever mentioned that Jared may have been showing signs of mental illness or having trouble at Pima College. They were too proud for that kind of disclosure, he said. But the idea that Jared Loughner grew up in an abusive home is ludicrous to him. A drummer for the band agreed with this assessment. "They treated that kid like gold," he told me.

Bills recollected this to me inside his sister's converted garage, near River Road, which was soundproofed and full of guitars and amplifiers. He showed me a Les Paul guitar that Randy had stripped and lacquered for him and repaired with some Bondo. "He did it just like he would a car, an awesome job. It's all primered."

When I was walking out the door, he told me that the stucco front yard planters inlaid with electric lights had been built by none other than Randy Loughner, free of charge. They were curiously bulged out on the sides and looked like pregnant Ls facing each other.

Before I got in my car I asked Bills why he thought the neighbors in Orangewood Estates could have gotten such a dim impression of the family if they were such loving parents to Jared.

"This isn't the kind of town where you really get to know your neighbors," he told me. "It's not like *Little House on the Prairie* here. I mean, come on."

SEVEN

IT ALL PLAYS IN

Ahaunting question: What might have happened had somebody close to Jared Loughner sought treatment for him, or if Pima College had referred his case to a county judge? The answer is forever unknowable, though some guesses might be attempted.

Loughner could have easily been stopped with a phone call. By hand-delivering the suspension notice to Loughner's home, Pima College was effectively notifying his parents that there was a grave problem. But a counselor also could have taken a step. So could a friend. So could anyone.

The state's committal laws are actually some of the most progressive in the country, stating that a person needs to be "a danger to self," a "danger to others," "gravely disabled," or an important fourth category that Loughner easily fit: "persistently or acutely disabled." The law also allows any "responsible person"—from a family member down to a complete stranger—to make an application for involuntary committal, which would have gone before a judge who holds hearings inside Kino Hospital.

Given Loughner's obsession with currency and grammar, his rambling delivery, and the odd tic in his eyes, a five-minute conversation would have made it clear that he most probably was suffering from paranoid schizophrenia. There would have been an order for treatment, and Loughner would have been kept at Kino Hospital at least overnight, and probably prescribed Thorazine.

Then it would have come down to a question of money. The state of Arizona has put its mental health safety net on a starvation diet, but unemployed fast-food employee (and legal adult) Jared Loughner would probably have qualified for federal help under Title 19 of Medicaid. His parents' assets would have had nothing to do with it. Even if he stayed at Kino Hospital no longer than a day, two things would have been accomplished: He would have had some conversations with a doctor, and he would have had access to drugs, including Thorazine. Whether these factors would have stopped him from being a killer is unknown. But it would have been far superior to the alternative, which was the indifferent hopelessness of West Ina Road.

His long-term future would have been much more uncertain. In the throes of economic depression, the state has sought to cut 260,000 of its patients from the Arizona Health Care Cost Containment System, which is the public health insurance apparatus. Though the name implies cheapness and bureaucratic heartlessness (who wouldn't love going into surgery knowing that "cost containment" was everybody's first priority?), the agency, known as AHCCCS and pronounced "access," was once considered a model program for distributing state and federal taxes to the sickened poor. That era is over.

Budget hawks like to say that once a government program gets entrenched dislodging it becomes immensely difficult. People's careers and salaries are now on the line, and they will create endless myths of apocalypse if the program's budget is ever threatened. But the corollary has become true in today's depressed Arizona. Once a cut is made to the budget that cut is likely to become permanent, and no amount of actual social disaster—such as a mass murder—can cause that money to come back.

For Arizona's tiny cluster of mental health advocates, the automatic appointment* of Jan Brewer to the office of governor was considered a ray of hope. Brewer's own son, Ronald Brewer, a diagnosed schizophrenic, has been locked up in Arizona State Hospital since a court found he was not guilty for reasons of insanity for committing sexual assault and kidnapping in 1989. Police said he forced his way into a woman's apartment and threatened to hurt her if she did not agree to a sexual encounter. "During the assault, she feared for her life and thought the suspect was going to kill her if she did not cooperate," said a Phoenix Police Department report.

The governor has mentioned this painful personal experience off and on through her career in the Senate and as a Maricopa County supervisor. When she took office as governor she proposed a reform of AHCCCS and new programs for the seriously mentally ill. But the legislature didn't go along, and Brewer eventually made $36 million in cuts, which meant those mentally ill people not already covered by the state's plan would receive nothing. People, that is, like Jared Loughner. There was still a suicide hotline with people answering, but no follow-up hospitalization. The health department has shifted its role from actually providing services to monitoring the contracts of the private companies like Magellan and Value Options that had been hired to soak up the federal Medicaid disbursements.

There is no legislative energy in Arizona to restore the lost AHCCCS money. I asked State Senate president Russell Pearce about it, and he acknowledged that "the state does play some role" in the treatment of the mentally ill because "government's role is to protect life, liberty and property." He went on: "It's a difficult issue because this man was not diag-

---

* Triggered by the appointment of then governor Janet Napolitano to be President Obama's secretary of homeland security. Arizona's constitution puts the secretary of state next in line; in the state's checkered political history, this office has been uncommonly important.

nosed. You can't deal with the unknown. The left always plays the blame game. Was he disruptive? Yeah. And maybe the parents had some knowledge, but there's nothing we could have done."

The Arizona legislature closed its first session after the Safeway shootings having deemed the Colt Single-Action Army Revolver the official state firearm and cutting $510 million from the state's health care budget, including services to the mentally ill. It also attempted to make it legal to carry a gun without restriction on a college campus, a bill vetoed by Brewer, who said the language was too ambiguous and might have made it legal to carry a gun onto a high school campus. There was almost no discussion at all about reforming the state's starving mental health network. Community Partnership of Southern Arizona, the agency that distributes the public dollars to mental health clinics in Tucson, had to lay off thirty people and eliminate twenty more positions—job losses that spread exponentially among its clinicians. Perversely, after the Gabrielle Giffords shooting there would be even fewer qualified professionals to stop a schizophrenic potential killer.

Like many lawyers in the country, Charles "Chick" Arnold has made a career of being a royal pain in the ass, but the ass he most consistently pains is that of the Arizona state legislature for what he considers to be its shameful neglect of the mentally ill. A lawsuit that bears his name, *Arnold v. Sarn*, required the state to provide a range of services. He also pushed hard for the 2002 expansion of Arizona's involuntary commital law that includes the vague but important category of "persistently or acutely disabled." I went to talk to him at his top-floor law office on Central Avenue, a boulevard several miles north of Phoenix's downtown and lined with seventies-era skyscrapers. This is the traditional power corridor for the state's legal mandarins.

Arnold is a short man who has a white-whiskered chin and a voice like a children's television host. He wore a tastefully colored tie and cap-toed shoes the day we talked; the conference room window framed a view of the nearly perfectly triangular Piestewa Peak, which used to be called Squaw Peak and has been renamed for Lori Piestewa, a Hopi Indian soldier killed in the 2003 invasion of Iraq. Just south of the building is the parking garage where an accountant named Ed Lazar was shot five times by mafia hitmen in 1975 before he could testify against Ned Warren, Sr., "the Godfather of Arizona land fraud."

Arnold has been watching the capital a long time, and he says there is no way this ineptitude would have happened under a more unified government. The attempted assassination of a U.S. congressmember and a mass murder in front of a grocery store perpetrated by someone who could have and should have been helped ought to have at least prompted soul-searching, and perhaps some steps toward mental health reform. "Before we got so polarized Republicans were just fine with this sort of thing," said Arnold. "There has been no dialogue or discussion. They are closed to this issue, and I think it has to do with the idea that government has no role here." The result is a confusing mess of which nobody can be proud.

In this way Arizona is again a reflection—an exaggeration, even—of the national posture. America's treatment of the mentally ill has lurched haphazardly through the years. In the English colonies of the eighteenth century, those who suffered from what we now recognize as schizophrenia were either confined to the homes or root cellars of their relatives or allowed to wander freely as long as they refrained from stealing or killing. These "lunaticks," as they were known, believed to have been driven mad by the moon, or simply cursed by God, became the prototypical village idiot of rural America, an outcast who steals from garbage piles and lives in a crude wooden shelter in the woods. The colonial legislature of Massachusetts ordered town selectmen in 1676 not to let them "damnify others," and the less fortunate were jailed or kept in jerry-built cages inside the charitable poorhouses, outside the view of polite society.

In 1841, a thirty-nine-year-old Bible teacher named Dorothea Dix went into the jail in East Cambridge, Massachusetts, to read scripture to the inmates, and was disgusted at what she saw—women and men out of their minds in cells where the temperature was barely above freezing alongside prostitutes and drunks. When she complained to the guards she was told that the insane were unable to perceive heat or cold. Dix felt herself outraged and devoted the next fifteen years of her life to poking her nose inside almshouses and county lockups, documenting the sorry state of care for the deranged, who she thought might see an improvement in functioning if they hadn't been treated like such organic trash.

She was not above sensationalist descriptions to prove a point. "The condition of human beings reduced to the extremist states of degradation and misery cannot be exhibited in softened language or adorn a polished page," she warned the Massachusetts legislature in a long report titled, in the parlance of the day, as "Memorial in 1843": "I proceed, gentlemen, to call your attention briefly to the present state of insane persons confined in this Commonwealth in *cages, closets, cellars, stalls, pens!* Chained, naked, beaten with rods and lashed into obedience." A professional and clean asylum—the name means "safety"—was the proper place for those who couldn't function normally. Ashamed lawmakers soon expanded the hospital at Worcester. Dix crusaded for the insane with the passion of a later generation of suffragettes. With so much to be done in this world, she remarked, it seemed that there must be *something* for her to do. Her advocacy took her all across the United States and Europe, and state legislatures relented, passing appropriations to build a series of state-funded asylums for those who couldn't take care of themselves.

Her work was contemporaneous with that of Dr. Thomas Story Kirkbride, a Philadelphia Quaker whose work with the insane convinced him of the need for enlightened and sanitary architecture in which to house them. He published *On the Construction, Organization, and General Arrangements of Hospitals for the Insane* in 1854, which outlined what would soon be called the "Kirkbride Plan" for the novel quality of its layout. Plenty of sunlight and high ceilings were called for, as well as separate diagonal wings for male and female patients arranged by room in the order of the severity of their illness, with all hallways within the clear sight of a central administrative post—similar to that of the guard shack in the prison cell blocks that would soon be copying the idea. A whole range of Kirkbride asylums were built in nearly every state in the country in the late nineteenth century, usually gothic fortress blocks surrounded by acres of lawns and gardens. A few dozen are still in use today, though the idea began to lose credibility at the turn of the century because of the massive costs involved, as well as critiques from cost-minded reformers that the rates of "cured" insanity were unchanged. Most Kirkbrides were abandoned and became horror-movie ruins.

The unattractive brain rot had been hidden behind state walls, where all manner of treatments were attempted—electroshocks, solitary confinement, and lobotomies performed by sticking an icepick into the frontal lobes, which turned violent inmates suddenly docile. Convincing a judge to commit someone became easy; many who were merely eccentric or obnoxious fell victim to relatives looking to push them out of the way. During World War II, the Mennonites and Quakers who refused to be drafted were typically assigned to do low-level cleaning work at the state mental hospitals. The filthy conditions they found there shocked their consciences. They spoke about it in public, and exposing the shoddy treatment inside these public institutions soon became a standby for journalists looking for a juicy story. In 1946, Albert Q. Maisel of *Life* magazine wrote with angry poetry and the indignity of a Dorothea Dix when he described state wards so jammed with bodies, feces, and tick-eaten mattresses that "floors cannot be seen between the rickety cots," and dreadful whirling nights in cells that were "merely black tombs in which the cries of the insane echo unheard from the peeling plaster of the walls." This was an experience many got to share. Within ten years approximately a third of 1 percent of the entire national population was housed inside a sanitarium.

The public mood began to sour on inpatient treatment. In 1963, the month before he was assassinated, President John F. Kennedy signed a bill to spend $3 billion to create a network of community health centers across the nation that would take the place of the discredited gothic asylum on the hill. "It has been demonstrated," he said hopefully (and erroneously), "that two out of three schizophrenics—our largest category of mentally ill—can be treated and released in six months." The development of chlorpromazine as a potential miracle drug for schizophrenia fueled the hope that "outside was better than inside" for those languishing in asylums, and the influential* novel *One Flew Over the Cuckoo's Nest* by Ken Kesey, published in 1962, helped this perception immeasurably.

The novel tells the story of Randle Patrick McMurphy, a new inmate in an asylum who is not really insane but faking it to make a criminal sentence easier. He fights petty battles with the power structure, represented by the odious Nurse Ratched, and is eventually lobotomized. Kesey wrote the novel based on his own experiences working the night shift at a facility in Menlo Park, California. By the time a movie version was released in 1975, winning five Academy Awards, including Best Picture, the specter of the asylum had come to signify all that was wrong with society—a spooky metaphor for power run amok—and a new generation of civil rights lawyers made their names and considerable fees by suing for inmates' freedoms. State legislatures found themselves happy to save money by firing doctors and turning their wards loose.

In just twenty years, from 1960 to 1980, a massive exodus took place from American mental institutions. The population went from half a million to less than one hundred thousand in a shift that came to be called "deinstitutionalization." Yet the result was not entirely humane. Distracted by deficits and the Vietnam War, Congress failed to provide funding for promised community health clinics, and sick people found they had nowhere to go. The population of the mentally ill homeless soared; active psychotics joined the legions of hard-core alcoholics and bums who begged for change on street corners or lived under highway abutments. Many were beaten to death; others eventually wound up arrested for crimes ranging from public indecency to murder. As it was in the days of Dorothea Dix, the cell block became the primary home

---

* As it happens, Jared Loughner listed this as one of his favorite books on his YouTube profile page.

for the seriously disturbed. Today the largest single mental institution in America is the Los Angeles county jail, where about half of the inmates on any given day are suffering from schizophrenia, bipolar disorder, or clinical depression.

Arizona's deinstitutionalization problem was as bad as anywhere in the United States. Cheap apartment blocks in central Phoenix and at the edges of Tucson became like minighettos for the insane. For those who couldn't afford subsidized rents, or were too disoriented to make payments, the desert and the streets were the only options. They roamed the sidewalks in greasy clothes, hands jittering, mouths agape. The down-on-its-luck north Phoenix neighborhood of Sunnyslope, once a colony of shacks for tuberculosis patients in the 1920s seeking dry air, became a haven for the new lungers of the 1980s: the seriously mentally ill who had no place else to go.

The current withering of care in Arizona signifies a new phase in deinstitutionalization, but one without the philosophical justifications. This is only rooted in the real-estate lifestyle depression gripping the state. The legislative leadership, including Russell Pearce, had to cut a bleak deal with the mental health lawyers putting pressure on them in 2010. Enforcement of *Arnold v. Sarn* would be suspended for two years, and in return the state would not pursue the repeal of a law that explicitly said they had to pay the bill for mental health services regardless of a patient's ability to pay. The law might still say that, of course, but the reality is exactly the opposite because of the lack of money. If you have no insurance in today's Arizona, it's just too bad. "We're in trouble here, and I don't see relief," said Arnold. "It's getting hard to offer hope as a response. There will be more Jared Loughner cases."

For H. Clarke Romans, the executive director of the National Alliance on Mental Illness of Southern Arizona in Tucson, it was understandable that Pima College should have wanted to simply banish Jared Loughner rather than deal with the harder question of how to help someone who was publicly disintegrating. He described Pima's response as: "Let's solve this problem by removing it from the area of our responsibility." This might also be seen as a miniature and local version of the state's current strategy of retreat and denial.

"From the get-go, unusual behaviors have been not accepted," he said. "This community inherited that worldview of mental illness. And so institutions are paralyzed in this inability to respond in a timely and consistent manner to people with mental illness. If on the Pima campus somebody were to fall down with a heart attack, everyone knows what to do—that's CPR. But Jared Loughner *was* having a heart attack. He was having little bits of heart attacks. He didn't have a massive one until the tragedy. In the ideal scenario, even if Pima wasn't equipped to deal with it, they could have conducted an outreach thing, even if they had suspended him. But schools don't want to know about these illnesses. They don't know how to do anything about them. It's not a polite conversation topic. People are more likely to want to talk about colon cancer. He was allowed to get sick because we as a society failed him."

There is a question, of course, as to how much responsibility a place like Pima Community College *ought* to have shouldered. A community college is not a replacement for parents, and Pima cannot offer much in the way of creating a sense of togetherness or intellectual adventure among its amorphous student body, many of whom are there to beef up their grades to get into a four-year state school, or because of a lack of cash or kids to raise or other circumstances at home that prevent them from going at it full-time. The bargain it strikes with its academic customers is not generally a warm one—write us the check, show up on time, and we'll get you the credit. Should such a place have had a speed dial to the county mental health court any more so than a grocery store or a car dealership or any other place of unsentimental commerce? The ordinary student or professor is not a trained clinician and is not qualified to distinguish between a person who is just being harmlessly eccentric or annoying, and someone with a serious mental illness on the edge of bloodshed. The real test is whether a person can effectively function from day to day, and that inability may only be obvious to the family or close friends, if any are left.

Even then, a small human connection can make a huge difference. On October 28, 2002, an eccentric student named Robert Flores walked into the College of Nursing at the University of Arizona with five pistols and 250 rounds of ammunition. He had already sent a terrifying suicide letter to the *Arizona Daily Star* titled "Communication from the Dead" that explained his anger over his failing marriage and the arrogance of people in the college administration. "I guess what it is about is that it is a reckoning," he had written, "a settling of accounts."

Flores went up to the second floor office of Professor Robin Rogers and shot her, apparently angry about being barred from taking a midterm examination. He then marched down to the classroom where the midterm was taking place. Members of this class had largely shunned him, because he tended to make belittling remarks to other students and acted generally weird.

He drew his weapon on Professor Cheryl McGaffic and asked, "Are you ready to have a spiritual experience?" He shot her and Professor Barbara Monroe. Then he turned to the class, and his eyes fell on two women in the front row who had been among the few in the nursing program who ever talked to him or tried to draw him out. "You guys get up," he said. "I want you to go calmly and slowly."

"What still amazes me is that he had that act of mercy inside of him," Laurel Steinbring told me. She was hiding in the back of the room and now works as a school nurse in Flagstaff. "He had enough bullets to kill each and every one of us."

Flores held the class hostage for another five minutes before deciding to let everyone else go as well. He watched them file out. Steinbring was among the last to have left. The initial decision to spare the two women who had forged a slight human connection to him had apparently made him change his mind about killing the entire room. His rage leaked away after that, and he took his own life after the last student was out of the room.

Nobody will ever know if Jared Loughner might also have been reached in extremis with a chance conversation. The critical time to have done so would have been in the days in the latter half of 2010, when his life was plainly falling apart, and he apparently gave up hope of finding a path out of his private mental hell. But nobody was around for him.

There are thousands of others like Loughner in Arizona, said Romans, people who have gotten neurologically unlucky and who have thrown themselves into a drowning pool of loneliness because they can see no other good alternative. The personal violence may never emerge, but the systematic violence of a cold, isolating world is always present. It is woven into the spreading city they inhabit. "Trust me, they are out there," he said.

❖

There was an enormous conjecture in the days after the Safeway shooting as to whether or not Jared Loughner was acting out a political agenda.

His targeting of the elected representative of the Eighth Congressional District of Arizona made the gunfire at the Safeway an intrinsically political act. But was he shooting at Gabrielle merely because she was a local authority figure and a famous person who happened to be nearby? Or was his desire to do violence to her rooted in a dislike of what she stood for?

Journalists combed Loughner's Internet rants for any clues to his ideology. He had made a list of his favorite books on his Myspace page, which was given an intensely close reading that first week. They included *Animal Farm, Brave New World, The Wizard of Oz, Aesop's Fables, The Odyssey, Alice's Adventures in Wonderland, Fahrenheit 451, Peter Pan, To Kill a Mockingbird, We the Living, The Phantom Tollbooth, One Flew Over the Cuckoo's Nest, Pulp, Through the Looking Glass, The Communist Manifesto, Siddhartha, The Old Man and the Sea, Gulliver's Travels, Mein Kampf, The Republic,* and *Meno.* Whether or not he actually read these books or just liked carrying them around is unclear. Conservative apologists leaped on the Karl Marx title as evidence that Loughner was a "leftist," while liberal bloggers jumped on Hitler's autobiography as well as Ayn Rand's *We the Living* as evidence of his nascent fascism. But none of this was correct.

A close look at his Internet writings shows that he was neither right nor left in any classic sense. His primary conviction was that a band of shadowy forces were manipulating ordinary people unaware of the deception. The ordinary world was not "real," and Jared Loughner saw himself as a hero who would uncloak the lies. He wanted to start a new monetary system of silver and gold, and he repeatedly told the administrators at Pima Community College that his classes didn't count anyway because he didn't pay for them with precious metals. Loughner was also convinced that the government was controlling its citizens through words, and that English grammar had been doctored to create a nation of sheep. "What is government if words have no meaning?" he asked Gabrielle at a 2007 forum, and she—understandably—didn't have an answer that pleased him.

The closest analog in the political world to this confusion of the real and unreal can be found within the ideology of the "sovereign citizen movement," a loose group of tax protesters and constitutionalists who believe the government of the United States and its paper currency is illegitimate because the "real" country has been taken over by a cabal, which has been using the bodies of its citizens as collateral to borrow money. The only real currency, they insist, is gold and silver, because its value is eternal and cannot be manipulated by governments or banks. Paper money is called "fiat money" and is inherently worthless, though it is gladly accepted at the day-long seminars that sovereign citizen gurus hold in rented hotel conference rooms. They also advertise their beliefs widely on the Internet.

Adherents who wind up in court have been known to file motions full of legal-sounding gobbledygook claiming that their flesh-and-blood personhood is different from the "straw man" entity that has been charged. They also accuse* the judge or their own lawyers of being

---

* In a May 25, 2011, federal court hearing in which he was ruled legally incompetent to stand trial, Loughner rocked back and forth and made a sudden outburst, apparently to Judge Larry Burns: "Thanks for the freak show. I saw her die in front of me. You're treasonous."

frauds. Some have changed their names. David Wynn Miller, a onetime Wisconsin tool-and-die maker and a guru of the movement, prefers to go by the name David-Wynn: Miller. He initially bragged to *The New York Times* that Loughner had probably been on his Web site, which purports to show how language has been the tool of a secret conspiracy for the last eight thousand years.

Such theories might be entertaining for a grad student who is impressed by Noam Chomsky. For a paranoid schizophrenic the beliefs of the sovereign citizen movement find a striking parallel in the "influencing machine" first described by Viktor Tausk in 1933—the unseen box that manipulates the world and that only the patient seems able to perceive. Like the protagonist of the movie *The Matrix*, the patient is awakened to the power that has hypnotized the rest of the world into compliance.

A few of Loughner's favorite books also speak to that fascination with conspiracy and the blurring of reality: Orwell's *Animal Farm* and Huxley's *Brave New World* in particular. His high school friends said that Loughner's favorite writer was the California recluse Philip K. Dick, whose sci-fi novels deal with dizzying scenarios that depict the hero's journey in attempting to sort out what is truly "real" and what is an illusion created by a giant conspiracy just outside his reach.

His diet of other media in recent years remains a mystery. He didn't write anything about the 2010 elections that has been made public. Only a few fragments from the documents found in his home on North Soledad have been released by federal prosecutors; they include the words "die bitch," "my assassination," and "I planned ahead." Jared Loughner's own writings reveal him to be a person explicitly fascinated with politics and government, though not in conventionally partisan ways. He believed that paper money was not real, and that only gold or silver were true means of transacting payment. He embraced the abstruse conspiracy idea that the English language was a means for government control of the populace, forcing him to communicate in ways that were already a means of robbing him of liberty. He was susceptible to being pushed, and the loneliness of his life left him with nobody to talk to about it.

There can be little doubt that Loughner was targeting Gabrielle primarily because she was a tangible representative of the government. Any person living in Tucson that autumn, even those who didn't watch the wall-to-wall television ads, would have been blind not to have seen the face of Gabrielle Giffords peering out everywhere, both sinister and benign, like the all-seeing eyes of Dr. T. J. Eckleburg in *The Great Gatsby*. She had become the most prominent local personification of "the government." There was no closer representation of federal power, or one that was more immediately accessible.

In fact, she was right down the street at the Safeway.

One of the most persistent voices against Gabrielle in her last reelection effort belonged to Jon Justice, the morning drive-time host on Tucson's most popular talk radio station, 104.1 FM. The call letters are KQTH, but in the old radio custom of coaxing rough sounds and meaning from the letters, the station refers to itself as "The Truth," which works if you gurgle it in your mouth. The implication is that other stations are not telling you the truth. *The Jon Justice Show* calls itself in its recorded intros "the only morning show in Tucson where *you have a voice*." The phrasing of this sweeper is also ambiguous. It could signify that other shows don't accept on-air calls from listeners (they do), or perhaps it only drives it home that Justice is the only local broadcaster able to put words to the latent feelings of the public, "your voice," therefore, being one of emotional ventriloquism.

I went to the studios of KQTH, The Truth, early one morning to watch Jon Justice at work. He was wearing a striped button-down shirt and has hair graying at the temples combed upward in front into a slight skater 'do. Justice was just getting over a month-long bout with a hematoma, which gave him an excruciating pain in his right side, preventing him from driving to the studio. He had been doing his broadcast by remote feed from the laundry room of his home in a subdivision on Tucson's northwest side. But now he was back at work and into the full Justice mode, which involves calculated fusillades of anger directed into the black nylon rectangle of his microphone. From here the sound of his voice is translated into a digital stream, then sent through an IP router to a transmitter where, after a brief profanity delay, it is translated again to an AES/EBU bit stream, then routed to a digital audio processor, and finally poured out the top of KQTH's, The Truth's, red-and-white striped tower off Wetmore Road in northwest Tucson, which at 729 feet is the tallest radio tower in Arizona. It also happens to be the fourth-tallest man-made structure of any kind in Arizona.

Today's outrage was a column in the *Arizona Daily Star* about a neighborhood zoning dispute. Some wealthy folks who lived in El Encanto—one of Tucson's first 1920s subdivisions, now blandly genteel—were upset that the managers of the El Con Mall—Tucson's first climate-controlled superblock, now eerily deserted and gasping its last—were leasing space for a twenty-four-hour Walmart, with its glassy front doors aimed toward their culs-de-sac.

Parochial squabbles such as this are common fare in Tucson's newspapers, but Justice heard within it the boot falls of an approaching army.

> This issue really isn't about the Walmart. It's not. It is about the individuals living in the neighborhood, okay? It is a lot of liberals, let's be honest. Walmart is a target . . . they have just been demonized to the point where there are many people who see it as the downfall of America. These are people, in my opinion, who don't respect the dollar. They don't respect capitalism. And we'll get into more of this a bit later with the *Arizona Daily Star* becoming basically an antigun lobbying group, because *it . . . all . . . plays . . . in*!

Justice gets up every morning at approximately 3:00 A.M. to surf the Web for fresh stories and finalize the rough script for the day's show, which consists of a stack of news stories on copier paper decorated with a yellow highlighter. The crucial factor for him is the narrative arc—the ability to connect one riff to another in a fluid way and make the whole four hours hang together in a more-or-less consistent wave of rhetorical energy. He seeks out the coupling points in stories, those bridges that can make, for example, Obama's decision to bail out the automakers not just relevant but intimately linked to a homeowners' association asking a resident to paint their garage a more pleasing shade of beige. The host guides the listener, strand by strand, through a web of assaults on their liberty, or, in this case, the call for zoning restrictions against a big-box store. As he likes to say: *it . . . all . . . plays . . . in.*

"From my rock radio days," he told me, "I learned the game of forward momentum and perpetuating an idea. I definitely have an arc that I do."

Today's four-hour crescent, for example, began with an update about an immigration law followed by a story about murder in Juárez, which led to an enterprise story in the *Star* about handgun deaths (this one was a money shot; the gray *Star* is a frequent target, and the slightest hint that guns are anything less than a birthright will send him into impressive pyrotechnic sputters), which leads to the Olympian outrage of the Walmart sliding doors, which elides into the 10:00 A.M. stopping point at another beloved punching bag, the University of Arizona and its new National Institute for Civil Discourse, founded in the aftermath of the January 8 mass murder, which Justice avers has nothing at all to do with people's civility, or the lack of it, and has everything to do with liberals wanting to confiscate guns. He was disappointed that he didn't have time for a coda, an AP story about a Hawaii representative who wanted to ban toy guns to keep kids from being shot by nervous police officers. The show is an intricate fabric of fear.

Off the mike, Justice told me that he has a weird instinct for when he is losing his listeners' attention on a given topic and knows how to skip to the next story without embarrassment to keep the spiel lively. He calls this "finding the exit ramp." Practiced speakers always know how to feel the room, but the distancing medium of radio means that whatever drift-off he might be feeling comes from his own mind, and perhaps the body language of his producer, Josh Dryer, who sits across the desk from him at the soundboard and occasionally injects a shot of his own disapproval into whatever Justice is decrying.

The studio is corporate bland, with a tight weave carpet and a view of a rooftop air-conditioning unit. On the wall is a flat-screen TV silently tuned to Fox News opposite a wood ornament of an American flag and the legend LONG MAY SHE WAVE. But the dominant visual element is a vinyl banner with the station's brand identity, The Truth, and the kilohertz frequency, in which the decimal point is a small star.

Justice's real name is Jon Logiudice. He was born in Southern California, grew up in San Dimas, attended a private Christian high school, and found work after graduation as a real-estate auctioneer and home inspector. This occasionally got him chased by dogs off the lawns of houses in foreclosure. As he tells it, he didn't much care about politics until he was hired to do talk radio at Atlanta's WKLS and discovered that he "was a lot better at yakking than at playing tunes." This led to a job at WKLQ in Grand Rapids, Michigan, where he earned a countrywide bubble of attention for what he now calls the "infamous dog-drowning stunt." He and his morning show partner announced in 2005 that they would take a shelter dog to a nearby pond and broadcast its ritual drowning live on the air the following morning for the listeners' amusement. Indignant calls flooded in to the station, and to 911, shutting down the boards temporarily. Justice said it was actually a public service, as he and his partner were trying to draw more attention to the dangers of leaving children unattended near water. Two kids had drowned in north-central Michigan the previous week. He got off chastened but was fired for unrelated reasons later. As his career advanced, his act became more explicitly focused on politics, but with a driving rock-and-roll rhythm.

"Ultimately for me, it comes down to entertainment," he said. "Can you be compelling and in a way that engages the audience? I don't do anything to shock people into listening. I try to talk about what I find interesting. There is an 'entertainment' value sorely lacking in talk radio. The more successful hosts can do the news but also put it in a way that's entertaining."

Tucson is the sixtieth biggest market in the country according to Arbitron, which is the ratings agency that determines how many people are listening* during a given hour, and therefore how much a radio station can reasonably expect to charge its advertisers. Little else matters in the business. The reports are released four times a year in electronic spreadsheets that are still called "The Book," because they used to come in the mail in a softcover binder. A crucial metric revealed in "The Book" is the TSL, or "time spent listening," which is the average amount of time a listener will stick with the program before switching stations or switching off entirely. For *The Jon Justice Show* the TSL hovers at about twenty minutes, which also happens to represent the historic average time of a driving commute from the northwest foothills to most points in the central arteries of Tucson. This is an elastic number, of course, depending on the distance between hearth and workbench, but the twenty-minute rule has been a local cliché for more than half a century. Tucson's spatial geography has a rough relationship to content: Justice tends to keep his discourses contained within twelve-to-fifteen-minute packages, which leaves room for the ads like cream at the top of the coffee.

The Jon Justice Show got a pleasant surprise in 2010 when Arbitron's spring book deemed it the second-most popular radio show in Tucson, second only to *Rush Limbaugh*. He has an average of 8,450 listeners

---

* Determining this is not an exact science. Arbitron recruits random listeners every quarter to get a sample size and extrapolate. The company recently introduced devices called Portable People Meters, worn on the belt like a pager. They can register a unique tone embedded within the broadcast sound of a particular show, a signature known as a "watermark," that is undetectable to human ears. But Tucson is still a smaller "diary market," which means the recruits still have to write down their daily diet of media each day and mail it in.

in Tucson for any particular twenty-minute hit. For a metro area of more than one million, that represents a small slice. But one truism of the industry is that listeners to spoken-word radio are many times more likely to keep on listening through commercial breaks than those tuned in to music, for reasons that are sensually intuitive. Language sounds a lot more like an advertisement, and the borders between talking and shilling are not as rough; the soporific half consciousness that radio can invoke is less likely to be disturbed. It is therefore a slightly more attractive medium for sponsors. Loyalty to the Justice oeuvre is also a big factor. As Justice's program director Ryan McCredden says, "The people who like it, *love* it." In a fractured media landscape, with the information roar coming from blogs, Twitter, Internet news, cable television, satellite radio, regular old television, what's left of newspapers, and two dozen other competing stations on AM and FM, this is a smart strategy—capture just one market, but capture it completely.

Because the Arbitron ratings depend so heavily on the listener being able to write down the correct station they favor, KQTH spends an enormous amount of time on the fiery audio bridges that connect the show to its advertisements. These recorded flourishes are called "imaging" within the industry. They usually last between five and ten seconds and consist of whooshes or heavy guitar and a basso profundo male voice proclaiming the name of the show and the kilohertz frequency, followed by "*The Truth*." "We push the imaging. It almost sounds more like a rock station than it does talk," said McCredden. "You're getting younger people who have never touched an AM dial. And we blow that younger demo out of the water. You can be more aggressive and make it sound young and cool and hip." The AM dial, where talk radio was born and still thrives, is generally regarded as the province of the middle-aged and the elderly; KQTH wants to reach into the college crowd and the young marrieds.

McCredden is a low-key professorial type from the small northern town of Thorp, Wisconsin, who did time at stations in Eau Claire, Madison, and Dallas before coming to Tucson. He won't go into his own politics in any detail, except to say that he doesn't think that people necessarily "need to have M-16 automatic rifles to go squirrel hunting." Conservative ideology is immaterial to what happens off the air in the studios of The Truth, in any case.

"As a program director you have to see through the politics and see what's entertaining," he says. "That's all that matters to me. I can go in to Jon and say, 'That was smart, funny, quick.' Period. 'I *completely* disagreed with you, but that was great radio.'"

The origins of modern talk radio are foggy, but one important early precursor was *America's Town Meeting of the Air*, a show on NBC radio that debuted in 1936. The host was George V. Denny, the dapper head of the League for Political Education who wanted to experiment with radio as a teaching tool and convened live panel discussions on newsy topics. Audience members at the Town Hall theater on New York's Forty-third Street were invited to come to the microphone and ask questions, some of which were zinging and rude. The show's signature lead-in was a pioneering example of radio imaging—a male voice that sounded like a newsboy shouting, "*Town meeting tonight! Come to the Old Town Hall and talk it over!*"

A disc jockey at New York's WMCA named Barry Gray repurposed this idea in 1945 when he set the mouthpiece of the studio telephone next to the microphone and broadcast listeners' phone calls. The effect was scratchy but sensational, and he started doing his after-midnight show live from Chandler's Restaurant on East Forty-sixth Street, interviewing whatever Broadway star happened to come strolling by after the theaters let out. Gray, who is sometimes called "the father of talk radio," was an outspoken liberal who routinely criticized Senator Joseph McCarthy on the air, and once got suspended for calling an aide to another senator "oily," a bit of scandalous ad hominem that would go totally unnoticed today. He was also a role model for a young Larry King, who broadcast from a houseboat docked next to Miami Beach's Fontainebleau Hotel.

The unraspy and rock-friendly sound of FM radio was introduced in the late sixties, and young listeners migrated there in waves, leaving the AM dial a ghetto for advertisers. Rip-and-read news and windy talk shows about gardening and baseball were a cheap way to fill it up with an older audience of insomniacs and sports hounds who would leave the dial in place for hours on end. But the renaissance came only in the tail end of the Reagan years, when the Federal Communications Commission repealed the Fairness Doctrine, which had required stations to broadcast an "opposing view" upon the request of an aggrieved listener. The door was open for unalloyed opinion. Small-market stations made an important discovery: their Arbitron ratings tended to soar in response to an especially angry or outrageous host. Moderate or deliberative shows perished like mosquitoes in November.

By far the most successful of the new hosts was Rush Limbaugh, an attorney's son from Cape Girardeau, Missouri, who worked as a PR man for the Kansas City Royals before taking a local talk show job in Sacramento, California, and then at New York's powerful WABC, where he was in an excellent perch to heap muscular ridicule on protesters of the first Gulf War and, soon after, President Bill Clinton. He has said that he never owned a pair of blue jeans—"and not just because of my size"— because he associated them with sanctimonious liberal college students. Limbaugh's style of mock pomposity mixed with an uncompromising read on the news was imitated by hundreds of acolytes. Early in his career at WABC he gave an interview on a television talk show in which he made a blunt statement about his technique: "I believe people turn the radio on to be entertained, to be entertained, to be entertained." His contract through the year 2016 with Premiere Radio Networks is said to be $400 million. His Book is leafed with pure gold.

The entertainment formula of Limbaugh, and those imitators like Jon Justice, is to keep hammering a master narrative of the universe. Every topic in the news is framed in the simple concept of "liberty," and those perceived to be outside it are automatically villainous. This sands down the edges of nuance and other distractions and makes the host *interesting*, with the dark appeal of the rebel or the superhero. "Most people have competing values in their head," said David Barker, author of the study *Rushed to Judgment.* "We simultaneously believe in egalitarianism and also individualism. So you frame an issue a certain way as to prime one value in front of another. And there is no counterargument."

The sliding doors at Walmart are a good example. For someone whose house is barely a football field away, it comes down to property rights—those big glass doors glowing at all hours underneath the bold blue logo have a distinctly unfriendly effect on the resale value of the house. But the issue can also be framed as an assault on Walmart's right to open a new store, which is an attack on the unfettered market, which is therefore an attack on the capitalist economy as a whole. Enthusiasm for any of the initiatives of the Obama administration might be framed as a socialist plot to take over the economy. One sliver of aberration is transmuted into the ugly whole.

This makes for an uncomplicated line of patter, if nothing else, and that is where the money can be found. There is little neurological pleasure in making compromises. Negotiation is a bothersome reality of life, which we all have to do far too often at work and at home. We don't pay thirteen dollars at the movies to see the villain talked or counseled out of his badness or appeased with a concession. That is the weakness we secretly loathe in ourselves. We go to see the bad guy get killed, slaughtered, *annihilated*, but, if you please, not before a sword-crossing spectacular worthy of *Beowulf.* Superheroes need a strong enemy to be superheroes. Otherwise, what would be the point of the show?

"We are not the analytic creatures that we appear to be," said Peter Stromberg, a professor of anthropology at the University of Oklahoma who has studied the medium. "We are primates. We like the feelings of highly arousing emotions. And that motivates us in ways that we don't like to acknowledge, like chimps spotting an enemy. As an entertainment medium, it is in the interest of talk radio to arouse people's emotions. It's a genre that renders random and confusing events into something that makes sense. A highly concentrated monomaniacal view of the world can become the 'key to the world.' The idea is secondary to the emotion."

The instinctual arousal that talk radio produces might be compared to the cadences of our parents' voices, he said. Or the music at a party getting progressively louder and more urgent. There is a pragmatic reason why stations like The Truth have borrowed so much of their imaging from conventional rock-and-roll radio.

"The listener comes to start thinking about the world in terms of a single organizing principle," said Barker. "There's good guys versus bad guys, and it starts to get like a religion." He added: "You can imagine how it's a short step, for a disturbed person, to the thinking that '*we have to do something about this!*'"

This seems to be extremely rare. There are only two cases where partisan media commentary probably played a contributing role in a killing or attempted killing. The first and best known was the actual murder of a host, Alan Berg, a caustic liberal Denver commentator who used to take great pleasure in making fun of The Order, a white supremacist group. Four men associated with The Order shot him to death in his doorway as he returned from dinner with his ex-wife in 1984. A more recent episode involved a convicted bank robber named Byron Williams, who allegedly loaded his car with weapons in July 2010 and headed to San Francisco to attack the offices of the Tides Foundation, an obscure progressive philanthropy repeatedly singled out by the Fox News star Glenn Beck as "thugs" who want to "warp your children's brains and make sure they know how evil capitalism is." Williams was pulled over for erratic lane changes on an Oakland freeway, got into a shootout with the California Highway Patrol, and surrendered after a twelve-minute chase. From jail, he told a reporter: "I would have never started watching Fox News if it wasn't for the fact that Beck was on there. And it was the things that he did, it was the things he exposed, that blew my mind."

Blowing the mind is an imperative of talk radio. Competitive pressures require the constant generation of low-grade outrage to tease out what H. L. Mencken once described as the suppressed desire in a reasonable man to "spit on his hands, hoist the black flag, and begin slitting throats." There is some irony in the ascendance of conservative talk radio, whose foundations were laid by the generally hostile view of the government among the Vietnam War protesters and liberal malcontents of the sixties. Taking rhetorical aim at the incompetence or cupidity of an elected official is a trope we recognize and even welcome—as familiar as the bad guy being blown away five minutes before movies end.

There is a blanket assurance in talk radio that one's interests are being looked out for, that some brave body is finally calling bullshit and speaking the truth to power. For the listener, there is no actual work required. No sacrifice is demanded from the audience. No need to get involved. No need to do the hard, incremental work of governing. Nothing except for the donation of twenty minutes of TSL and accepting, along with a chorus of ads for cut-rate mortgages and gold-hoarding stocks, the willingness to entertain a view of the universe that is, at its core, a conspiratorial and paranoid maze, with the listener always cast as a hapless victim, the pawn of an invisible machine.

There is nothing new about this in America, of course. Alexis de Tocqueville observed in 1840 that newspapers in the young American democracy were more prone to shriek than to persuade. "Style will frequently be fantastic, incorrect, overburdened, and loose,—almost always vehement and bold," he wrote. ". . . The object of authors will be to astonish rather than to please, and to stir the passions more than to charm the taste." Richard Hofstadter noted in his classic 1964 *Harper's* essay "The Paranoid Style in American Politics," anticipating partisan talk radio by twenty years, that the search for an omnipotent villain—whether it be Masons, Jews, Catholics, Illuminati, foreign-born immigrants, or financial speculators—has been a robust vein of thought in the United States almost since its birth, and that a proven method of self-advancement is to magnify it. He writes: "The paranoid spokesman sees the fate of conspiracy in apocalyptic terms—he traffics in the birth and death of whole worlds, whole political orders, whole systems of human values. He is always manning the barricades of civilization."

This message finds friendly soil in places like Tucson, where social capital is already low and where the lack of cohesion among one's neighbors produces a higher than average degree of suspicion of one's fellows. Channeling that latent fear and loneliness into the outrage of the day, the host becomes a superhero.

In the last hour of the broadcast, Jon Justice moves from the sliding doors at Walmart into an extended riff about how the reaction to the attempted assassination of Gabrielle Giffords and the calls for civility have really been all about a hidden agenda: the federal government wanting to roll back gun rights.

> I ask all those individuals who are using January 8 to push for more gun control—*where ya been?* If you care so much for gun control, what about all those homicides that took place last year, and the ones which took place at the hands of people who had weapons? You weren't crying out for gun control then. You never are. . . . They are trying to play off the emotions when we have almost daily shootings that occur, and they never speak up and say anything.

He goes on with an explanation:

> The mental health issue doesn't align with what they're trying to accomplish. Sure, it might be the proper avenue to go and look if you're going to look at anything that could have stopped what took place on January 8. Did Pima Community College do everything it needed to do? You know, what was the mental state of this individual? Did people miss anything along the way? Let's examine that! Oh *no no no.* That flew for a moment, only because it was the right way to look. Right up until individuals said, "Yeah, that's not really working out for us, we need to go the gun route and the incivility route, because both of those issues are those that people will actually latch on to. Those issues will ultimately help us in our

leftist agenda in getting guns out of people's hands, limiting their freedoms, and demonizing the voices of dissension that *we don't like!*" Nine-thirty, time for your ABC news update on The Truth.

After the break, Justice goes to the phones and takes six calls in a row, all of whom are in enthusiastic agreement with him.

There is Brett, who wonders why Jared Loughner's mental state wasn't forwarded to federal officials for some kind of background check. "Even if he failed a background check, there's no saying he couldn't have gotten a big knife and still killed, or, you know, done even more damage to Gabrielle Giffords with a well-placed stab to the heart."

There is Ken, who says, "There's a deeper problem, and it's something the liberal left has implemented themselves. Things do not get entered into the record. There's this whole stance on privacy of the individual. . . . If there had been a simple track record of what this guy was like mental health–wise, problems in school, there's no possibility that he could have passed the entry requirements to buy a weapon."

There is Rick, who says, "Every time I hear articles from the *Arizona Daily Star*, which is so far left it, God, it drives me nuts, every time I hear this antigun stuff it reminds me I'm now a paraplegic in a wheelchair. . . . I'm very vulnerable, and all this crap I read makes me realize I need to get to Diamondback and cover my back pretty quick." (Diamondback is a local gun store.)

There is Carl, who says, "The left decides everything is a problem with a gun, but they don't take into account the thousands of times per year that people's lives are saved because of a gun owner. Until they decide to put that into the equation, they might as well go on talking to themselves."

And finally there is Phil, who goes down a road that Justice does not like. "We might want to inform your audience, your listeners, that this is how Hitler got started. He registered all the guns, and then he went and confiscated all the weapons from the citizens."

Justice leaned in to the black rectangle without expression. "Well," he says, "I understand the point, but you use the word 'Hitler,' and I do an eye roll and tune out. We do live in a country where we won't get that far. We have enough conservatives and enough gun rights advocates that that will never occur. I do appreciate the phone call . . . *kinda*."

The call screener is a twenty-five-year-old assistant producer named Ross Williamson, a graduate of Arizona State University's Walter Cronkite School of Journalism, who sits in a small room across the hallway. He has a small chin beard and is wearing a shirt with a Cincinnati Bengals logo. Those who dial in to the Justice show talk to Ross first, whose first blunt question—"What's your name and what's your topic?"—ensures that they have a coherent point to make that might interest Justice before they get logged in to a program called, as it happens, Assistant Producer, which cues up their name and a brief description of their topic onto Justice's computer screen for his perusal. If the caller goes down a greasy slope into the offensive, that gets flagged, too. Justice takes about ten calls every hour, and the vast majority of invited voices are in hearty support of what he's just said. Occasionally a cranky dissenter is gutsy enough to ring in, and he enjoys the takedown. Among shows like this the rate of listeners who actually call the show is known to be a tenth of 1 percent. The day of the Giffords shooting calls flooded in from all over the country from people listening to the show on streaming Internet.

Fear is what drives Jon Justice, and he says so without hesitation. He has been unceremoniously fired from multiple stations—a common fate in talk radio—and the awareness of his own fragile professional universe has given him a great deal of motivation to stay employed and make good Book. He resolves to do each and every show as though it were a tryout, which is what drives him to get up at 3:00 A.M. to take in a glutton's diet of news stories. He avoids the nakedly ideological sites, like the Cato Institute or NewsMax, and prefers to take his information from reasonably straight sources—CNN, Fox, and the newsy links on the Drudge Report—and judge whether it plays in with the master narrative of a sustained and interconnected assault on liberty. "My own take," he says, "is always going to be more instinctual. The first impulse is usually the right impulse." Despite what is sometimes said about him in Tucson's liberal quarters—that he is a mountebank who lacks true conviction—he affirms that he always believes what he is saying into the microphone, if for no other reason than that a limp delivery would be palpable to the listeners.

"Lack of caring will always make a bad show," he told me. "I always prepped the same way that I did when I was terrified. That results in a lot of leftover material."

I ask him if he's said anything that he regrets, and he pauses half a second before saying no, nothing in a grand sense. He was glad he challenged Sheriff Clarence Dupnik for blaming vitriol "from people in the radio business, and some people in the TV business" for the Giffords shooting. What fuels his insecurity are the smaller things. He once pronounced hyperbole as "hyper-boil," for example. Another time he talked about a higher court squashing a ruling when what he meant was quashed.

Such goofs are nothing, though, compared with the nervousness he would feel if he received that strange telepathy that his listeners were beginning to shut down, to cease being upset about the news and thereby entertained for at least twenty minutes of morning TSL, and possibly longer. "If I saw people dropping off," he told me, "that's when I would question what I was doing."

EIGHT

"I AM ARIZONA"

One of the nation's foremost authorities on American political assassination happens to live in a condominium barely two miles from the Safeway. He invited me over one Sunday afternoon, into a living room that was decorated with a mishmash of Indian and Western art: Hopi-style pots, an 1873 Winchester rifle, a colored Navajo saddle blanket. James W. Clarke is a professor emeritus at the University of Arizona and the author of *On Being Mad or Merely Angry*, a book-length study of the psychology of John Hinckley, who tried to kill President Reagan in 1981, as well as *American Assassins*.

A big part of this latter work was trying to understand and categorize the varied motivations for those who have attempted or succeeded at assassinating major political figures, from John Wilkes Booth to those of the present day. Clarke drew a lot of heat from his colleagues for his conclusion that insanity was almost never the sole motivating factor behind a person picking up a gun and going after an elected official. To say that the political noise in the autumn of 2010 didn't influence Loughner's decision to shoot Gabrielle Giffords is, for Clarke, "pure nonsense." He almost certainly was pushed by what he heard around him.

"The toxicity of this campaign was beyond anything I've ever experienced, and I've lived here thirty years," said Clarke. "I don't think the kid had a clear political rationale. It may not have been defined in liberal-conservative terms, but he was clearly antigovernment, and the antigovernment rhetoric was a major part of the campaign against Gabrielle Giffords in this last year. You could not drive across town without seeing these 'Burma-Shave' signs on the side of the road that told you how she was going to cut your Medicare. The political white noise provides a facilitating context, especially for someone outside the conventional social structures. Such things can be thinkable."

For one spiraling into a paranoid schizophrenic view of the world, said Clarke, "Giffords *was* the government doing all these bad things."

Clarke did not intend to develop an academic specialty in assassination. He grew up in the small coal-mining town of Elizabeth, Pennsylvania, floundered in his classes through high school, and made it into a local liberal arts college only by a fluke: The admissions director wanted to do a favor for Clarke's father, a respected lumber dealer. Before he earned his Ph.D. at Penn State he got drafted into the U.S. Marines and, while helping guard the brig at Parris Island, became appalled by the behavior of some of his fellow marines, who seemed to enjoy humiliating the prisoners. "I began to think, What makes a person this mean? Why would they enjoy torturing people this way?"

He had cause to remember that thuggery during his first job, which was as assistant professor of political science at Florida State University in 1968, the year Martin Luther King Jr. was shot in Memphis and Robert F. Kennedy was shot in Los Angeles. The conventional line on both shootings was that they were the deeds of "madmen" and "lone nuts" that had nothing to do with the state of affairs in America. That seemed like a too easy answer to Clarke. These killings had taken place within a social fabric, he thought, emerging like pinpricks from both the segregationist fervor of the South and the swirling chaos of the 1968 Democratic Convention. The life circumstances of the killers, too, almost certainly played a role in their decisions to act. Clarke had been an urban sociologist of the James Q. Wilson mode, but he abandoned that career and spent the next decade traveling from courthouse to courthouse during the summers, pulling old trial transcripts and police records from the various political killings that have stained American history since the end of the Civil War. And he found patterns.

Clarke developed a basic taxonomy of assassination, divided into four parts: a Type I person, which includes people like the Southern avenger Booth and the Puerto Rican nationalists Oscar Collazo and Grieselo Torresola, who tried to kill President Truman in 1948. They commit their deeds for purely political reasons; they believe themselves to be acting like selfless martyrs in a cause. Type IIs include people with an overwhelming need for status and acclaim—the basic narcissist looking for headlines. Examples include JFK's Lee Harvey Oswald and Sara Jane Moore, who shot at and missed Gerald Ford in 1975.

A Type III personality is consumed with psychopathic hatred toward self and society and wants to injure both by the most outrageous display of bloodshed possible. Such people include the enraged Italian immigrant Giuseppe Zangara, who shot at Franklin D. Roosevelt in an open car in Miami and accidentally killed Chicago mayor Anton Cermak instead, as well as Arthur Bremer, who shot and paralyzed George Wallace in the parking lot of a shopping center in Laurel, Maryland.

Finally there are Type IVs, the true psychotics, who show severe delusions of their own importance and a slippery hold on reality. The best-known example is Charles Guiteau, who shot President James Garfield in a train station in 1881 and thoroughly enjoyed the press coverage of his trial, waving to spectators and composing a babbling poem entitled "I Am Going to the Lordy," which he read from the scaffold before he was hung.

Based on Jared Loughner's angry denunciation of his federal court hearing as a "freak show," and his insistence that he is not the one who is crazy, Clarke judges him to be close to a Type IV. Yet one leaked detail of the investigation is particularly significant to him and may eventually challenge that designation as a psychotic. The FBI had seized Loughner's laptop computer, found out what he had been looking at on the Internet, and then told *The New York Times* that these Web pages had included information about the death penalty, the mechanism for lethal injection, and the biographies of famous American assassins. That meant that less than eight hours before he would take a cab to Safeway with a Glock 19 in his pocket to shoot a well-known congresswoman he was reading about the likes of Lee Harvey Oswald and Arthur Bremer, a pantheon he would soon join. Admiring the deeds of other famous political killers is a common theme among those contemplating their own burst of public vengeance.

"This gives them a certain sense of historical continuity," said Clarke. "In almost every modern case, assassins have researched the lives of prior assassins, and even seen them as role models. Sirhan Sirhan did. Hinckley did. Bremer did. Timothy McVeigh. Even Eric Rudolph. The Columbine kids had a fascination with Hitler. If you have no other means of getting attention, a violent interaction with a famous personage will get you that."

Clarke got into trouble with some in the mental health community by insisting that all these notorious figures emerged from a particular social context that had influence on their thinking and behavior. Even while mentally ill, they were still in dialogue with the outside world. The English poet John Donne said, "No man is an island, entire of itself." And no insane assassin operates in a complete vacuum. The voices they hear are not just in their heads. There is always a part of their reasoning that remains tethered to the culture around them.

"I challenged the blanket assessment that this has no political context and was all about mental illness," he told me. "My take on it is all about the criminal responsibility. I don't care how fucked-up they are. If they are able to plan an attack against a political figure in a public place, that to me suggests they knew what they were doing was wrong, and there could be severe consequences, and they decided to move ahead with it."

He acknowledges feeling some discomfort with his own life's work. There is no way to explain assassination without going into granular detail about the sad lives of its perpetrators. To document and publish these stories is to create a body of biography that may become part of the next killer's delusional canon. When he received a phone call from *Arizona Illustrated*, a local show on the PBS affiliate Arizona Public Media, in the days following the Safeway shootings, Clarke found himself saying, "I'm sorry. I just don't want to talk about the guy who did this." He changed his mind after a friend of his, a fellow volunteer at a soup kitchen, practically begged him to do it. "You *have* to say what you think," said this friend, and Clarke relented. "To write about these people is not to rationalize or to forgive," he told me. "It's to understand and explain."

In his view, the best historic comparison to Jared Loughner is that of Arthur Bremer, the pathetic son of a Wisconsin bread truck driver who was the subject of shunning and ridicule throughout his junior high and high school days. He wrote that he considered opening fire with a .38 caliber revolver at a downtown Milwaukee intersection before being distracted by news of the 1972 presidential campaign and deciding to eliminate either Richard Nixon or George Wallace so the world could witness, as he put it excitedly in his diary, "SOMETHING BOLD AND DRAMATIC, FORCEFUL & DYNAMIC, A STATEMENT of my manhood for the world to see."

Bremer had compared himself to Gavrilo Princip, the diminutive Serbian nationalist whose killing of Archduke Franz Ferdinand helped set the stage for World War I. His diary full of ranting and hopelessness was the source material for the 1976 movie *Taxi Driver*, which was a major inspiration for John Hinckley (he tried to assassinate Ronald Reagan in a bid to win the admiration of Jodie Foster, who played a teenage prostitute in that movie). The triumph of media genealogy: An assassin begets an assassin.

On the way out of Clarke's condominium, where he has lived since the early 1980s, I asked him if there might have been other environmental factors at work besides the nastiness of the recent election. Was there anything specific to Tucson, Arizona, that may have also contributed to Jared Loughner's helpless drift?

"All assassins have a history of social disconnection," he said. "And the neighborhoods here are some of the coldest and most distant that I've ever experienced. My wife is from Santa Rosa, California, and she's said the same thing. There's no backyard conversations here."

He waved his hand to the north, into the collection of Foothills houses beyond that he has lived nearby for a quarter of a century, and he knows almost none of the people who live within eyesight.

"I don't find this to be a family town at all," he said.

I recalled reading about Timothy McVeigh, the ex–U.S. Army soldier who blew up the federal building in Oklahoma City. There was a crucial period in his life when things might have gone a different direction. He was home from the army and sleeping on his parents' couch in his hometown of Lockport, New York. He had trouble getting a date. The only work he could find was as a low-wage security guard at a local zoo, a humiliating comedown from his service in the Gulf War. He turned to antigovernment rants as a way to find some meaning in a life that was starting to seem pointless. "Is a civil war imminent?" he wrote to a newspaper. "Do we have to shed blood to reform the current system? I hope it doesn't come to that, but it might." He had a brief mental breakdown and started making wild bets on Buffalo Bills football games, harboring a growing resentment against authority figures. McVeigh eventually drifted to a friend's trailer outside Kingman, Arizona, where he planned what he hoped would be the first bombardment in a war against the federal government.

Nothing clicked for him, said a journalist who followed his trail. If some higher purpose had just been there for Tim McVeigh, a good job perhaps, or a girlfriend, he likely would have turned down some other road.

Serial helplessness is an especially bitter thing to a new adult male between the ages of eighteen and twenty-two, when good things ought to be happening and aren't. The world unfolds, but to what end? There is wild biological hope brewing inside, though people turn their eyes.

Jared Loughner was almost certainly a schizophrenic, but he was still making an attempt to live with what shabby options he had been given. He quit marijuana and tried to join the army. He stopped binge drinking. He enrolled in Pima College, showed up for class, and tried to write poetry that people would enjoy. He tackled books that challenge the intellect and ask penetrating questions about man's existence. He was trying to ask those same questions in his own way, and even when he was at his most garbled, he was hunting for a listener who understood his point of view. He voted in elections, went to hear his congresswoman speak, and volunteered to help out at a book festival.

But nothing was clicking for him—nothing at all. He was drifting away from his parents and had severed relationships with most of his friends from high school, who were off making happy progress on their own. He had not sought any help for a sickness that was consuming him. Girls had avoided him. People made fun of him when he posted things online. His question to his congresswoman was incomprehensible and embarrassing. He carried the Constitution around as a battering ram. He got kicked out of community college in a humiliating way, by three uniformed cops, in full view of his father. At one point, according to media reports, he offered to pay former friends just to hang around with him and keep him company.

His whole universe was bounded by the bland comfort of chain stores, where the only key to love is money. He had worked at Peter Piper Pizza and Mandarin Grill, been fired from Quiznos, and stomped away from his manager at Red Robin. The best job he had had was at Eddie Bauer. He favored the food at In-N-Out Burger. He bought the gun at a Sportsman's Warehouse. He bought the ammunition at Walmart. The night before January 8 he had photos of himself developed at Walgreens, and he spent his last night as a free man in a Motel 6 before calling a taxi from a Circle K convenience store. He committed the most significant deed of his life under the logo of a Safeway.

After his name went out over the news that afternoon, nearly every mental health care provider in Tucson got on the phone with the office and had the staff review their databases for any signs that a Jared Lee Loughner, age twenty-two, had sought treatment from them. One of these executives admitted to me that his reaction upon hearing the negative had been one of *Thank God!* The institutional embarrassment would have been fierce. Better not to have wound up under the gun like Pima College; better not to have had anything at all to do with this toxic free radical.

I went down to see Dan Ranieri, of La Frontera. I asked him about the relationship between schizophrenia and environmental context, and he put his feelings to me in strong terms.

"In spite of what people say, that this was the solitary act of a crazy person, I have no doubt that some of the vitriolic stuff that's been going on contributes to that," he said. "This can be a difficult town. There's certain parts of the country, and Arizona is one of these, where if you grow up there you don't necessarily have a social network. There's very little in Tucson that pulls everyone together. People may or may not know their neighbors. There really aren't connections. That doubtlessly contributed to it."

Into this vacuum of the fractured human bonds and the incessant fear of poverty has rushed the gaseous hope for a decisive fix-it-all solution, the emergence of a bold, cold superhero who will stand up to the aggressor and thrash the living hell out of it. We call this craving one for "liberty," but it is really a form of enchainment to our own well-tended loneliness in the deluxe desert. If a genuine avenger cannot be found, there are plenty of ambitious contenders whose war cry is temporarily convincing. We love their bandolier of magic bullets and their willingness to shoot them for us.

"People are essentially abdicating their influence to shape things to a handful of really crazy politicians," Ranieri told me. "You can't expect people with narrow agendas to solve our problems."

✤

The most enduringly popular public official in Arizona—one whose influence is absolutely inescapable—is Maricopa County sheriff Joe

Arpaio, and when he acts like he is irritated, which is often, his lips draw to a fine line and his dark eyes harden.

He leans forward across his desk and speaks in a theatrical growl to me, in the accent of his native Massachusetts. "I thought illegal immigrants donating their organs would be a big story. Nobody printed it!"

Publicity is like oxygen for Arpaio, and he was mystified by this turn of events. A press release had gone out two days before proclaiming the news that fifteen illegal immigrants had volunteered to donate their organs for transplant. Not a single newspaper or television station touched it. This probably spelled the end of the publicity road for his I.DO! program,* in which inmates at the jail were encouraged to sign papers donating their hearts, eyes, kidneys, and other vitals to medical use in case of their deaths.

The failure to squeeze a story from this tidbit made for a sour morning in the executive suite of the Wells Fargo building, where Arpaio, aka "Sheriff Joe," aka "America's Toughest Sheriff," aka "America's Worst Sheriff" (as *The New York Times* once called him), keeps his offices, along with a sizable PR staff. Another recent press release proclaimed that a conservative booking agency had named him the sixth most desirable talk-show guest in the nation. That one, too, had been greeted by crickets.

"So I'm a publicity hound?" said Arpaio. "So what? I want everyone to know all over the country—when you move here, *watch out for the sheriff*. Everyone in this county knows who their sheriff is. I'm doing great things for the inmates. And now they're willing to give up their organs!"

Arpaio is seventy-eight years old but looks much younger. He has clung to power for nearly two decades and shows no sign of relaxing his grip. He is best known for a series of camera-friendly stunts that local journalists used to find inescapable, and that the occasional traveling European television crew still finds of some use, when they want to do a

---

* Short for "Inmates who Donate their Organs."

segment that vamps up the caricature side of the American West. Every written profile of him has included a Homeric list of his tough-guy deeds over the last two decades and, regrettably, this one has to include it, too, because understanding the sheriff's appetite for fame is also to see how Arizona's voters reward those who play on fear, no matter how bad the actor and no matter how ineffective the actual results may be. Despite several corruption scandals in his office and damning evidence that his posturing has actually made crime go up, he is still the most popular elected official in Arizona, one whose endorsement is eagerly sought by other office seekers.

The sheriff is most famous for forcing several hundred jail inmates to live in a series of army surplus tents in a fenced yard, in a place called Tent City. The day he opened this outdoor compound was August 2, 1993, a day when the temperature rose to 113 degrees, and televised images of the sweltering inmates and the no-nonsense sheriff went worldwide. The exposure was never again this good, but it didn't stop Arpaio from publicizing countless other punitive gestures. He took away coffee, salt, pepper, television, cigarettes, and pillows from the inmates. The only underwear issued was dyed pink. Those inmates who volunteered for the "chain gangs," who picked up litter from the side of the highways, were assigned to wear black-and-white jumpsuits that looked like leftovers from a Hollywood costume warehouse. Food consisted of nearly inedible surplus bologna and stale bread—to save taxpayer money, Arpaio said. His appetite for publicizing these sideshows is bottomless and pathological (more on this in a minute), and there will seemingly never be a time during his tenure when the press releases and the investigations into his political enemies will stop.

I had been one of his many enablers, having written a few stories about him and his antics when I was a reporter at *The Arizona Republic* a decade ago, and I went to see him again a few weeks after the Safeway murders. His corner office on the top floor of the Wells Fargo tower looked exactly the same: a shrine to Sheriff Joe. Framed copies of his two ghostwritten autobiographies. A fake Arizona vanity license plate

that said MY WAY.* A tall wooden sign advertising Tent City with a pink
neon light that says VACANCY. Printed copies of the latest news stories
about him were stacked neatly on his clean desk.

He gave me a look of glowering appraisal over that giant nose, and
then asked me the same curious question that I first got ten years earlier.
"So, Tom, wouldn't you feel *bad* if somebody popped me because of what
you wrote?"

I told him I thought that was unlikely. This is one of the sheriff's
favorite greetings. He loves it when people fear for his safety, and he loves
being able to tell them how he isn't afraid of the hoi polloi. One of
his chief deputies once wrote a fawning memo begging him to use a team
of bodyguards; this memo was promptly "leaked," as though it were
yet another press release.

"I should have been dead a thousand times over if I worried about
what the media says about being killed," he said. "Everyone says, 'Aren't
you worried about what happened to the congresswoman? Aren't you
afraid of being popped?' I'm not. It's unfortunate that elected officials
have to go through this."

There is not a conversation with Arpaio lasting longer than sixty
seconds that he does not steer back to himself: his total lack of fear; his
overwhelming popularity; his relentless persecution by Phoenix's alternative weekly newspaper, *New Times*; the thousands of flattering profiles
that have been done on him by international media; his book sales; his
pink underwear; his tents; his cheap food; his crusade against illegal
immigrants; his biannual flirtations with running for governor or senator (he never does); his professed lack of caring what you write or say
about him.

"I *loved* it when you blasted me," he told me. "My polls went higher!
Everybody said, 'Leave our sheriff alone. Get off his back.'"

The tough-hombre routine has a touch of Yosemite Sam. His child-

* The song of that title is also his cell phone ring tone, and the one he has told his wife
to play at his funeral.

like pleasure at "taking heat" from his critics and being intrinsically "controversial," his unapologetic megalomania, the briefest nods he gives that he doesn't really think in his heart that there is any true public safety benefit in taking away pillows and issuing pink underwear, and that it is just an extraordinary hurdy-gurdy show—all of this has given him a strange free pass within the remnants of the Arizona power structure, even though the novelty wore off a long time ago. *That's just the sheriff being the sheriff,* people say. But they have to deal with him. His rock-solid electoral base is the legions of senior citizens who live out in Sun City and Leisure World, and ringing them are the legions of bark-skinned social conservatives who see no contradiction between revenge-based jail policies and the creeping abuses of government they would otherwise loathe. And then there are those who just find him badass and entertaining. One poll showed that he had local name recognition of 94 percent. Four major presidential candidates have toured Tent City; Senator John McCain always treats him like an archduke. When Janet Napolitano was the U.S. attorney for Arizona, she found herself in the unenviable position of having to oversee a federal investigation into the systematic abuses at Tent City, and she, too, let him slide.

The belief among more skeptical voters and lawmakers in Phoenix is that the Joe Show is just a local quirk, another roadside curiosity of the alienated Southwest that doesn't really affect the bottom line.

Except that it does, and the damage to Arizona has been real. The sheriff never showed much interest in Mexican immigration until 2005, when he sensed—correctly—that it was becoming one of the big populist issues of the coming decade. Maricopa County deputies were soon making surprise "sweeps" through heavily Latino portions of the city, stopping random drivers for the most minor of infractions and asking for identification. "We are quickly becoming a full-fledged anti–illegal immigration agency," he bragged. But the busts only netted several hundred ordinary border crossers and not one of the "people-smuggling kingpins" that Arpaio said he wanted to bust. He refused to coordinate these roundups with any other police department, even when he ran them in another jurisdiction. One night he raided the Mesa city hall looking for illegal immigrants working as janitors without bothering to let the city of Mesa know about it. One dismal fact of life in American law enforcement anywhere is that cops are basically tribal. They profess otherwise in their public statements, but they secretly can't stand it when the FBI comes in and manhandles their case away from them, and they *hate* it when another local agency thinks they can do it better. Institutional pride is often stronger than justice. This is part of the reason why many investigations die in the filing cabinet. Cops guard their findings from one another like family jewels, out of both insecurity and buried spite. The immigration carnival made this dysfunction even worse.

The rates of violent crime in the Phoenix metro area started to climb, as deputies were too busy stopping Latinos with defective license plate lights to investigate rapes, robberies, and homicides. In 2008, the *East Valley Tribune* ran a five-part series that showed how the sheriff's response times to 911 calls were plunging. The *Tribune*'s stories, which won that year's Pulitzer Prize for explanatory reporting, also found that Arpaio had been spinning his crime statistics wildly.

One basic gauge of any police department's efficacy is a percentage called the clearance rate, which is a ratio of investigations that are opened against how many are cleared by arrest or a determination that no crime has taken place. The county's dismal clearance rate of 18 percent by arrest was made to look palatable because of a provision called "exceptionally cleared," which should mean that a suspect's identity is known but no arrest can be made because of a circumstance beyond the control of the police, such as lack of evidence or a constitutional problem. But after the immigration sweeps took effect, this clause was invoked three times as often as an arrest was made, often without any investigation. The unavoidable conclusion of this report was that Maricopa County had become a more dangerous place because of the sheriff's policies. It wasn't just bad policing, it was fake policing.

"Why am *I* the bad guy?" Arpaio responded when I asked him about this. "Why are you saying *I'm* wasting resources when something is a Class Four felony? We're doing thousands of seizures of drugs, and you say I'm wasting resources? This is a crime suppression operation. Tell me a police department who arrests eighty-seven people in seventeen hours."

There was more fungus hiding underneath the theater of the tents and the night sweeps. Arpaio had long feuded with the county Board of Supervisors who control his budget, and the clash grew operatic in 2006 when he and his ally, then county attorney Andrew Thomas, indicted Supervisor Don Stapley on charges of failing to list business interests on a disclosure form. The case ended in disaster. An outside prosecutor concluded that there was no way the case could be brought to court because the investigation was so tainted with politics. "The vast record is littered with behavior so egregious that a reasonable person's sense of fairness, honesty and integrity would be offended," she wrote. Arpaio and Thomas also accused a superior court judge of bribery and obstruction of justice but presented no evidence. The judge then sued the county for $4.75 million. Critics charged that the sheriff was using the arrest powers of his office simply to go after anyone who stood in his way.

All this cost the county dearly. A financial review showed that Arpaio's office had channeled approximately $99.5 million that was supposed to be used for the jails to these profitless investigations, as well as to his immigrant sweeps. "Over the past several years, MCSO has lost sight of its most essential priorities," claimed the Goldwater Institute, a conservative think tank that finally became upset over the unchecked gobbling of taxpayer money. The rising rate of violent crime and the costly diversion of manpower for the ineffective sweeps make it an agency in need of reform, the group said.

Arpaio told me he intends never to retire, no matter what his critics say. I asked him about what kind of vision he has for Arizona's future, and he paused.

"I'm kind of proud of this area," he said. "It's not like Springfield, where you have old houses that are dilapidated. It's so modern. I like modern buildings, modern highways. There's a big airport, the fifth largest. You have nice sports facilities. All this has happened since I've been sheriff. It's a modern metropolis. I have so much confidence in this state. Every day, I'm on national TV. Every single day."

He had a miserable childhood in Springfield, Massachusetts. His mother died giving birth to him on June 14, 1932, and he was raised by a stern and distant father who had emigrated from a small town near Naples, Italy, to run a grocery store. The future lord of Tent City frequently got struck with a belt by cousins and uncles for petty misbehavior—he says he can't even remember what he did to deserve it—but he stops short of calling it child abuse.

"There was a lot of discipline," he has said. "In those days, you got strapped if you did something wrong."

His father, Nicola Arpaio, didn't have much to say to young Joe Arpaio or know what to do with him. "He used to come home after a hard day's work and fall asleep in the chair," Arpaio once remembered to me. "So I didn't have a father that would take me out to play ball or those kinds of things. He was always tired. So I didn't have that type of childhood." His high school classmates described him as withdrawn and incredibly shy, and still profoundly troubled over the absence of his mother.

The first time Arpaio ever realized that his father was proud of him was when he managed to get quoted in a newspaper story.

After working as a beat cop in Las Vegas and Washington, D.C., Arpaio had joined the U.S. Drug Enforcement Administration and was stationed in Turkey. He helped arrest four peasants guarding a cache of raw opium and gave a quote to a reporter about it. UPI picked it up as a color story, and it ran in the back pages of several hundred papers, including—most crucially—*The Springfield Morning Union*, where Nicola Arpaio was able to spot it. The old man clipped the story and, as Arpaio found out later, showed it to dozens of people around town.

"My father was proud, I know, when I made international news," he told me in 2002. "I could see when I got home that he was proud of that. . . . I just wish my father was still alive to see *this*. I think he would have been proud of how I became internationally known."

Arpaio had a long career with the DEA, where he was not universally liked. His fellow agents started calling him "Nickel Bag Joe" for his willingness to arrest even the most pathetically low-level drug customer for the sake of a bust. He also became known for his penchant for calling up reporters and trying to gin up stories about the latest drug seizures, when bags of marijuana and cocaine are customarily laid out on tables for the cameras like slain deer. After time in Mexico and Turkey he picked Arizona as a warm place to retire, and arranged to be transferred to the Phoenix bureau, as the agent in charge. There was a big ceremonial party at the Mountain Shadows Resort when he retired in 1982; he then helped his wife run a Starwood travel agency, which advertised, among other things, trips to the moon on a spaceship that had yet to be built.

After seven years of dull retirement, he grew angry at Maricopa County sheriff Tom Agnos for rebidding an inmate transit contract held by his wife's company. Arpaio thought about suing but instead decided to run against Agnos, who had been the subject of strong criticism for botching an investigation into the murders of seven Buddhist monks in a temple on the west side of town. Agnos's deputies had arrested the wrong men at first and had interrogated one all night long until he "confessed." Arpaio campaigned as a fresh, clean G-man and won handily. One of the first things he did was take a walking tour of all the county jails and personally introduce himself to the deputies, so that "people would know who their sheriff was." Then came the tents and the stunts. And people now know who their sheriff is. His best relationship is with this amorphous concept of "the public."

"Friendship: I've never really understood what that word means," he once told me.

One of his top deputies, Lieutenant Brian Lee, came into the room at the sheriff's request. Lee once worked in detention, and he is now on the PR staff; he's in charge of the Twitter feed, among other things.

"Should I put it on Twitter that I'm going to Vegas?" asked the sheriff. It was another of his speaking engagements. He seems to prefer that immigration activists protest him outside these luncheons; when they do, a press release goes out.

"Sure," said Lee. "We'll say something cutesy like 'Demonstrators can get some gambling in after they protest.'"

Arpaio seemed annoyed yet again, and makes his eyes go narrow. There were regular picketers outside the Wells Fargo tower, he told me. "You'll see them out there each day. Calling me Hitler. There's a guy with a beard, he runs the whole thing. I guarantee you, if that guy killed me, everybody would be second-guessing. 'You should have known; he was following you around.' Every day he's out there! This society we live in, everybody's afraid to do anything because of being sued, because of civil rights, and on and on. I'd like to go out and grab him. People are afraid to say anything because of the high-tech society we live in."

Sure enough, there was a lone protester outside the building holding a sign that said Arpaio Thugs—Game Over. As we talked, a few motorists on Washington Avenue honked in support. A few others gave him the finger. He wouldn't give his name, but he told me of Arpaio: "He puts people out in the desert in 120 degrees, gives them food they choke on. What kind of person is that? This guy's a sadist. What does that do to Arizona's reputation? It's torture. Period. End of story."

The insane have a way of dying inside Arpaio's jails, and the county has lost a series of wrongful death suits as a result. One man who was forced into a restraint chair had his neck broken and was paralyzed from the arms down. Another asphyxiated to death. The *Tribune* found that at least sixty inmates had died in a four-year period because of lack of medical care. But it should be said here that most of the abuse has not happened in the famous Tent City, which is usually a disappointment for the foreign journalists hoping to find a Grand Guignol of sweat and misery. It is instead a glorified service yard full of gravel surrounded by razor wire, where crushing boredom is the main hazard. A giant indoor common room with cafeteria tables and weak air-conditioning is open twenty-four hours. The weather is indeed miserable: Temperatures can drop below ten degrees on the coldest winter nights, when five thin cotton blankets are the maximum allotment. Summers are predictably tough. The tents are welded metal frames planted on concrete slabs. Each one has twelve bunks and a mounted giant electric fan. Inmates here are on a work-release schedule, meaning they are let out daily to go back and forth from their jobs. Quite a few are repeat DUI offenders.

Inmates whom I spoke with on a pleasantly mild winter day all said they would rather be in Tent City than inside "The Hole," which is what everybody calls Durango Jail, where the detention officers are meaner and the air stinks. One computer programmer who was in for a five-month sentence for domestic violence told me the disgusting food had caused him to lose twelve pounds in three months. "I would say," he told me carefully, "that this place is one of a kind. It is enigmatic. But in this jail, the tents are luxury. If you've got to be in jail, I would rather be here." The only academic study made of its effectiveness indicated that an inmate was about 62 percent likely to reoffend once released—about exactly the same rate as in the prior administration. Arpaio had allowed no more studies after that one.

He also didn't want to talk about the Safeway shootings when I brought it up, though he mentioned that Giffords seemed like a nice person and that it was a shame.

"Why aren't they concerned about *my* safety?" he wondered. "I see these signs, ASSASSINATE ARPAIO. It's sad, but nothing surprises me anymore. You look at schools, people getting wiped out. It's getting out of hand. Strange phenomena. I'm not blaming the media. They have a job to report. But unfortunately, it's not unusual, what happened in Tucson. But it's going to happen again, no doubt."

This turned into a lament about what had been done to him in effigy at a Tucson rally more than two years earlier. Somebody had brought a piñata with the head decorated to look like Arpaio's face and a group of younger protesters had clubbed it with sticks, separating the head. Pima County legal defender Isabel Garcia held the head up and received some applause.

"I didn't see a big uproar about *me*," Arpaio complained. "Where was the outrage? Cutting the head off a piñata. . . . Hold on, I've got a file about all this." He went out into the hall to make sure I had the press clips, which turned out to be about the avalanche of criticism unleashed against Garcia in the wake of this incident.

We talked again about the immigration sweeps and whether they may have made Arizona a more dangerous place.

"I have a strange philosophy," he sheriffed, "that I *enforce the law*. I didn't get elected on this. I got elected on pink underwear and all that.* I don't need this. Why do I need this? I can get publicity in many other ways. I have a strange concept: I can get results. I can back up what I say. Since I have a gun and badge, I can do something about it.

"Let me tell you something," he went on. "The day I die, you won't even know how to spell my name. Secondly, what the hell am I doing this for? The publicity is going to be gone when I leave. Why do I let anybody know what I'm doing? I told you before, I don't run a CIA operation. I want to let people know what I'm doing. I've got Italian TV visiting me next week. I've had over four thousand profiles run all over the world. Who else can say that?

"You came here to talk about Gabrielle Giffords, and we got on to me. But *I am* Arizona. I left a dent here. A legacy. And if I didn't, who cares?"

---

* He said this last part in a dismissive way, which is just one of the many subtle tip-offs he seems to give his interlocutors that he, too, acknowledges on some level the pure worthlessness of what goes on in Tent City.

NINE

IMMIGRANTS, GUNS, AND FEAR

The *patrón* keeps a plaque from the Rotary Club on his office wall. He is a devout Catholic, and he is a reliable donor to Republican political candidates, because he doesn't much care for runaway spending on social programs. He is a believer in hard work and the American dream.

His business is putting up high-end homes—really gorgeous custom mansions that front the mountains—typically with generous acreage surrounding the property and with lots of careful desert landscaping, granite countertops, earth-toned walls, and large, luxurious bathtubs. The *patrón* likes to install solar panels on the roofs. The average cost is about $3 million, and they are occupied by players in the top socioeconomic crust of Tucson, either those who did very well in their careers with Chase Bank or Raytheon, or, as is usually the case, imported their money from elsewhere.

Every one of these beautiful Foothills homes was built with the help of illegal labor up from Mexico, and the boss has been hiring them steadily for nearly a quarter of a century. He could not make the numbers work without these unauthorized carpenters, masons, and electricians, and he agreed to discuss it with me on the condition that I keep him anonymous. We sat in his small office cube in Tucson, and he spoke with candor about how he bends the rules.

"I break certain laws," he acknowledged, "but I try to keep it to a minimum, and I suppose I try to justify it certain ways. I compare it to a white lie instead of an outright lie. If you couldn't find legal ways to stay in business, somehow you would try to justify breaking laws. Our minds let us justify things. There is a strong desire to be successful in business, and your mind lets you stretch things to fit what might not be right."

The *patrón* speaks no Spanish himself but has a trusted assistant—a native of Mexico who was once an illegal migrant himself—who translates the boss's job-site instructions to the workers and also helps him find new members of the crew, who come through word-of-mouth recommendations from brothers and cousins. "There's always ways to hire them in some manner," he said. "Creative ways." The pay is in cash every week, and it is about 60 percent to 70 percent of what a bona fide American worker would get. The expenditure is kept mostly off the books. He uses a lot of subcontractors and suspects that a percentage of their workforce, too, is migrants from Guatemala, Mexico, and Honduras.

Getting around the law is easy enough for a subcontractor. The law says that the employee has to provide some documentation: various combinations of a driver's license, a permanent resident card, a birth certificate, a social security card. But the Form I-9 that bosses must file only states that the documents "appear to be genuine and to relate to the employee named." A bad, blurry photocopy becomes good enough when the roof needs to get tarred. Subcontractors aren't forgery detectives and don't try too hard to develop those skills. If the migrant has made up a social security number, it can take months or years to detect. The online system called E-Verify has cut down on the problem somewhat, but an employee can still get around it by using a stolen or borrowed identity, even one that is shared among many friends at the same time. Only a fraction of American employers use E-Verify, in any case.

Over the years, the *patrón* told me, he has probably employed about 250 different individuals who are obviously migrants without papers, though nobody acknowledges it out loud. They are always nice guys, he said, with big families and polite children. And they work diligently for cut-rate wages. Their leavings are high quality—perfectly laid flagstones, concrete poured well, walls that meet at exact right angles. "If I compare them to the American guys, the numbers who work hard is much higher," he said. "Is it because they can't stay here? I don't know. American kids just plain don't want to work as hard."

Neither do they want to work as cheap. Putting up a wood frame for a two-thousand-square-foot home is about $480 with the typical crew of migrants, a business agent told the *Tucson Citizen*. But if legal union-wage carpenters were on the job, the cost would multiply by a factor of four, to $1,920. The customer gets a much cheaper house for the same quality, the contractor keeps his costs lowered, the migrant gets a wad of cash to spend as he likes, and virtually nobody is in a position to complain except the union carpenters and the ideologues. It has always been that way in Arizona, where the biggest fight at the 1911 constitutional convention was over the employment of Mexican workers, which the unions hated and the copper giants loved.

The uncomfortable fact is that the prosperity of the modern state of Arizona has been built by the sweat of those who are pulled up here from across the border by the economic force that transcends all politics to shoulder the low-status jobs we quietly offer them, even while loudly professing love of law and country. This is the invisible Arizona hypocrisy—a wink and a nod that has ensured that the pools get cleaned, the hotel sheets are crisply laundered, the golf courses are mowed, the strawberries are picked, and the roof beams are nailed tight.

The city of Tucson blatantly tried to emphasize this in a 1977 booklet for potential employers that touted the cheap labor pool heading up from Mexico. "Employers who have established plants in Tucson say that our Mexican-Americans are easy to train, will follow instructions, are more loyal and equal or exceed the productivity of workers in other parts of the country," said one sentence. The guide was quickly withdrawn amid cries of racism, even though the economy depended on the supply of cheap workers. It was not just fields and roofs. By that time, almost a fifth of the line workers at the Hughes Aircraft Company plant were Mexican American, with an unknown number of them lacking papers.

This persistent human undertow, almost geological in its strength and permanence, has existed in Arizona since before the Civil War and will continue to exist through the current paranoia—for as long as Mexico has an abundance of people and the United States has a hunger for consumption. Today's immigration hard-liners complain about the fiscal burden on the state, in the form of deadbeats waiting for treatment in the emergency rooms and rows of non–English speakers packing the classrooms. Stories are told of cruel practical jokes: an Anglo man walking slowly through a hospital waiting room with a rent-a-cop's badge prominently pinned to his shirt, chuckling to himself as darker-skinned people headed for the exits, abandoning sick family members out of fear of *la migra*.

Yet the hard numbers do not support the assumption that migrants are a drain on the system. They are actually an occluded asset, according to a University of Arizona study. The costs associated with care at hospitals are slightly less than an annual $120 million and the expenses to the overburdened school system are about $544 million—a figure dwarfed by their contributions in buying goods and paying for services ($4.41 billion), paying state tax revenues ($318 million), and contributions to state economic output ($28.9 billion), according to a 2007 study. Border crossers also pay billions of dollars into the social security system that they will never stick around to collect. "As fourteen percent of the workforce, immigrants make significant contributions to Arizona's economy," concluded economist Judith Gans. "There are also specific fiscal costs associated with immigrants. But, by virtue of their contributions as workers to Arizona's economic output, their overall contribution to the state's fiscal health is positive."

They would never be here if it weren't for the many figures like the *patrón*—employers willing to look the other way and make a deal. Most of the hiring in Arizona is done by the big vegetable farms outside Yuma and Willcox, but small businesses like restaurants and hotels play an important role. The *patrón* feels like Immigration and Customs Enforcement has bigger shrimp to fry and wouldn't bother coming after him, though his fellow home builders had been on edge recently over a raid the month before on a chain of restaurants called Chuy's Mesquite Broiler. Federal agents had reportedly rounded up kitchen and dining room workers who did not have correct papers and accused the owners of paying cash under the table.

Though the *patrón* gives money to local Republican political candidates, he feels like his party has gone off the rails on the subject of immigration, and especially with their hullabaloo surrounding Senate Bill 1070. To him the century-old practice of cross-border labor commerce is merely the invisible hand of the market at work. A healthy real-estate economy needs affordable carpentry in order to work. The suggestion that migrants ought to be allowed to become citizens or even remain here on the job has become anathema within the Republican Party, and not just in Arizona. Those who support guest-worker programs are accused of promoting "amnesty" for lawbreakers. "Secure the borders" became the rallying cry for anybody even moderate who sought public office, including Gabrielle, who made it a centerpiece of all her campaigns.

During Senator John McCain's run for the GOP nomination to the presidency in 2007, he took withering criticism within his party for making the following statement at a Florida debate: "We need to sit down as Americans and recognize these are God's children as well, and they need some protection under the law and they need some of our love and compassion." A sentiment that seemed well in line with the traditions of Christianity and antidespotism, but it got McCain nowhere at all. Before long he was chest beating with the toughest of them.

McCain's initial position is a good summary of how the *patrón* feels. He knows that some of the migrants out there get ripped off by the contractors, being promised payment at the end of the week that never materializes and with no remedy because nobody in this mix is going to go to the police. The *patrón* may not strictly obey the immigration laws of the United States—laws he considers unjust and meddlesome—but he would never dream of stiffing a worker of his pay. "Being moral, being good to people is important. I couldn't see taking advantage of them. If our government said, 'You should start shooting every illegal you see,' it wouldn't be something you could do. We have to figure out a way to get along with immigration rather than getting rid of it altogether. What are we going to do? Build one of these gorgeous walls that there'll be a door in it the next day? It's so sad, because they are trying to find a better life for themselves and their families. They risk everything for their families. They're sending almost all the money back. How can you deprive someone of that?"

The tradition of using hired labor from Mexico is a long one. Recruiters called *enganchadores* went into Sonora and Baja California in the 1910s to entice subsistence farmers north of the border, where they ran cattle, dug mine tunnels, and picked fruit for bargain wages. Copper mines flourished with the help of cheap labor, but the camps were largely segregated. In fact, the borders of Arizona might have been drawn differently without this racial tension. Republicans in the U.S. Senate wanted to admit the territories of New Mexico and Arizona as one southwestern superstate in 1906, which would have increased the GOP's strength in Congress. The government in Santa Fe was dominated by Latinos of high birth and wealth whose ancestors had been living there for more than two centuries, which was unpalatable to the arriviste Anglo settlers in Arizona who overwhelmingly rejected it in a vote. A gratified South Carolina senator called their decision "a cry of a pureblooded white community against the domination of a mixed-breed aggregation of citizens of New Mexico, who are Spaniards, Indians, Greasers, Mexicans, and everything else." The reality was that it had taken place after the implementation of a "literacy test" that disenfranchised most of Arizona's Spanish speakers. So the result was foreordained.

The rest of the Arizona constitution was basically a liberal one, thanks to the Democratic-labor alliance then in power. It guaranteed workmen's compensation for injuries, an independently elected mine inspector, an eight-hour workday, bans on child labor and polygamy, as well as freedom of speech and the press that was even more strongly emphasized than in the U.S. Constitution. But there was anti-immigrant sentiment at the convention. Several proposed provisions would have seriously hurt the chances of Spanish speakers to find a job in the new state. One said noncitizens couldn't be employed on public works projects, and another would have prohibited anyone who couldn't speak English from working underground. And no company could have more than 20 percent of its workforce composed of "alien labor."

No force in Arizona was more racist at the time than the unions. If you couldn't holler in English down the mine shafts, they claimed, then you couldn't understand blasting commands and were a danger to everyone (the safety records of the mines showed not a single fatality had been caused this way). These anti-immigrant motions were quashed by business interests, but they exposed an institutional hypocrisy in Arizona that has not abated to this day: the willingness of ranches and big industry to adopt conservative social policies while quietly encouraging Mexican labor and the consequent breaking of the law.

Most of the hopeful wage workers crossing through the Arizona desert don't intend to stay long. This is only a difficult port of call: The biggest job pools are located in Chicago, New York, and urban Texas. Yet the portion of the line that the U.S. Border Patrol calls the "Tucson Sector" became a favorite crossing zone in the first decade of the century as a result of a deliberate strategy to steer the traffic through some of the worst country possible. A plan approved by then Immigration and Naturalization Service commissioner Doris Meissner in 1994 foresaw this swelling of human movement in the Arizona desert.

"When the Border Patrol controls the urban areas, the illegal traffic is forced to use the rural roads which offer less anonymity and accessibility to public transportation," said the report, adding: "The prediction is that with traditional entry and smuggling routes disrupted, illegal traffic will be deterred, or forced over more hostile terrain, less suited for crossing and more suited for enforcement."

Everyone knew that the best places to sneak across the border were hidden within the cities of El Paso and San Diego. If high fences, powerful lights, helicopters, and determined teams of agents were deployed there in the cities to clamp down, the trekking bands of migrants and the professional guides called "coyotes" would move into the depopulated ranch country—and especially into the wastelands of Organ Pipe Cactus National Monument and the Cabeza Prieta National Wildlife Refuge. The name *cabeza prieta* means "dark head," for a distinctive black peak around which the land turns into a bewildering hell in the summer, with temperatures routinely above one hundred degrees.

"We did believe that geography would be an ally to us," Meissner told *The Arizona Republic* six years after the plan was approved. "It was our sense that the number of people crossing the border through Arizona would go down to a trickle, once people realize what it's like." There were fourteen migrant deaths in the Arizona desert the same year the plan was approved. It has since become a matter of routine for hundreds to die there each summer. The group Derechos Humanos reviewed medical examiner reports and concluded that 253 had perished of thirst, sunstroke, or homicide in the period between October 1, 2009, and September 30, 2010. Even in a down economy, the jobs are still there, quietly tugging, and the migrants keep risking their lives in search of them.

I spoke to one of those who survived the journey, a man in a cheap leather jacket named Rigoberto who was up from a small town in Honduras. He was standing in the predawn at a day-labor pickup spot outside the Southside Presbyterian Church on Tucson's Twenty-third Street. In front of us were the lights of the freeway and a direct view of "A" Mountain, the volcanic cone that soldiers fighting under the banner of the king of Spain had used as a lookout against the Apache in 1776. Its original name, Cuk Son, had become smoothed into the name of the town. One clue to the rotten economy was that we waited there on the sidewalk for a good part of the morning and only one pickup truck rolled by in search of a body for hire. He wasn't even a contractor; he was a guy whose house had been foreclosed upon, and he needed some extra muscle to cart out the junk.

Rigoberto did not get that job; three faster men beat him to the unrolled window. He is forty-eight years old, moving a little slow. He wires what spare money he can to his wife and four children, selling his labor to anyone who can pay the going rate of eight bucks an hour. Home is a small one-bedroom apartment into which he squeezes with three other men and pays $150 for the privilege. His biggest complaint about the United States is the food, which tastes too sugary on his tongue.

There are factories in Honduras that sell shirts and underwear to big American discount stores, but they tend to favor younger laborers, and the pay is about eighty cents an hour. Rigoberto could have tried to break in there, but he wanted the high pay and adventure of coming north. "As humans, we want something new," he told me. "It is an experiment. Life is about trying something new." He got here by taking a bus up to Chiapas in Mexico and then illegally jumping onboard a freight train. He lashed himself to the top of a boxcar with his own belt to avoid being tossed off on the curves. The journey though Mexico, from train to trail to other trains, took more than three weeks. And then he found himself in the border town of Nogales, Sonora, where he joined a night caravan of migrants heading north across the desert. They marched through grassy flats for about two days before they were met by an empty van on the side of the highway, which took him to Tucson and his brother's apartment. This was a relatively easy passage. Nobody died or was robbed.

Rigoberto told me he was preparing to leave the United States after three years of laying tile on rich people's patios not because he had been harassed by the police but because the jobs were so spotty. The crash in the housing market had socked him as hard as anybody. He knew all about Senate Bill 1070, which obligates local police officers to question the true nationality of suspicious people they happen to pull over. The law was not yet being enforced in Tucson, partly because of court challenges and partly because of resistance among city officials. Rigoberto also said he was aware of the general climate of rancor surrounding undocumented immigrants like him, which was confusing, because he wasn't here to cause trouble. "Criminals are people who kill," he complained. "Not people like us."

A retributive piece of work like Senate Bill 1070 found root in Arizona not just because of the U.S. Border Patrol's disastrous strategy decisions, but because the state's heavy population of Latinos—now 29.6 percent and rising fast—has never really developed a mature political structure that might have quashed it in a legislative committee. Such a mean-spirited bill would have had a significantly rougher time seeing daylight in Sacramento or Austin or Santa Fe, and that is because California, Texas, and New Mexico all have older networks of Latino influence that ensure enough presence at their capitols to make compromises necessary. But in Arizona, the last part of Mexico to be absorbed into the United States, the voting strength of Latinos remains a slumbering giant.

Less than half of the people who identified themselves as Hispanic on the 2010 census are registered to vote, and efforts to get them to the polls have been lackluster. In some elections the turnout has been 10 percent or less. "This is somewhat near where African Americans used to be: numeric strength that doesn't carry to the ballot box," said local pollster Margaret Kenski. Of the ninety members of the legislature, eleven of them are of Latino heritage. In a state where Anglos are about to become a minority, that is saying something.

I went to talk about it with Richard Elías, a Pima County supervisor with a sweeping view of history. He also happens to come from one of the oldest families in town, and one which has been here longer than just about every Anglo migrant to the area. His ancestor Juan Elías was one of the architects of the 1871 Camp Grant Massacre in which hundreds of Apaches were mercilessly slain. Elías took me down to the family business,

Old Pueblo Printers, to meet his eighty-three-year-old father, Alberto Elías, a genteel journeyman who has run off wedding invitations, funeral programs, and posters and campaign literature for various politicians—including Gabrielle—out of the one-story building for more than four decades. This used to be the offices of a weekly Spanish-language newspaper called *El Tucsonense*, which ceased publication in 1963. A few of its issues were displayed in frames. Outside in the back is a metal shed where the lead pigs for the linotype used to be melted down for scrap.

Alberto told me that the older Latino political presence in southern Arizona tends to get overwhelmed by interests in the state capital of Phoenix, where the disorganization and lack of community is even greater. The transience and lack of human connectivity that is the hallmark of twenty-first-century Arizona sociology has also affected the 30 percent of it that happens to have ancestry in Mexico or Central America. There is that same pragmatic get-rich-quick mentality, as though the place were for rent rather than for purchase. That comes with a certain amount of fatalism toward the affairs of state.

"We don't become outraged as a group," said Alberto. "The power base is where? Phoenix. We have no way to control that."

The strong cultural institutions that used to bind Mexican Americans together in Tucson started to fall apart after World War II, he said. "There were different ways of living, different ways of eating." The rise of the automobile had a segregating effect. Up through the end of the forties, many properties in white neighborhoods had restrictive covenants against a sale to persons of "African, Mongolian or Mexican descent," and realtors often wouldn't deal with Mexicans even after these covenants were ruled illegal. The northern end of the oldest colonial-era neighborhood, Barrio Viejo, was ripped out in the name of urban renewal and replaced by the bland slab of the Tucson Convention Center and a spookily deserted office complex called La Placita Village. Mexican Americans were encouraged to buy or rent tract homes in the vast open spaces south of Twenty-second Street, creating a psychological dividing line. The spatial togetherness of Mexican Americans that dated to the eighteenth century was dispersed and drowned into wide avenues and strip-mall stores—a fate similar to that of the Anglo monoculture that encompassed it. Lengthy friendships and shared purposes became a bit harder to maintain. "The relationships you create translate into business relationships, which translate into friendships, which translate into networks," said Richard.

The suburbanization made the social fiber much weaker and tended to foster rivalries between small factions who lived apart from one another and had conflicting interests, said Lydia Otero, the historian who is also a professor of Latin American Studies at the University of Arizona. "There's a lot of personal problems that get in the way of larger political organizing," she said. "The initiative to get involved about big things just isn't there. It's a general malaise."

Part of the result was a lack of strong establishment leadership. There were certainly examples of *individual* leaders. Elías himself. Congressman Raul Grijalva, the son of a migrant worker, who graduated from the U of A, ran a neighborhood center, and put in long hours on the Tucson Unified School District board and the county Board of Supervisors. Former city manager Joel Valdez. City councilman Roy Laos. But there was no clear institutional path to success that might be emulated among new generations. The Catholic parochial schools and colleges that had helped earlier generations of American immigrants find success through education were not robust in Tucson. "They don't have the structural power to help them," said Richard, "and we haven't done a good job finding people who are going to replace them."

Alberto said he was heartened to see nationwide marches in the spring of 2006 protesting a restrictive change to federal immigration policy: a hundred thousand walked in Chicago and half a million in Los Angeles. A corresponding event in Tucson turned into an angry circus after members of a fringe anti-immigration group called Border Guardians burned a Mexican flag, provoking physical confrontations and several arrests. Within four years the energy was depleted and the mood was markedly resigned. Senate Bill 1070 passed through with a comparative whimper, without the scale or the outrage of that earlier protest, and without an energetic drive to register Latinos to vote. The willpower had leaked away.

"People are scared," said Alberto. "The kids are scared. They browbeat us every day. Our people are browbeat. Let me go a step further. When ICE comes in and does a raid, they come in with masks and automatic weapons and embedded media in their vans. People get terrorized by that. We had elderly people saying, *Estoy permaneciendo en la casa hoy* [I'm staying in the house today]. The fear factor has leaked in."

"It was a matter of the subconscious," added Richard. "We don't want to get caught up in all that."

Underlying all the paranoia on both sides is an overwhelming demographic fact: Arizona is a state where the white people are getting older and less numerically potent and the brown people are more youthful and growing stronger. Data from the 2010 U.S. Census showed that there are now more Hispanic children than white children in the state, complementing what was already a 180 percent jump in Latino citizens over the previous two decades, the majority of them completely legal. If current trends continue, the state founded on race and the railroads will actually be a majority Latino state by the year 2015. And even if an economic hiccup puts that date back a year, or even several years, it will not change the inevitable growing up of those who are already here. The tides cannot be yelled back.

This is the metatrend now poking at the Arizona collective unconscious, and perhaps the tough-talking laws represent the gasp of a majority that perceives on a molecular level that there is a price to be paid for the luxury and privacy enjoyed through the years. These punitive laws could read as a form of sublimated guilt. Monuments of the immigrant underclass in Arizona have been pleasantly merged into the landscape thus far—the roofs and pools of the Foothills homes and the perfectly grilled steaks a silent testament to their effort. But now the masses are swelling, and their visibility is unmistakable.

In Tucson, for example, 60 percent of the young people are minorities. The enrollment in the largest school district is 68 percent Chicano. But the senior citizens of Arizona are more than 80 percent white. Ronald Brownstein of the *National Journal* has called this an oncoming conflict of "the gray and the brown." He writes: "Over time, the major focus in this struggle is likely to be the tension between an aging white population that appears increasingly resistant to taxes and dubious of public spending, and a minority population that overwhelmingly views government, education, health, and social-welfare programs as the best ladder of opportunity for its children." Brookings Institution demographer William Frey points out that Arizona is a bellwether for the rest of the country, which is likely to experience the same kind of growing minority presence in the decades to come.

The coming demographic shift will inevitably translate into a political shift, and it will make the long-awaited Latino awakening inevitable, said Richard Elías. In a democratic society there can be no hegemony of racial leadership when the numbers of the governed are tipping far out of balance with their governors.

"There are new Chicano leaders all over this community," said Richard Elías. "Every day they are growing up. They are twelve, fourteen, sixteen today. These are leaders we won't be able to stop if we wanted to. No wonder they're scared of us. If they keep up the anti-immigrant legislation, if they keep treating us like *las cucarachas*, it will be inevitable. There is no way to avoid the numbers."

Russell Pearce, author of Senate Bill 1070, is missing the ring finger on his right hand. It was shot off many years ago by a Latino suspect he was trying to arrest.

Pearce once called himself "The John Wayne of the Legislature," and many have called him "the shadow governor of Arizona," because the person who holds the constitutional office, Jan Brewer, rarely answers questions about the problems facing the state and is known for her maladroit public deliveries.* All of the philosophical energy in the spring session following the Safeway murders came from Pearce's agenda, which revolves primarily around cutting taxes and expanding gun ownership rights, and, most of all, stopping illegal immigration, a subject with which his interest is obsessive. Even after the splash of SB 1070 he was getting ready to introduce even more legislation that would wrench immigration powers away from the federal government and give them to the state.

I talked to Pearce in the middle of the 2011 session and asked him about what his long-term vision was for Arizona's future. The conversation quickly turned to his pet subject.

"We have our challenges, but Arizona is a great place," he told me. "The neat thing is, we're not a small state anymore, we're a big state. What I see going on here is important not just for our state but for the nation. As you know, we have this illegal alien invasion that's destroying this country. Are there good people among them? Sure. But you have the child molesters, the drug dealers, the gangbangers, they are coming in too. . . . I see Arizona in the lead of saying 'Enough's enough.' We need to change things. I've been proud to be in the front of this parade. . . . We don't need to stand by and listen to the mouthpieces and incompetents in the federal government. That Arizona politicians think they can ignore the damage to the taxpayers and our country is outrageous, and it is malfeasance. The future is bright. We are waking up to the interests of the taxpayers. It's like the Revolutionary War, when they pleaded to King George, and then they wrote a letter saying, 'Get your boot off our throat.' We are going to take back this nation, and the first place we're

---

* Including, most famously, thirteen seconds of awkward silence during the only debate of the 2010 governor's race. When she spoke again after the pause, she said: "We have did what was right for Arizona."

going to do that is Arizona. The future of Arizona is as bright as I've ever seen it. We're lowering taxes, reducing regulations, and creating safe neighborhoods."

Russell Pearce is a grandnephew of Joe Pearce, one of the last survivors of the band of enforcers called the Arizona Rangers. Russell grew up poor, did a little cowboy work in the ponderosa plateaus near Ash Fork, and then found work as a Maricopa County sheriff's deputy in 1970. Seven years into his career he was on patrol in the heavily Latino neighborhood of Guadalupe when he came across three kids drinking beer outside a store in the middle of the July afternoon. He went to go take the beer away, and one of them made the unwise decision to order his Doberman pinscher to attack Pearce, who started to beat the dog away with the butt of his flashlight. Another of the kids snatched the deputy's service revolver from its holster and pulled the trigger. The bullet struck Pearce on his right ring finger and bounced into his chest, where it lodged near his spine. Blood poured from his hand, but he still managed to wrestle one kid into the back of the squad car and then give a car chase after the others, who were still in possession of his .357 Magnum. The youths were rounded up by other deputies. The shooter received a five-year prison sentence.

Pearce later became a lobbyist for the sheriff's department down at the capitol and discovered he had a taste for politics and bill writing. When he was promoted to chief deputy for newly elected sheriff Joe Arpaio in 1992, he took notice of an initiative at the Arizona State Prison in Florence to put overflow inmates into canvas tents. Though Arpaio hotly contests this version of history, Pearce has always said Tent City was his idea. He left the sheriff's office in Arpaio's bad graces, got elected to the Arizona legislature from a conservative Mesa district in 2001, and got to work on a legislative program to stop what he calls "a national crisis, an epidemic" of surreptitious border crossers coming up from Mexico taking American jobs and committing crimes. He tried to pass a version of Senate Bill 1070 in 2005 and kept at it until his colleagues finally relented five years later, and Brewer—in the single most important act of her career—signed it. A delighted Pearce retired the randomly assigned bill number in honor of the accomplishment, in the spirit of a sports hero's jersey number.

More than ideology may have been at work. Laura Sullivan of National Public Radio reported that the bill's content was approved in advance by Corrections Corporation of America (CCA), the nation's largest private prison company, which stood to reap lucrative per diem payments from all the migrants held behind bars before their deportation hearings. CCA already has a significant presence in Arizona as the operator of three prisons. This company and Pearce are both members of the American Legislative Exchange Council, a regular gathering of state lawmakers, large corporations, and trade associations that says it is dedicated to "principles of free markets, limited government, federalism, and individual liberty" and does not make a list of its members public. At one of the ALEC meetings in Washington, D.C., Sullivan reported, the bill was circulated for comments and shaping from the private prison giant. After it was enacted in Arizona with the help of thirty-two cosponsors (the majority of whom were ALEC members or had received campaign contributions from CCA or associated groups), there was happiness among those who stood to profit most from the harsh new law. During a conference call with investors, the president of the Geo Group, which lobbies for the prisons, said: "Those people coming across the border and getting caught are going to have to be detained and that for me, at least I think, there's going to be enhanced opportunities for what we do."

Pearce told me there was no influence from the prisons on the bill that made his national profile. "Never spoke to them. Never talked to any of them," he said of his alleged contacts with Corrections Corporation of America. "ALEC is made up of public people and private people. Anyone with an IQ can see this is an absolute fabrication." He pointed out that he had introduced a version of the controversial bill beginning in 2005 and methodically for every year thereafter—long before the meeting in question took place in the Washington Hyatt.

What drives his political passion, he says, has nothing to do with the old injury to his hand or any dislike for Latinos or the welfare of corporate America. Not even the fact that one of his sons, Maricopa County Deputy Sheriff Sean Pearce, was shot and wounded in 2005 by an undocumented Mexican immigrant while serving a search warrant at a Mesa trailer park. It is rather the dedication to the rule of law, a concept that he holds sacred. "That's why I went into law enforcement," he told Robbie Sherwood of *The Arizona Republic*. "I don't believe someone has the right to break into your house. I don't believe someone has the right to break into your country."

Pearce comes from an old family from the Church of Jesus Christ of Latter-day Saints, and has attended lectures given by a curious figure in the Mormon pantheon: a former Salt Lake City police chief named W. Cleon Skousen, a speaker on the far-right circuit during the sixties who made warnings of a Communist takeover from within, the same line of reasoning of the John Birch Society. He wrote a book called *The Five Thousand Year Leap* that asserted that the Constitution was inspired by God and that its Framers were guided by the Bible. The founding of the United States, he said, instantly represented more progress in civilization than had been made by any others in the previous five thousand years of the earth. Skousen also authored a school history textbook called *The Making of America* that portrayed happy slaves in the South and used the term "pickaninny" to refer to young black children. This choice of word resulted in a huge kerfuffle in Arizona in 1986 when Governor Evan Mecham publicly defended his friend Skousen and the use of the slur. Skousen died in Salt Lake City in 2006 but was reelevated from obscurity by talk show host Glenn Beck, whose enthusiastic recommendations of *The Five Thousand Year Leap* sent it rocketing to the top of Amazon.com bestseller lists. Pearce himself is a frequent speaker at Tea Party rallies.

Yet his hard-line stances were too much even for many conservative Mormons in his home legislative district in the suburb of Mesa. The LDS church has always emphasized the integrity of the family unit, and many feared the immigration crusades would tear apart the border-straddling Latino families and alienate an entire culture. Opponents filed enough signatures to force a recall election against him. At this writing, Pearce was trying to rally national support to fend off the challenge and stay in office.

He had also been hoping to follow up Senate Bill 1070 with a raft of other laws that would have made Arizona an even tougher place to be an illegal immigrant. They included one to strip all infants of migrant parents of their automatic U.S. citizenship—the so-called anchor baby exclusion in the Fourteenth Amendment to the Constitution. Another would have made it a state crime for immigrants to drive a vehicle or attend college; another would have required school districts to collect data on their illegal students; yet another would have required emergency room doctors and nurses to immediately call the police if any migrant showed up with a broken arm or a bleeding head wound or for any other reason. He had knocked a lot of heads on his own side to try to get these bills through, though the debate was held mostly behind closed doors. "There are very few actual conversations down there anymore," said the official state historian, Marshall Trimble. "They don't really know each other. This is the same thing that's happening nationally. I see Arizona as a microcosm."

I went down to Arizona's capitol complex—which is now physically owned by a private investment group—to hear the fate of these bills when they reached the Senate floor. Not for the first time, I marveled at the low quality of the architecture, which emanates little sense of grandeur or ambition. The heart of it is a squat three-story building about the size of an average midwestern courthouse, built in 1912, and topped with a dome covered in bright copper leaf. It has been largely emptied out to make room for a so-so history exhibit. It all goes downhill from there. The blocky Senate and House chambers flank the front lawn like twin lobes of a brain, products of the dismal era of the internationalist style of public buildings in the late fifties, all soaring rectangular glass plates facing outward. Covering them up is a bizarre engorged lacework of tufa stone, non–load bearing, as if the architect was embarrassed by the poverty of the façade and wanted to hide it with a curtain. Between the chambers is a carpet of concrete and a patch of heroically struggling bluegrass.

In back is the biggest travesty of all, the nine-story Executive Tower, a brown dwarf of a skyscraper erected in 1974 to house the top state offices with every dignity that becomes a medical-dental plaza. The governor's office is on the ninth floor, a bulged crown at the top, which gives it the vague appearance of a forehead. When Evan Mecham was in office he once claimed that the attorney general was bugging his conversations by aiming a microwave listening device at these wrap-around tinted windows.

My grandmother had spent most of her career here as an administrative employee working for the state examiner and the State Highway Department. There have been periodic conversations about trying to bring more class to the seat of government, but the discussions have gone nowhere and are especially dead now that the state is broke and has sold off its own grounds to a leasing company anyway.

The last real opportunity to do something distinctive was in 1957, when part-time Scottsdale resident Frank Lloyd Wright, late in his life, presented a series of drawings* for a new capitol that would have nestled inside the red sandstone peaks of Papago Park like a thunderbird sunning itself. The governor's office would be in the bird's head and the outstretched wings would have housed both chambers of the legislature. State officials objected on technical grounds: The state's constitution specified that the capitol had to be in Phoenix, and the eastern set of mountains Wright had in mind for his dramatic setting had not yet been annexed into the city. But the real reason was that this creation would simply cost too much.

The lackluster cubes of the Senate and House were built the following year, and few have felt sentimental about them ever since. "My first choice would be to bulldoze them down and start over," Republican

---

* A rough model was Wright's Marin County Courthouse, which winds around grass hills like a serpent.

senator Jake Flake once told *The Arizona Republic.* "We don't have an Arizona Capitol people can be proud of."

I found a place in the crammed third-floor Senate gallery and listened to the debate, which was influenced by a letter that sixty Arizona CEOs and the presidents of five chamber of commerce organizations had signed. Like nearly everyone in the Arizona power web who has anything even slightly less than radical to say on this issue, the letter's authors first made an unequivocal (and ass-covering) denunciation of the plague of illegal immigration: "We agree with you that our borders must be protected first, and now . . . Arizona lawmakers and citizens are right to be concerned about illegal immigration. But we must acknowledge that when Arizona goes it alone on this issue, unintended consequences inevitably occur." These being: boycotts, lousy image, canceled contracts, and loss of tourist revenues. The debate was better held in the U.S. Congress, they reasoned.

A cultural quirk of the Arizona State Senate is that the most intriguing public exchanges usually take place after the votes are tallied, when a member can stand up, holding a microphone like a pop idol, to "explain my vote." There was a lot of explanation that day as Russell Pearce's pentateuch of bills went down to defeat. One of the CEO letters had been addressed to Senator John McComish, who stood up to say that he agreed. "These immigration bills are a distraction," he said. "They could be potentially, if we were to continue with them, a detriment to the growth of our economy, and they are something people don't want us to be focused on. . . . It seems obvious to me that it's time for us to take a time-out on immigration."

Sylvia Allen stood up. She is a stocky conservative Mormon realestate agent from the town of Snowflake who once earned notoriety in a hearing for saying that more uranium mining should be permitted near the Grand Canyon because the earth is six thousand years old and has managed to survive in the time when there weren't any environmental regulations. She has also blamed Arizona's long drought on too many pine trees sucking up the water.

"If the state of Arizona doesn't think they have a problem, they are sadly mistaken," she said. Her voice rose to a near shout. "We have problems in our state created by people who care less about honoring our laws and are reaping the benefits of our lifestyle that people before them paid the price to do. And it's *wrong* that we do not turn this back on them," she said. "Instead *we're* the ones who are wrong, and we're the ones in trouble, and we're the ones who are called racists!" But then she voted against Pearce's omnibus bill, saying she hadn't had time to study it.

Pearce was noticeably perturbed, and chastised the Senate from the head table. "I stand on the side of the citizens and not a bunch of businessmen who wrote me a letter," he said. "We have become the envy of this nation, with twenty-five states writing legislation modeled after 1070. And yeah, we might be in court again. They always sue. Do anything they can to stop enforcement of our laws. . . . Being sued on 1070 by our own government. The states have never, ever, ever been preempted. And I'm going to correct it here one more time. This is not a federal issue. It's a states issue. Once they cross that border, it's *your* neighborhoods, *your* education, *your* health care, *your* citizens that are impacted. It's *you* that pay a price. And it's your responsibility, *you* who took an oath of office to defend these laws and protect our citizens. You can't keep passing the buck to someone else."

I couldn't get in to talk to Pearce the afternoon these bills went down—"the mood here is not good," an intern apologized via text message—so I went out into the Senate lobby where Representative Frank Antenori of Tucson was peering out the windows and through the curtain of tufa stone to where a group of demonstrators were chanting "*Sí, se puede!*," the famous rallying cry of César Chávez when he organized poor migrant farmworkers in the sixties. Some held placards that said PEARCE, WHAT DID WE DO TO YOU? and WE ARE HUMAN.

"What gets me," said Antenori to a security guard, with disgust, "is why are they chanting in Spanish? Why aren't they chanting 'We want to be Americans! Help us be Americans.' They aren't helping their cause."

I went over and introduced myself, and we talked for a while. He told me about a book he'd written about his participation in a battle during the first Gulf War, in which a unit of Special Forces encountered an armored unit on a deserted highway, and it ended up a bloodbath for the Iraqis. "It wasn't a fair fight," he acknowledged with a smile. Then we talked about Arizona's notions of personal liberty.

"This state is divided basically into two groups," he told me. "The people who want to be left alone, and the people who want to stick their noses into everybody's business. The silent majority and the activists. Those who want to be left alone say that 'I don't want to cut my grass, I want to be able to park my car on the lawn,' and then there are those who say 'You can't park there. And you have to cut your grass.'"

Russell Pearce agreed to speak with me over the phone the next week, and we talked about the Arizona Rangers a little before getting into the politics of the moment. When I asked him if the legislature was spending too much time promoting gun freedoms after the Safeway killings, as many on the Democratic side have suggested, his pitch and pace intensified. I had to scrawl ferociously to keep up with him.

"That's one of the most asinine statements I've ever heard," he said, and then offered a postmortem of recent mayhem, which he says was caused by illegal immigrants. Twelve Phoenix police officers killed. The case of Kelly Tracy, a sixteen-year-old Gilbert High School student on her way back from band practice who was wiped out by a drunk driver without correct federal papers. Rob Krentz, a rancher down near Douglas whose murder in the brush in 2010 was widely blamed on Mexican drug runners, though no solid evidence had emerged.

"We've got drug traffickers, carjackers, child molesters all coming in," he said. "We wouldn't have these problems if we were doing the job we were supposed to. What is his substitute for freedom? I don't believe there is one. Why do you call bad guys 'bad guys'? Because they are! They don't follow the law. We put people in the position where they can't defend themselves. If someone had been there at that Tucson event who was mentally prepared and properly equipped, they could have saved lives. *Guns save lives*. Nobody has a right to tell me I can't defend myself, that I can't defend my family. Nobody has a right to take that from me. We have a God-given right from the Founding Fathers. I'm *offended* by those people who think they can take my rights away from me because of a bad guy. He's saying he has a right to be doing these issues which are important to other people. I have a constitutional duty to protect life and liberty. I'm offended at those who would dismiss that."

The Safeway shooting has nothing to do with the state of Arizona, he said. Nothing at all.

"What does the Virginia Tech attack have to say about Virginia? This is a *nut*. It's a sad occasion, and it breaks a lot of hearts. I always got along with Gabby. A liberal. She's getting a lot of credit for things she didn't do, but that's a part of life. We never had a cross word. It's kind of interesting that we pick out this act and make it a relevant issue when we ignore Rob Krentz's murder, how we choose to elevate certain issues because we have an issue behind them. This was *a nut*. And the gun nuts are going to promote this to promote their liberal agendas. In a free society there are risks, and those risks are worth it. You're always going to have a deranged guy out there."

Carrying a handgun provides a secret thrill that gun owners almost never discuss. Hiding one on your waist gives you a bounce. The feeling of firing a shot sends a jerk and a controlled spasm up the arm, like pounding a nail with a magic hammer. Soldiers in combat firing at the enemy have described a sensation similar to that of sexual arousal. The handgun is the leveler of bodily advantage, giving a weakling the authority to end the life of an Olympic athlete and the moral coward the ability to destroy a Pericles.

Just holding one calls a person out of an everyday stupor, frees him from the mundane disappointments of existing, reminds him that he, too, can, and perhaps should be, a superhero. For a brief time after college I worked as a sheepherder in the La Plata Mountains of southwestern Colorado, which was a job that involved spending a lot of time on horseback. The feeling of commanding that swift animal from up high was quite a lot like the feeling of holding a loaded pistol, a sense of calm and control. This patriarchal John Wayne power is not really deserved—it is not even yours—but it *seems* deserved, which is equivalent.

"Now *this* is what Congress would love to get rid of," said Charles Heller, as he opened the gun safe in the hatchback of his Pontiac. "Your fully functioning, full-capacity, semiautomatic Springfield armory, forty-five caliber."

He took out the gun and showed it to me. We were parked outside one of the ranges at the Tucson Rifle Club, which amounts to a few shade ramadas built in front of a set of bulldozed embankments. It is about forty miles west of the city, on the edge of the Tohono O'odham Indian reservation. Heller sells advertisements on AM radio for a living, but his real passion is guns—or rather, the blessings of personal liberty that supposedly come as a package deal with being able to carry one.

Heller is a friendly looking man, earnest, blond-haired, open-faced, slightly rotund, with a slight gap between his front teeth. Three ballpoint pens are clipped neatly in the pocket of his blue cotton shirt. He wore a billed cap commemorating the sunken USS *Arizona*. Heller works as a concealed weapons trainer in his spare time, but, more important, as the secretary of the Arizona Citizens Defense League, a nonprofit group of gun enthusiasts dedicated to the proposition that gun ownership is a cornerstone constitutional freedom that should never be impinged.

It has been a long time since I've shot a gun. Years ago, in Utah, I had bought a .22 caliber Beretta pistol (a virtual copy of the one from my father's closet that I once looked at with dangerous adolescent fascination) for camping trips out to the desert, vague "protection" against critters and possible human trouble. It made one hell of a loud bang when I fired it at dry wash banks, but the slugs were the size of chocolate chips and would have had no knockdown power. In a bad situation its primary use would have been as a noisemaker. I got rid of it a long time ago.

Heller gave me a five-minute refresher on the basics of safety. Treat guns as if they were always loaded. Point the muzzle in the direction that is safe. Keep finger on the frame of the trigger until you make decision to fire. Know what your target is and what's beyond it. Always maintain control of the weapon.

Outside the shower, Charles Heller is always carrying at least one loaded gun tucked away on his person. He wouldn't tell me the exact number that he owns, but during our afternoon together I saw at least four, and he produced them by reaching into his button-down shirt and withdrawing them from obscure regions of his upper body. "I've lightened the load over the years," he told me. "I'm down to about seventeen pounds of steel on any given day."

Carrying all this weaponry fosters a new awareness of one's place in the world, he said. "When you put a gun on, it changes you. You feel exposed. But that quickly goes away. What it does is put you into a heightened state of awareness."

Think of doing a mundane activity, he told me, like brushing your teeth or watching television. Your mental state is relaxed and your movements are somewhat unconscious. This is "Condition White," a lowered sense of your place in the world. Wearing a gun puts you up into a state he calls "Condition Yellow"—just a little more alive, a little more mentally primed, a little more observant of the expressions of those strangers around you. Heller has been eating in diners when an argument breaks out either at the cash register or at a nearby table, and he will turn around and affix the noisemaker with a certain confident look. That telegraphed the fact that he is packing a gun and is ready to pull it out, which, he says, tends to have a calming effect.

He much prefers to live in Condition Yellow.

"I don't *not* carry," he said. "If I have an ability to use my skills to prevent violence and I don't, I'm worse than useless. I'm constantly aware of what's going on, and now I make it a sacred part of my obligation to be cognizant of what's going on. I don't see myself as a junior cop or any of that kind of crap. I want not to be harmed."

We sat on a bench in the shade and Heller told me the brief story of his life. He had grown up in western Chicago, the son of a World War II veteran tank commander who still kept a .45 caliber revolver left over from the war. The ten-year-old Heller was already fascinated with BB rifles and begged for permission to shoot the heavy pistol. His father responded by stripping the entire unloaded weapon down to its parts, tossing them on the bedspread, and saying, "When you can put it all back together, you can shoot it." Heller eventually managed the feat with no help from anyone, and when he could demonstrate to his father that he could make a total disassembly and reassembly, he was allowed to go down to a range on Mannheim Avenue and shoot the Colt for real. "That thing made a music so sweet I have never lost the tune," he told me. The heft of the weapon absorbed most of the recoil; it was like taking a hard bump in a vehicle with extremely good suspension. A fluid motion rather than a jerk. Heller bought himself a two-hundred-shot repeating Daisy BB rifle and set up his own range in his father's basement, getting good enough to ventilate a pie pan at sixty yards.

Chicago's gun laws irritated him to the point that he moved to Arizona in 1994 because of his inability to legally carry a gun within city limits. "Any government that doesn't allow me my gun rights doesn't deserve my tax dollars," he told me. Arizona does, in fact, have some of the most liberal gun laws in the country. State Senator Lori Klein made a public announcement on the Senate floor that she carried a .38 Special in her purse, two days after the Safeway shootings. "I pack," she bragged. On another occasion, *Arizona Republic* reporter Richard Ruelas asked to see her pink .380 Ruger. "Oh, it's so cute," she said, and pointed it directly at him. He wrote of seeing the pink laser-dot sight on his chest. When gun safety experts criticized her for exercising poor judgment, she said she could not have accidentally shot him because her finger was not on the trigger.

You can carry a concealed weapon in Arizona without any permit or special training or a background check for felonies. This means that a weapon can be stuffed in your waistband, or in a boot, or under your armpit in a special holster, and no one is the wiser. Alaska and Vermont are the only two other states that allow this with no questions asked. There is no waiting period to buy a gun, meaning you can walk into any store that sells them and walk out in thirty minutes after only a federally required check for any past convictions. California, by contrast, requires ten days. There are no provisions barring the mentally ill from buying guns. Prior misdemeanors won't get in the way either, as they do in more than twenty states. And there is no state limit on the amount of ammunition that may be carried in the part of the gun called the "magazine," where the bullets are lined up in a stack for ready firing. A twenty-eight-year-old man demonstrated the laxity of the state laws when he showed up to protest a 2009 visit by President Barack Obama carrying a pistol and wearing an AR-15 assault rifle slung across his chest. He did this for no other reason than because it was legal, he said. "In Arizona I still have some freedoms left," he told a reporter for the *Republic*.

Arizona's liberal gun laws are, in part, derived from the proliferation of firearms inside the state in the years following the Civil War. The big handgun manufacturers like Samuel Colt of Hartford, Connecticut, needed a new, postwar market for their factories' output. The new farming and mining settlements out West were good places to sell weapons to whoever was buying. The Texas historian Walter Prescott Webb has written that the Colt six-shooter was responsible for the defeat of the Comanche Indians, as it could be rapidly and accurately fired by someone mounted on a horse, unlike a breech-loading rifle. The mythology of the frontier gun culture grew up almost as fast. Colt did much to tout his guns as tools of Western conquest, even engraving elaborate depictions of battles on the cylinders of his pistols.

The dime novels and Western movies of the 1920s strengthened the association. The onetime Philadelphia dentist turned author Zane Grey took residence near Payson and became a sensation with novels such as *Riders of the Purple Sage* and *Under the Tonto Rim* that portrayed romantic dilemmas solved with a heroic burst of gunfire. By the mid-1900s nearly a quarter of all Hollywood movies were being set in the mythic West of the past century, featuring clean cowboys like Tom Mix* and Gene Autry. Columbia Pictures built a movie set outside Tucson for the 1940 shootout movie *Arizona*, and the fake town was later turned into a theme park called Old Tucson, which would eventually become the second-largest tourist draw in the state, behind only the Grand Canyon. An elderly Wyatt Earp, then serving as a consultant to Hollywood directors, told newspaper writers all over again about the 1881 carnage in the alley behind the O.K. Corral in Tombstone, Arizona: essentially a petty dispute between two rival bands of thugs over the control of silver bullion robbed from stagecoaches. Acting as city marshal, Virgil Earp and his brothers Morgan and Wyatt (formerly known as "The Fighting Pimps," for their fondness for brothels) had been trying to relieve the Clanton and McLaury faction of their pistols—Tombstone then had stricter gun laws than all of Arizona has today—when the shooting started, leaving three dead.

The long-ago gunplay in the transient mining towns of the nineteenth century entered the American vernacular and became part of the self-reinforcing image of Arizona as a land tamed by the gun, giving lawmakers a quasihistorical and sentimental reason to keep the laws easy on firearms dealers. The streak of libertarianism that has always colored the state's political culture helped bolster this identity.

The relative dearth of gun laws persuaded Charles Heller to leave his life in Chicago and move here, where he got married and grew a network

---

* He was killed in a 1940 car accident north of Tucson swerving to avoid a construction barrier, and flipped his car over twice, knocking loose a suitcase full of money and jewelry that hit him in the back of the head. The wash was renamed Tom Mix Wash in his memory, and a monument there with a metal sculpture of a riderless horse says: "In memory of Tom Mix. Whose spirit left his body on this spot, and whose characterization and portrayals in life served to better fix memories of the Old West in the minds of living men."

of friends. He worked as a radio host doing swap-shop shows, taking calls from people advertising furniture and cars and other used goods over the air. That led to a job selling advertisements for the radio station KVOI, which is owned by a company called Good News Communications. He also became an instructor for a concealed-weapons class and joined the Minutemen, the volunteer group of armed citizens that roams the American side of the border looking for illegal aliens in the arroyos. Heller has trouble walking long distances because of a torn *meniscus musicus* in his knee, and so he ran the communications shack, which was a converted shipping container, fitted with air-conditioning and a citizen's band radio, set in one of the more remote locations on Kings Ranch near the border. His job was to stay in touch with the field teams and keep the U.S. Border Patrol apprised of their locations. The teams prowling the brush used to find the bodies of dead migrants as a matter of routine— this was known as a "Code Black"—and also people who were dehydrating and crippled. More than a few lives were saved by the Minutemen, he says.

Because he sold airtime for a religious radio station, I had assumed Heller was a born-again Christian. I asked him if he identified himself as such, and he gave me a wide, gap-toothed grin. "Hell no, I'm Jewish!" he said. "I do not accept Christ as savior."

He went on to tell me that he believes in God and reads the Torah and likes to irritate his many Christian friends sometimes by repurposing a quote from one of St. Paul's letters: "I can do all things through Leatherman." He patted the all-purpose folding tool of the same name that was dangling from the key ring near his belt.

There was a specific reason why those car keys were not in his pocket. Anyone who keeps both pistol and keys in the same pocket is one day going to put an accidental bullet in his upper leg, or in the vicinity. At a political event once he stood directly behind Arizona governor Jan Brewer with a loaded pistol under his jacket, though not for any sort of hostile reason. He carries a gun virtually every minute of the day, and he might have saved the governor's life in case a Jared Lee Loughner should have emerged from the crowd. "Remember, all guns are loaded all the time," Heller said, then added wryly, "but in my case, they *really* are."

Heller puts his core philosophy this way: "The firearm is a symbol of freedom for me and a tool of its enforcement. We went racing past tyranny a long time ago. We have been mugged by the state. Now there are four boxes that protect our freedoms. There's the mailbox, the ballot box, and the jury box. The backup system is the cartridge box. You don't want to get to that point, where your message to the government is over a rifle sight. That's called Libya. I am not looking to set up an apocalypse. Places like that have always been more dangerous places to live. Look at Russia. You had to mind your Ps and Qs or you would get taken away. We ought not think about safety; we ought to think of freedom."

The handgun business is one of the only major manufacturing industries in the United States that operates with no federal safety standards. After an enormous amount of lobbying, and with fierce opposition from the National Rifle Association, Congress mandated a computerized background check of felonies, court orders, domestic violence complaints, or other similar criteria for anyone who buys a handgun from a licensed dealer. The "Brady check" was named for President Reagan's press secretary, James Brady, who, like Gabrielle, suffered a devastating head wound from a would-be assassin's bullet. Jared Lee Loughner passed his Brady with no problem; he was flagrantly crazy but not yet a convicted criminal.

The check, which is phoned in by a store clerk and typically takes about five minutes to consummate, can be evaded simply by going to one of the frequent gun shows that operate in convention centers and hotels, where legal transactions can still occur between private individuals with no snooping or interference by anyone. The "gun show loophole" is closed in only six states. Arizona's gun shows are particularly notorious, as they are said by law enforcement officials to be a major source for the weapons that keep Mexican drug vendettas aflame. There is also a lot of collateral damage this side of the border. The Centers for Disease Control has estimated that there are about thirty thousand gun deaths per year in the United States, with slightly more than a third of them homicides and the rest suicides and accidents. Detailed causality studies are hard to come by. In 1996 the CDC saw its $2.6 million budget for gun research eliminated by Congress, with an order that no funds "be used to advocate or promote gun control."

"Look there," said Heller. He pointed to a father climbing into the high cab of a GMC Sierra pickup truck with his grade school–age son. The two of them had just finished an afternoon of shooting and were heading home. The father was blank-faced but tipped a hand to Heller, who tipped it back as they rolled out of the dirt parking lot. "We have a culture of people being nice to each other and driving nice vehicles and treating each other with respect," he said. "That is the real culture of Arizona."

Heller is an exceedingly temperate man in the way he handles his guns and his personal movements. His house has one fire extinguisher for every room. Two ride with him in his vehicle, which is a silver compact Pontiac Vibe with a CB antenna on top. There is a gun on his headboard when he sleeps at night and a gun in the pocket of his bathrobe. He limits his drinking to one beer at home every Saturday night, and then on St. Patrick's Day he allows himself a single tumbler of Bushmills whiskey, which he sips very slowly through the night while working at his desk. He has been depleting the same bottle by tiny annual increments for more than a decade. He had to go to Hawaii for business the week after our meeting, and he wasn't looking forward to it, because that state prohibits the carrying of firearms. He also could not, of course, take his Glock onboard the airliner, so he would be carrying a tall wooden walking stick cored with steel rebar.

"September eleventh is never going to happen on my watch," he told me. "I'm not looking for it, but if I'm in the middle of it, I want the tools to deal with it."

He professes no great love for guns *qua* guns. "They are inanimate objects," he said. "I don't give a rat's ass. It's a tool." One of his students once asked about the painted black finish of his Glock 23 and how it affected the appearance of the weapon. I don't know, said Heller, let me see. He took the gun over to a cinder-block wall and scraped it back and forth, making scratches and marring the finish. Wow, he announced as he examined it. I guess it looks terrible. In nearly four decades of carrying a weapon he has never once fired one in anger or been in a situation where one might have been useful.

"But if that problem happens," he assured me, "there is no other answer. It's an acknowledgment of your power over life and death in your hands and the respect to use it wisely. The reason I carry a gun is, I hate violence. I notice that around armed and confident people, there isn't a lot of violence. You don't look like food when you have a weapon."

Predation is the crux of the whole question. The act of owning a gun is almost a theological statement. It carries an assumption that the universe is hostile and capricious. It assumes that society's safeguards or God's providence will not be sufficient to protect us from Darwinist terrors, and that a person must have access to the easy ability to remove another's life forever and without question, in a decision that might contain within it all the deliberation that three seconds can afford.

The sole operational purpose for a handgun is to condemn a human being to the darkness of death. They are not practical for hunting. When used in anger, they are not meant to be discharged at the legs or hands in order to "wing" a bad guy in the style of *Red River*. Never point a gun at another person unless you intend to shoot, goes the old safety maxim, and do not shoot unless you intend to kill.

This gets to the truth of the matter, which bears restating. The only true purpose of a handgun is to hammer a two-ounce foreign object into the fragile meat of the brain, the irretrievable treasure chest of personality, memory, and comprehension. Beyond the euphemisms of "self-defense" and "home protection" lies this unalterable truth that no amount of political niceties should ever try to conceal. This fact should be the starting point for any discussion.

Whatever limp debate about guns there has been in Arizona since the killings has been focused on the extended length of the magazine that Jared Loughner used, that stuck out of the bottom of his Glock like a stool peg, grotesquely long and able to give him thirty-one rounds to inject into the soft meat of people without a pause. He had two more in his pocket and probably would have killed even more people at La Toscana Village if the cheap aftermarket brand he had purchased had not jammed. An ordinary clip carries ten rounds, and it was a matter of federal law that anything bigger was illegal for sale between the years 1994 and 2004. Congress let the ban expire, and while several states— including California, New Jersey, and New York—have banned them locally, Arizona has never shown much enthusiasm to do so. "I don't think it has anything to do with the size of the magazine or the caliber of the gun," Brewer told reporter Howard Fischer after the shootings. "The guy is a madman. Our justice system will hold him accountable." Sales of the extended magazines soared in the days after the event to those frightened that another ban might be coming down. There is said to be a seventy-five-year supply of them already in the marketplace.

I asked Heller why anyone would need one of those long magazines for "home protection," and he said: "If you're out in the middle of nowhere and confronted by drug mules, and they're carrying heavy weapons. If you only want to fire it over their heads as you're running away, you're going to want that. If something serious happens, you want as much on you, so you won't have to reload. Why do we make Corvettes that can go up to two hundred miles per hour? My point is that it's your decision to have it—it's not the government's business to tell you that you can't have it. That would be the ultimate expression of punishing the innocent for the acts of the guilty."

We go over to the outdoor range, which consists of a concrete pad covered with a tin roof. In front of us are about three rectangular acres of dirt, and the back end is an earthen berm about twelve feet high, which had been shored up there years ago. By now it must contain enough embedded lead to shield a nuclear reactor. We have the place practically to ourselves on this winter day, and after getting the verbal okay from the one other shooter for us to walk "downrange," we drag out a wooden frame holding a stapled portrait from the shoulders up of a blackened man-shape—the classic anthropomorphic target. At least this, too, is honest.

Heller hands me the same scratched-up Glock 19 that he once blasphemed against a brick wall to make a point—which also happens to be the same type and model of gun used by Jared Loughner to instantly steal the lives of half a dozen people and violate my friend's cranium with a cheap piece of lead and copper.

"All right now, put five in the head."

I feel nothing so much as a complete poseur right now as I stand and point it at the rounded shape of a human head. After several moments of hesitation, I squeeze the trigger. There is some resistance, and then, click, *pow*: a thunderclap. The barrel leaps in my hand like a snake come to life; an empty shell flicks outward and to the right. A neat round hole has appeared in the silhouette. I had expected to smell burning powder but can smell nothing but warm desert air. The powder is smokeless.

I squeeze the trigger again, and the firing pin falls against the back of the .40 caliber cartridge.

What happens next takes place in one twenty-thousandth of a second. The pin dimples a tiny circular disk on the back of the cartridge called a primer, which is made of a mixture of lead, barium, and antimony compounds. It creates a small white flash when struck. That tiny spark ignites a larger deposit of nitrocellulose doped with calcium carbonate. Also called the old British name guncotton, nitrocellulose is basically wood fiber soaked in nitric and sulfuric acids, and it burns to nothing within a few milliseconds, creating a concentrated temperature of about fifty-four hundred degrees Fahrenheit inside the barrel, as well as a gaseous head wall of nitrous oxide and carbon dioxide trapped behind the cartridge. This space becomes—instantly—an airtight chamber, because the heat causes the brass cartridge shell to expand. This enormous pressure launches the copper-jacketed slug out of the shell at the speed of twelve hundred feet per second. The copper-coated slug is about the size of a large cherry pit, though much heavier. As it travels forward, slender grooves carved on the inside of the barrel twist it into a spinning motion, which gives it stability in flight the same way that a spiral flick on a football makes it fly straighter. These grooves leave tiny distinctive scrapes on the bullet by which it might later be positively matched to the barrel in a criminal investigation. The bullet passes through the paper target and burrows into the dirt bank at the end of the range.

Invisible particulates from the primer settle onto my hand and arm. This is the "gunshot residue" that also turns up in forensic tests—it can disclose whether the person has recently been firing a weapon.

Let's try an experiment, Heller suggests. He fits me out with a plastic holster on my left hip and hands me the Glock, which had been loaded with ten rounds of .40 caliber ammo. Then he takes a .38 caliber pistol over to a neighboring stand about ten feet away. He wants me to wait until he starts shooting at his own target. Then I am to calmly and deliberately draw the Glock from the holster, switch it to my good right hand, take careful aim, and put two bullets into the head of my target.

I understood where this game was headed. This was in service of his master point about an armed citizenry being a safe citizenry. If anybody—man, woman, or teenager—had been at the Safeway crowd packing a concealed weapon very much like Loughner's, the kid would have been neutralized and bleeding on the cement within the first few seconds of gunplay. An extremely questionable scenario, and one that raised far more doubts than answers, but we were about to role-play it here.

When I hear the crack of Heller's gun through my earplugs, I calmly do as I had been instructed: draw, transfer, aim, shoot twice. And in this brief interlude I feel an intense sickness in my stomach. For a second I am *at* the Safeway under the fake Italian arches amid the potted geraniums and the American flag and the smell of mesquites and air-conditioning and the sudden eruption of pops. People are falling down dead all over, and I was in the superhero role, suddenly and completely tasked with saving them all: saving Gabrielle, saving my friend Gabe and the little girl.

My field of vision turns a slight shade of pink. I feel the reverb of the weapon like an ice pick between my shoulder blades.

"Not bad," says Heller, coming over to inspect the target. I can't tell if his impressed tone of voice is genuine or just him playing the role of encouraging instructor.

He points at one of the fresh holes. "Now that one would have gone right through the brain stem. I want you to note that Loughner shot for fifteen seconds. That took only five. I timed it."

He adds, with a mildly critical note, "I did, however, get off six rounds before you shot. Man, I wish I had been there at that Safeway. . . . Hey, sit down for a second. You're a wreck."

TEN

THE MEN FROM NOWHERE

A rizona's belief in itself as a bastion of liberty is part of what makes it a uniquely easy place to do business. The lack of a well-established hierarchy makes it possible to get a lot done in a hurry. "Bring enough cash and have a big enough set of balls and you can get anything done in this town," said one political consultant friend of mine, as she was shopping for a new pair of high-heeled shoes at the Camelback Esplanade.

I heard the same thought expressed in different terms from Keven Ann Willey, a Tucson native who worked as the editorial page editor for the *Republic* before moving on to *The Dallas Morning News*. I dropped in to see her in Texas a few years after she moved and asked her, offhand-edly, what struck her the most about her new state's political culture. She answered that it gave her a real appreciation for the lack of fetters in Arizona's power structure, because in Texas, when you come in wanting to accomplish something, you are typically asked a hundred questions by the civic gatekeepers about who you know and what family do you have here and what is your track record and how can we trust you? People are not generally frisked like this in Arizona.

A recurrent theme in state history up to the present day is what might be called the "man from nowhere syndrome," in which a stranger rides into Arizona with a little bit of money and a salable idea and is able to do some good, or make a fortune, or do great damage, or a combination of the three in a very short period of time. Arizona has always welcomed this speed seduction; it is, in fact, part of what the economy has depended upon for more than a century. Fast cash with few questions. The blank white sheet of Arizona is a magnet for second-act seekers and dreamers and those out to find, as Western author Bret Harte once called it, "a fresh deal all around." The loner with a compelling story might be considered the ultimate archetypal figure of Arizona. Their motives have ranged from honest city building to contracted larceny and the somewhere in between. This is a repeating pattern, stuttering through the years.

There was Black Jack Newman, a striving immigrant from Poland whose name was long and complicated, and people found it easier just to call him the "new man" around the mining town of Globe in the 1890s. He staked thirteen new copper and silver areas down Bloody Tanks Wash and named the new settlement Miami for his girlfriend. There was James Reavis, a real-estate agent and Confederate Army deserter who took the railroad to Phoenix and showed off documents from the eighteenth century proving that huge portions of the new state—along with water and mineral rights—actually belonged to him, because of a deed he had acquired from a colonial land grant from the king of Spain to one Don Miguel Nemecio Silva de Peralta de la Cordoba, aka "the Baron of Arizona." Reavis confiscated easement payments from railroads and silver mines, and started making life hell for ordinary settlers before an inspection by the surveyor general showed "the Baron's" documents had all been written with steel-tipped pens instead of quills, and could not have come from the Spanish royal court. There was Richard C. Flower from Boston, who brought investors out to a barren stagecoach stop where a vein of gold was said to have been discovered by the son of the emperor Montezuma, and for a good show there were nuggets that had been scattered on the ground only a week before. This was just one of the "salting" schemes that probably generated more cash than the actual working mines of Arizona in the nineteenth century.

In more recent days, Gary Martinson, a North Dakota home builder who liked the easy winters and Old West image, has erected close to two thousand of his resort-style Bison Homes around the Mogollon Rim. There is Jim Click, a former linebacker for Oklahoma State University who came out to Tucson when he was twenty-seven at his great-uncle's request, took over the languid Pueblo Ford at the corner of Twenty-second Street and Wilmot, rechristened it Jim Click Ford, and blanketed prime-time television with his earnest Oklahoma drawl. He is today one of the city's biggest philanthropists. There was sports impresario Jerry Colangelo, who came out from Chicago as an assistant basketball coach with two hundred dollars to his name to manage the expansion Phoenix Suns. He would go on to help build the downtown baseball stadium and own part of the Arizona Diamondbacks. There was the suntanned charmer Ned Warren, who found a paradise of incompetent regulation and cheap land in Arizona in the seventies. With a letter of endorsement signed by Senator Barry Goldwater he sold bogus desert homesites that had no water, sewage, or roads, bundled these contracts together as "paper," and then sold these, too, as investments—a scam that prefigured the great 2008 mortgage bubble. Drunks in East Phoenix taverns were paid to put their names on mortgages on land they would never see. The paper was stacked together and auctioned off, and the companies quickly went dark. Warren's "Great Southwest Land & Cattle" cost his suckers $5 million.

One of his spiritual inheritors was Charlie Keating, the Cincinnati antipornography bluenose who saw an opportunity to get rich in the banking deregulation of the eighties, bought a thrift called Lincoln Savings and Loan, and used its federally protected assets to invest in all manner of junk bonds, as well as in Keating's beloved Phoenician golf resort, where the swimming pool tiles were made of mother-of-pearl and the gardens were built by natives from the Kingdom of Tonga. There was Duke Tully, hired as the publisher of *The Arizona Republic*, who wore army medals to cocktail parties and told pulse-fluttering stories of his combat days in Vietnam, until his own newspaper exposed him as a liar who had never served in the military. Sam Nanini had come out of Chicago with a large reserve of questionable money and built "the greatest community anyone has ever seen" near the corner of Oracle and Ina, where La Toscana Village and its Safeway would soon stand.

Perhaps the prototypical Man from Nowhere is John McCain, a veteran Navy pilot and former Vietnam POW who met Cindy Hensley at a Honolulu military reception in 1979. She was the daughter of the man who held the license to distribute Anheuser-Busch beer in the Phoenix metro area. McCain became a vice president of public relations for his father-in-law, quickly made friends, and was running for an open congressional seat within two years. He frequently got lost driving himself to campaign rallies. When faced with the question of why he hadn't lived in Arizona for long (never a particularly tough question here), he answered that his longest previous mailing address was in the Hanoi Hilton, and that ended that.

Arizona is not unique as a place where a stranger can ride in and tell a story and make a new home: Such an activity is worn deeply into the leather of the United States, and perhaps even to all rooted civilizations everywhere. This has certainly been a cherished activity of my own. The state of Arizona, however, has always been a much easier milieu to get away with it on thin credibility, and in this way, it serves as a trompe l'oeil of the national narrative of extreme liberty.

Men from Nowhere who hope to do big things generally need a fixer on the ground, however—a guide to lead them through the brambles and toward the honey. And one person who has been known to get that contract is Charles Coughlin, probably the state's top political consultant and lobbyist, who is known for his blunt capability to get jobs done as much as for his easy profanity and willingness to use a theatrical temper in service to his ends. One lobbyist who knows him well told me that interests on one side of an issue sometimes put him on retainer just so he can't work for the other side.

There is a private consigliere like Charles Coughlin ensconced in an obscure off-site office in every state capital city in America. There were probably Coughlins in the courts of Medici Italy or during the last days of the Qing Dynasty in China, when shifting faces on the throne was a matter of routine but where the semipermanent knowledge of how the wheels really turn is kept at a safe distance from the palace, where it might be lost to a change in popular sentiment, or an invading rival, or the ax blade.

His consulting firm is called HighGround, whose meaning might not always be the moral interpretation of the phrase. More relevant is what "high ground" means in military terms: the best land seized first, from which arrows and missiles may be rained on enemies. Its offices are in a beautifully restored twenties house on a street in a once tatty central Phoenix neighborhood. There is no sign outside and no obvious address posted. You'll miss it if you don't know what you're looking for. Inside the dark-paneled sitting room are a few antique couches and a poster of Coughlin's smiling face in a parody of the famous artsy blue-and-red campaign poster for Barack Obama. CHANGE, says the legend, FOR A TWENTY.

He came in apologetically late, having just driven in from a rough meeting in the town of Florence, where he had been representing a Canadian mining company called Curis Resources, Ltd., which is seeking a permit to pump acid for copper ore inside the city limits. This was not the easy knock they thought it was going to be, even though Florence has shown a historic willingness to be flexible with what happens inside its borders. Beginning in the late eighties, the city council began pushing the boundaries outward, so it could encompass the Arizona State Penitentiary and six other federal and private prisons on its edges. Approximately twelve thousand convicts—none of whom use the parks or can cast a ballot—boosted the city's official resident base by a factor of three and automatically triggered the flow of millions more dollars in grant money. The joke goes that Florence is now the state's largest gated community. But Coughlin was having a hard time convincing the city to revise its general zoning plan to accommodate a copper mine.

He pulled up a leather chair in a side room, and I asked him about what's been happening in the legislature, with all the emphasis on guns and go-it-alone immigration laws. He smiled in approval. "It's a Western questioning of authority," he said. "We confront all the questions, there's nothing we won't talk about. The extremes do get all the attention, but there's a healthy dialogue in this state. I love it. I was talking to Paul Senseman* about this very thing, and he said, 'We're behaving exactly as we should, Charlie. We were the last state on the American continent. We're questioning our older brothers and sisters.'"

Coughlin is sometimes called Governor Jan Brewer's Karl Rove—the brains behind the pomp. He served as her campaign chairman and the head of her transition team. A Phoenix television station found that nearly a dozen of his clients and associates ended up with positions on boards and high up in cabinet departments, a record that only boosted the perception that Coughlin enjoyed a direct pipeline to the ninth-floor governor's office. His list includes heavy hitters like the Salt River Project, the Fiesta Bowl, and Corrections Corporation of America, operator of several private prisons in Arizona, including the Central Arizona Detention Center in Florence, which temporarily houses migrants without papers. And he often gets desired results. As it happened, the governor gave her quiet approval to the acid-pump mine in Florence just a few months after Coughlin's tough knock.

When Sarah Palin came to Phoenix for a rally for Senate Bill 1070, Coughlin helped her write a speech. The one applause line that she insisted stay in the text above all others—"Mr. President: do your job, secure the

---

* The governor's longtime aide, who frequently answers questions directed at her.

border!"—turned out to be the one that got all the press, noted Coughlin, admiring her instinct to find words that resonate. He claims not to have heard from her ever since she bought a $1.7 million McMansion behind a set of gates in north Scottsdale, out amid the resort country.

Retaining his outfit is like having an instant ground game for those who lack the patience or time to build a social movement the old-fashioned way, but Coughlin said that simply paying the firm for representation or perceived access never guarantees a favorable outcome with any elected official—from the governor on down. "The perception is that they'll automatically do what we want them to do," he said. "That's just not the case." At the minimum, though, "we get a straight answer" from those in charge. And as for the quickie outcomes, money alone never guarantees anything. "I've seen a lot of people blow huge sums," he said, "and get fucking nowhere."

The aggressive posturing to his rivals, the threats and the querulous phone calls, were more a matter of personality than strategy, he told me.

"It's in my nature," he says. "I fight passionately for what I believe in. If I did something wrong, then go ahead and lynch my fucking nuts. . . . Maybe I bullshit myself about this, and the trouble with this business is that you can rationalize any behavior, but you try to work out what are the higher goals of perpetuating an ideal of how government should work."

Coughlin may be the closest thing to a working institutional memory that exists anywhere in Arizona's flickering political culture, but he himself once rode in from the approximate country of Nowhere. Though he shares a first and last name with the thirties' right-wing radio priest, Father Charles Coughlin, as well as a home state of Michigan, there is no blood relation. He grew up the son of an Ann Arbor lawyer who represented auto parts manufacturers. Dinner-table conversation at the Coughlin house always revolved around which automaker was getting screwed and which union kingpin was enriching himself. He came to Phoenix in 1984 in his early twenties after a chance meeting with John McCain in Cleveland, who was there as a favor to do a campaign event for a congressional hopeful named Matt Hatchadorian. Coughlin was so impressed with McCain's verbal delivery and his story of surviving torture in a North Vietnamese prison that he offered to come out to do fundraising work for McCain's successful run for Senate that following year. And then he decided to stay.

"What appealed to me about Arizona was the notion that . . . you felt like the opportunity was limitless," he once told the *Arizona Capitol Times*. "You could see as far as the horizon could go, and you could be whatever you wanted to be."

Coughlin found a job with the suburban city of Mesa. He was soon being asked by private carting companies why the garbage rates to the citizens were set so high. They encouraged him to go down and make a case at the state Senate, where he was politely told to go talk to the Senate president, Carl Kunasek. "I didn't know shit," said Coughlin. "I just went to talk to Carl." This turned out to be "an easy knock," to use one of Coughlin's later favorite expressions. He walked right in and made a case. The genial Kunasek took a liking to the brash kid from Mesa who wanted to pry open a basic government service for competition. Within five weeks Democratic governor Rose Mofford had signed a bill that mandated that cities over 150,000 in population allow up to seven carting companies the right to operate. "That cost the city $3 million, and I had to get the fuck out of town," said Coughlin. But finding new work was not a problem.

That episode was an object lesson in a formula that can bring riches to the insightful: *If you don't like the law, change the law.* The world is not fixed; its rules may be selectively modified, and a man who can figure out how to build his tollbooth in one of the many slot canyons of the law is a man who may retire early.

Coughlin was a top adviser to Governor Fife Symington, the great-grandson of steel titan Henry Clay Frick, who had first come out from Maryland as a Luke AFB cadet, made a lot of money developing real estate—that quintessential Arizona business—and resigned from office in 1997 after being convicted of financial chicanery. It was another national embarrassment for Arizona, which had suffered in the previous decade from the spectacle of Governor Evan Mecham* and the FBI sting operation called AzScam, in which multiple legislators were captured on videotape taking bribes from an actor posing as a casino operator. "There isn't an issue in the world I give a shit about," Representative Bobby Raymond told his interlocutor. "I do deals. My favorite line is 'What's in it for me?'" It became the signature quote of the episode.

Coughlin regained his influence in the governor's office after Symington's resignation, after serving as head of the transition team for Governor Jan Brewer. He also works for initiatives, candidates, and corporations. The farrago of allies he has made over a quarter century means guaranteed face time for his clients. He is not above turning on a ferocious temper for effect. I was once the target of it, when I covered Phoenix city government for the *Republic*: He hollered at me over a story involving a faked memo over a Walmart zoning variance. This came just hours after a conversation in which he told me he was trying to be a better person and not "an asshole," as he acknowledged he had been many times in his past.

Transgression, repentance, and then more transgression have been running themes in his career. Former Senate president Jane Hull grew irritated with his hardball tactics and told his then boss, Grant Woods, that he was persona non grata at the legislature. He had to make sneak visits to the third-floor antechamber of the Senate where all the lobbyists hang out. And there was a low moment in the 2010 governor's race be-

---

* A Pontiac dealer from Glendale who was a perennial candidate until 1986, when his unequivocal message against taxes caught the imagination of voters, many of them recent arrivals in Arizona, in an exceptionally low-turnout Republican primary. His administration was marred by his choice to rescind a state holiday for Martin Luther King Jr., which earned the state a high-profile national boycott. He later told a group of black Arizonans: "You folks don't need another holiday. What you folks need are jobs." He was removed from office after failing to report a $350,000 loan, among other misdeeds, becoming the only U.S. governor ever to be impeached, indicted, and the subject of a recall all at the same time.

tween Brewer and Attorney General Terry Goddard when he responded to vague rumors about Brewer's health by blog posting an old FBI transcript from the AzScam days in which one witness offered up the rumor that Goddard was gay. This was an ancient zinger against the late-married Goddard, and Coughlin quickly removed the post, but not until it got decent play as a story and forced Goddard to assert, once again, his heterosexuality. Brewer wouldn't apologize for the actions of her surrogate. "I didn't say it," she told an AP reporter. "Why would I apologize if I didn't say it?"

The man who did say it said he was indeed very sorry. "We have heard from some people who were offended by our blog post yesterday," Coughlin wrote. "For that, we apologize. Our purpose was to point out how ridiculous it has become that blogs and other irrelevant speculation are being used to create rumors that the media takes seriously." Well, then.

The lack of a mature Arizona political structure has given its men from nowhere an easy ride into the twenty-first century, and it only got easier after a change was made to the law in 1999 providing public funds for candidates to run for office. The Clean Elections law* was meant to defuse the power of big corporations, but it only made it even easier for newcomers to run campaigns on peanuts and bypass the gritty climb they might have been asked to make in other regions: the tedious work of volunteering on campaigns, running for school board, doing favors, making concessions, learning names, understanding points of tension, knowing where the streets lead, learning to make peace and get things done, and then—and only then—making the jump to the state legislature or Congress.

Arizona's system tends to give more weight to extreme positions than it does to established political virtues. The Tucson district that includes the Foothills and La Toscana Village is represented by a retired merchant

---

* Some key provisions of this law were struck down by the U.S. Supreme Court in June 2011.

marine captain named Al Melvin, who moved to the master-planned community of Saddlebrooke six years before running for office for the first time. Campaigning against "liberals," "bureaucrats," and "illegal aliens," he knocked out veteran business-friendly moderate Pete Hershberger in the 2008 primary and cruised easily to victory. He has since pushed to make Arizona a repository for nuclear waste. He also praised the courage of fellow senator Lori Klein for reading a letter aloud in the Senate from a substitute teacher in Glendale who claimed that his Latino students all "want to be gang members and gangsters" and "hate America and are determined to reclaim this area for Mexico"—a description that the school district investigated and concluded was fantasy.

Another one of that vanishing breed of moderate Republicans in Arizona is Chris Herstam, a former legislator who is now the vice president of government affairs for the law firm of Lewis and Roca. The lobby has the architecture of intimidation common to white-shoe Phoenix law firms. There are towering walls of gray slate squares and tasteful, expensive-looking Asian prints on the walls, subtle reminders of all the money confiscated in previous judgments in favor of the firm's clients. I went to see him in the Lewis and Roca conference room, and he shared with me the shifting numbers. Republican registration was at about 36 percent, down several percentage points from the midforties. Democrats were holding steady at about 30 percent. But registered independents were at 31 percent, up from 16 percent. At the rate they were traveling they would be the dominant political party in Arizona without even being a party.

Perversely, though, their growing presence was making Arizona government *less* independent. Those who joined the independents tended to be those disgusted, or at least disenchanted, with the core message of their party, which meant that those left within the party structure were the hard cores and those most dedicated to an extreme candidate in the open field of a primary. "The rabid ideologues show up and vote no matter what," said Herstam.

Making matters worse is the lengthy general election season mandated under Arizona law. Primary day is in the last week of August, which tends to be sizzling hot, and also a day when enough people have planned their vacations and won't be around to go to the polls. Arizona is also under the mandate of the 1964 Voting Rights Act to ensure minority representation. The method of doing that has been to create serpentine districts that swallow as many Latino voters as possible so as to guarantee a victory for a Latino, typically a Democrat. Those votes that normally would have gone to an Anglo Democrat are split off in this way, and the moderates are diluted in a Republican district, creating a legislature guaranteed to lean conservative, unrepresentative of the fuzzy middle and what Coughlin acknowledged was a "sinecure for the left" in a "permanent minority."

All of these factors combine to create a map where, out of thirty legislative districts, perhaps two or three are any sort of real contest in the general election. Most of them are cakewalks for the primary victor, who in recent years has tended to be the loudest in the primary. Independents voting in the general election find they have no real choice. Such a scenario does not reward anyone who professes a belief in the art of compromise or shared solutions, which does not have quite the pulling power. Arizona's electoral system—in both legal structure and sociological reality—tends to bestow its laurels on the angry and drowns out the less passionate voices. And it rewards the Man from Nowhere, who appears like a superhero ready to slay beasts and restore order.

Traveling a far distance in a short time, particularly at the ballot box, is an enduring feature of Arizona public life. When I asked Coughlin about it, he grew animated.

"That's worthy!" he said. "That's a uniquely American thing! Maybe it's a vestige of a bygone American era. It is arguably a good idea. I could argue that. If you have a good idea, you have a shot out here. I love that."

✴

Harold Bourquin doesn't know who this "guk" really is, but he has been chasing the guy's shadow for months now. The traces are everywhere: on cinder-block walls, electric transformer boxes, playground equipment.

Just three letters scrawled in orange marker—*guk*—probably not his initials but some obscure code. Borquin can't stand it.

"I'm one of those who wants to be proud of where he lives," he told me. "And this leaves a bad taste in my mouth. I want people to see Maricopa for what a good little town it is." He sprayed solvent on the letters, and the ink immediately began to bleed in orange streams down the utility box.

Borquin is a member of the Graffiti Abatement Team for the city of Maricopa, Arizona, which wasn't even a city ten years ago. There is reason to say that it isn't even a city now. But there are fifty thousand more people in the desert than there used to be, due to the work of a few major home-building corporations—KB Home, Pulte Homes, and D.R. Horton among them—who went on a spree here in the first decade of the twenty-first century, erecting Brobdingnagian master plans of boomerang streets and snout-nosed homes in what had been cotton flats the year before. People could pick their favorite model out of a catalog and, for almost no money down, move in six months later to a new home that smelled of fresh glue and caulking. The population rocketed from 1,230 to 45,000 in a single decade, giving it a dazzling 4,000 percent rate of expansion and winning it the title of America's fastest-growing town, according to the Census Bureau. It was the perfect symbol of Arizona's promise: a paradise of middle-class homeownership in a new landscape of privacy and convenience, made possible by hydrology and lots of empty land.

But a dark side materialized almost immediately. Many of the people who relocated here—nearly a third of them with subprime loans, by one estimate—foreclosed after the mortgage crash of 2008. Maricopa became checkered with brand-new homes standing empty. Swimming pools turned green with algae. Weeds grew tall in driveway cracks. And some of the town's immensely bored young people started making graffiti hits on the abandoned property, thinking that nobody was paying attention.

"Places where the homes weren't selling got hit harder than other places," said Bourquin. "It does show a trend. There was an upswing in the community showing its frustration."

He doesn't get paid anything for erasing guk's mess. It is strictly a labor of civic love he performs twice a week, a purely volunteer effort for the city's Code Enforcement Bureau, which found the money for a Dodge pickup, a supply of solvent, and regular buckets of cover-up paint from the Sherwin-Williams store all keyed to the specific color schemes approved for each subdivision by the various homeowners' associations. Most of them are a light shade of brown. The city desperately needed the cleanup. "It looked like inner-city Detroit around here, and I can say that because I'm from Detroit," said Brian Duncan, the head of code enforcement.

Bourquin wears a golf shirt with the city's big M logo on the breast and carries a city ID card around his neck. He has plenty of free time these days, as he was laid off two years ago from his job as a division manager for Paddock Pools and has been having no luck finding a way to be reemployed. He used to be in charge of installing a special kind of acrylic pool deck coating doctored up to look like flagstones or brick. But the swimming pool business is directly tied to the housing market, and Harold's job was one of the casualties.

So, too, is the current value of his house, for which he paid about $252,000 and is now worth closer to $152,000. His mortgage is now close to "upside-down," which means he might owe more than the house is worth. People in Maricopa typically aren't shy about discussing the value of their homes anymore. The meltdown put almost everyone here in the same pickle. This sensitive topic is now more a matter of gallows humor than a taboo. Some of those who turned in their keys took out their frustrations on their onetime dream house. Bank officials found a number of fist-shaped holes punched in the drywall and occasionally the granite countertops or the toilets ripped out. One man scattered a large bag of birdseed in the kitchen, perhaps hoping that rodents would come for the feast. Another abandoned family dwelling became an underground "fight club," where a few locals would gather to stage hand-to-hand brawls. "These homes were built at the wrong time," local Realtor Steve Murray acknowledged. "There probably could not have been a worse time to build them and sell them. They are now probably fifty to sixty percent upside-down."

Times had felt significantly rosier for Bourquin in 2003, when he and his wife had picked a model called "Chuparosa" out of a Pulte catalog. "My sister Jackie is a real-estate agent, and she said, 'Maricopa is the place to be. You'll get the most bang for the buck, and when you resell you'll get the best price.' That was the big push—you could get a whole lot of house."

Getting a whole lot of house has been the desire that has sustained Arizona's economy for decades, and Maricopa's story is like a blown-up cartoon version of what happened to the whole Southwest when the real-estate market collapsed. Some quick history: This was little more than a dusty railroad crossing at the northern edge of the Ak-Chin* Indian Community reservation, mostly notable for being on the way to someplace else. Founded as a watering stop on the Butterfield stage line in 1871, it changed places three times before the Southern Pacific Railroad made up its mind and erected a permanent depot in 1887. Through most of the last century it was a desert dot with a tavern and a Circle K frequented mainly by ranchers and Latino seasonal workers hired out by nearby cotton growers. In the late eighties the real-estate entrepreneur Mike Ingram of El Dorado Holdings began buying up land for around five hundred dollars an acre and making building rights agreements with home builders.

None other than Charles Coughlin of HighGround was brought in

---

* The name means "place where the water loses itself in the sand." The Tohono O'odham Indians who settled here had developed a technique for trapping the meager rainwater within loose sand where they could grow crops.

to campaign for a five-cent sales tax to widen Arizona 347, the only road into Phoenix and its plentiful suburbs twinkling with jobs. The road passed over what can charitably be called not the most scenic patch of desert in Arizona—a flat dun expanse prone to dust devils, its monotony broken only by dried-up tamarisk and some volcanic rocks.

Coughlin won that tax increase for Ingram's widened road and didn't come back for ten years. And he was astonished at what he saw at the end of its four lanes. Arizona 347 was now called John Wayne Highway. Gigantic instant neighborhoods like Cobblestone Farms and El Dorado had gone up in a hurry, and a rump city government was quickly chartered, just to have an agency to issue housing permits and do some semblance of planning. The local water company drilled wells down to one thousand feet. At the height of the craze more than seven hundred permits were being executed—or "pulled"—every month, and city officials guessed that three human beings were being moved into Maricopa every hour. Cotton growers found it easiest just to sell off their land; one family now just grows a decorative kind of wheat that is lacquered and sold to arts-and-crafts chain stores like Michael's.

Planners began to talk about extending the city limits all the way down to Interstate 8, some twenty miles to the south, and making the city a major link in the urbanized corridor that would eventually unite Phoenix and Tucson into one giant megalopolis in a little more than two decades. Maricopa was sold in the short-term as a tidy, slumless, middle-class community for a young family to get started on a reproductive adventure, as well as a paradise for "flippers"; that is, fast-buck investors who acquire a home in a hot area and then sell it quickly at a profit.

Nothing at all would have happened without the road widening. One durable rule of commuting is called "Marchetti's Constant," after the Italian physicist Cesare Marchetti, who postulated that ever since man's Neolithic beginnings, he does not like to tolerate spending any more than an hour and a half every day moving away from the home. This was the ideal foot range for a man to hunt, find food, build alliances, and attract mates and still be a safe distance away from the cave. As it happened, Maricopa was located about a forty-five-minute drive from the heart of Phoenix, and even less from Sky Harbor International Airport. It fit a subconscious preference as well as a more modern truism of suburban real estate: drive until you qualify.

"In perspective, what we're doing here is the reality for Arizona," said assistant city manager Roger Kolman, "and for the rest of the world."

What the home builders did not leave behind in Maricopa was any sense of a connected physical environment or people in relationship with one another. The only nearby jobs paid minimum wage or barely more at the Fry's grocery or the Native New Yorker deli. City hall was a set of double-wide trailers welded together and mounted with A/C compressors; it looked like a canteen the military might have erected in Iraq. The only public park was a couple of baseball diamonds and a soccer field on the far eastern edge, where children always had to be driven. Medical issues required a forty-minute drive to Chandler, as there was no hospital. No sidewalks connected the megabarrios. Community life simply did not exist.

"The houses probably grew faster than the social fabric," acknowledged the town's second mayor, Anthony Smith. "The connections that people would get either by having local jobs or just by staying home were missing. We need to find sustainability as well as infrastructure." In that spirit the city has put on some public events, including a salsa festival in April, some Fourth of July fireworks, and a carnival with kiddie rides called Stagecoach Days held in October.

Tooling around Maricopa can give you vertigo. It is easy to get lost amid curving streets with names like Smyth Farms Circle and Oxbow Lane, and the houses are all of the same monotonous Sunbelt ranch vocabulary, holding the same approximate low-six-figure values. Few people were walking the streets when I visited on a hot day in early May, and *nobody* ever goes to the grocery store without a car.

After enough time in Maricopa one begins to get the impression of a classless society more thoroughly executed than anything Karl Marx could have envisioned. No house is too extravagant and nobody's house is too ramshackle (the homeowners' associations see to that). All of it in every direction is comfortably middle-class, totally middlebrow, and without physical extremes. A democratic median. "It does kind of seem like everyone's equal here," Bourquin said. "Everybody's the same. Nobody is more important than anybody else."

He spotted another electrical box with taggings and abruptly stopped the truck. I would have missed it completely, but Bourquin's eyes had become sharp for this sort of thing. The box had been claimed not by the elusive guk but by another artist, who had left letters as unreadable to me as kanji. Bourquin went to work on it with solvent and philosophized out loud. "Some people just want to be heard," he said. "Some people are just kids in love. Some people are making a statement to the world. But hey, draw a picture, write a poem, sing a song, but don't do it this way. It's a kid trying to send a message to someone, but it makes no sense to us."

He covered up the rest of the mark with a paint known as "Maricopa Gray," the most well-used color in his palette. The team goes through a bucket at least every week. Bourquin rarely notices any symbol that seems to be gang-related, and while the defacements happen on a nightly basis, usually between two and four o'clock in the morning, they amount to cosmetic damage, like acne on a cheek. But they offend his code of decent behavior. He grew up in a house with a Latino mom and an Anglo dad, where there were old-school manners and no foolishness was tolerated.

We got back in the truck and Bourquin steered us out to the highway and almost to the border of the Ak-Chin reservation, where he turned down a dirt road that paralleled an irrigation canal full of water and a six-foot cinder-block wall. This was the back end of Maricopa Meadows, which, like all of the subdivisions, was built inside walls fortified like Renaissance villages. Household trash is sometimes tossed over these walls, Bourquin told me. Once he found an abandoned truck back here that turned out to have been stolen. On the other side of the canal were tract homes for the Ak-Chin reservation that had been built in the seventies by the federal Bureau of Indian Affairs. They were rectangular and stucco-sided, with carports, and looked a lot like identical models that I had seen on Indian reservations all over Arizona. I realized, too, that they looked an awful lot like the homes just on the other side of the subdivision wall, also mass-produced and made of similar cheapjack materials: concrete pads, gypsum walls, clay-shell tile.

Bourquin spotted another outraged slash of paint on the outer wall, and this one wasn't hard to see. Big purple letters reading: CANNABIS— LEGALIZE IT! Bourquin opened the drum of beige paint that had been color-coded for the Maricopa Meadows Homeowners Association. The words were on the coarse surface of the cinder-block wall, so he had no choice but to cover it up with a beige blast from an electric paint sprayer. Sweat glistened on his forehead as he created the new square. The temperature was about ninety-five degrees outside, with not a hint of clouds, just a brownish haze collecting over the hardpan desert to the south. He always kept the truck engine running so the A/C would be fresh.

We got going again on the road beside the canal. Bourquin saw some kids swimming in it and rolled his window down, telling them sternly to get out, that it was dangerous. They nodded acquiescence, and we kept going. The subdivision wall opened up, and I could see one of the oddly shaped pieces of land, too low in the floodplain to sell, that the developer had seeded over and tried to turn into a minipark. A "tot-lot," in the parlance of the exurbs, with plastic playground castles planted there to make it kid-friendly. Bourquin told me, angrily, that it was on the playground equipment where he found the most disgusting graffiti: male and female genitals and the nastiest words, some carved with a knife.

The foreclosure mess had hit his own block pretty hard, he told me. A lot of neighbors moved away quickly, one of them in the middle of the night. When gas crept up to nearly four bucks a gallon, it became unreasonably expensive to keep making the ninety-mile drive every day up to the Valley and back. He hated to see these people go and give up like that. He learned to spot the subtle signs of a vacated house: shiny cobwebs near the front door; dried oil patches on the driveway; a fine layer of dust on the outside of the windows; shades always drawn.

For whatever its virtues as a financially welcoming place for young pregnant couples just venturing out with a two-bedroom, Maricopa's instant launch had physically encouraged the isolationist impulse: not merely the occasional desire for privacy but as a total way of life, fixing it on a set of rails even when the inevitable urge to mingle starts to creep in. The built landscape works to defeat that. The systematic isolation may work for some. It does not for others.

The writer Samantha M. Shapiro spent a depressing week in Maricopa during the worst part of the foreclosure crisis in 2008. "There was nowhere to go and no one on the street," she wrote. "The brick walls on both sides of my house meant I couldn't see my neighbors and they couldn't see me. So I began to spend my evenings at Fry's, the supermarket in the main strip mall on Highway 347. Fry's had couches and wireless Internet and a flat-screen TV—and, more important, people. As it turned out, I was not the only person in Maricopa who thought Fry's was a pretty great place to spend an evening." She met a group of teenagers who congregated on the couches near the television for lack of anywhere else to go, as well as a nineteen-year-old store manager who told her: "The only thing good is Fry's. Without Fry's, I wouldn't have met anyone here. It's just slit-your-throat-and-wrists boring."

Bourquin is a joiner by temperament, and even when he was still working at Paddock Pools he made an attempt to get to know the people around him. He bought a water filter from one neighbor and struck up a friendship. His wife runs a jump-rope after-school program for girls. But he acknowledges that it takes effort and doesn't occur by magic. "Everyone goes around here in vehicles, usually by themselves," he said. "It makes it hard to get together. It takes effort. It isn't something that's going to happen by itself."

Maricopa had recently been experiencing an unexpected renaissance, thanks in part to the plummet in values. "All these Canadians with gym bags full of loonies and spending like drunken sailors," in the words of one broker, discovered that you could get a lot of house in Maricopa and started buying vacation homes for bargain prices on short sale. Realtors began decorating their Web sites with maple leaves, and there is now a Maricopa Canadian Club that meets for beer and rodeos in the winter. In the hot summer months the houses get weedy, dusty, and possibly graffitied. Hence a new recession-era trade: the "concierge services," which are basically a housewife or an out-of-work handyman who will keep a watch on the house while the absentee owners are away.

There are also homes in Maricopa, bought to be flipped, that have never once been occupied by a human being, some of which are sold in casual auctions in front of the Pinal County Courthouse. About 70 percent of the closings are for full cash payment on the spot, a level of white-knuckle speculation far out of reach for the ordinary family.

The ridiculous bargains were an enticement for Sarah Palin's daughter, Bristol Palin, who put down $172,000 for a four-thousand-square-foot home in Cobblestone Farms. The purchase generated a lot of press, as well as speculation that the address was a possible beachhead for a Palin run for Congress, as Arizona's whipsawing political culture never much minded a newcomer. Realtors were flooded with calls for the next few weeks, not necessarily because of the tabloid interest in Bristol but because of the stunningly low price the twenty-year-old paid for a lot of house. She told an interviewer that she had no friends in Arizona and knew no one here except her infant son.

Pinal County was full of people in transition. According to figures from Arizona State University, one quarter of its population was moving either in or out in the calendar year of 2005. The lack of continuity means that a newcomer can make long political strides. The sheriff is an ambitious transplant from North Adams, Massachusetts, named Paul Babeu, who campaigned in 2008 on a platform to get rid of the photo traffic-ticket machines on the sides of the roads. He has since refashioned himself into a crusader against illegal immigrants and "drug cartels," calling Pinal the number-one pass-through county for both menaces. The resulting publicity landed him as a frequent guest on Fox News.

Babeu has since purchased dozens of semiautomatic assault rifles for his deputies and run night operations with snipers in the desert, even though his county is seventy miles from the border. "It's all lethal force only, and we go into that environment knowing that we're likely expecting an armed threat from these people," he told reporters. But precious little evidence emerged to support this. One of his deputies claimed to have been ambushed in the desert by a gang of armed Mexican smugglers who rained bullets down on him; a state investigation failed to find cartridge shells in the area that might have been fired in the way the deputy described. An analysis by Dennis Wagner of *The Arizona Republic* found that barely 2 percent of Arizona's immigrant arrests were made in the county, and marijuana seizures were also paltry compared with the actual border counties'. But Babeu remained popular among core constituents in Maricopa, and especially in the northwestern portion of the county, which has seen virtually no violence that can be linked to cartels.

"The real thing about Arizona is that we're all afraid," said Bill Hart of Arizona State University's Morrison Institute for Public Policy. "The culture is changing, the economy is in a shambles, people's futures are not ensured. And so it's a springboard for ambitious politicians on all levels to play on that fear."

The lobbyist Chris Herstam once told me a story about sitting in the tenth-floor conference room at *The Arizona Republic*. Several dozen of the high-income decision makers in town had been invited for an informal talk on the health of the economy and the state's reliance on people from the rest of the United States who come to Arizona to buy a home. The half-acre-and-a-pool economy had been thriving in the first few years of the new century, and the employment rate was healthy, but they concealed a decline of jobs in other sectors and the painful inability of the university system to handle an influx of lower-income students.

"I'm concerned about this nondiversified economy," Herstam told the room. "The market rises and falls. If there's a major drop, we're going to be in trouble."

At this, the local chairman of Bank One, Mike Welborn, spoke up.

His out-of-state bank had acquired the assets of Valley National Bank and, as such, he was the heir to the seat once occupied by the legendary president Walter Bimson, whose philosophy of making promiscuous low-interest home loans to young families in the forties helped secure the phenomenal growth of the Phoenix metro area.

"Quit saying that, Chris!" he allegedly said.* "You are wrong. That is the thinking of the past. The stock market will continue to rise through our children's lifetimes. We are in a new era in this country."

"All I could do," recalled Herstam, "was say, 'Mike, I hope you're right.'"

The belief in forever ascendant home prices was perfect shorthand for the old Arizona story, which stands for admirable attributes in the national character: a love of family, a yearning for independence, an optimism about the future, a desire to own a little postage stamp of the world. But the city of Maricopa had also been founded on that national story, and it had been thrown up quickly and on dangerous assumptions of cheap gasoline, endless water, a stable economy, and homes built in a hurry that people would always want.

Are such places doomed to physical and spiritual decay? Arthur C. Nelson of the Metropolitan Institute at the University of Utah has predicted that up to twenty-five million suburban homes across the country will be vacant by 2030, the fruits of irrational hope. What will invariably happen is that single-family dwellings will be split up into rental apartments, with separate entrances and new plaster walls, much like the Federalist town houses of older Eastern cities. Feckless exurbs like Maricopa—in the absence of effort—would be at risk for becoming the slums of the coming decades, because nobody would want tacky

---

* Welborn is now the CEO of P. F. Chang's, a chain of Chinese restaurants. I called to ask him about this exchange, and he said he did not recall it. "You're on the right wicket," he said. "I knew a lot of people who believed that: that the construction industry would always grow and people would always migrate here. But I never bought into it."

houses in a nonplace. The most recent U.S. Census revealed that one of every six housing units in Arizona was standing empty. A University of Arizona economist told reporter Howard Fischer that the surplus would be enough to handle at least ten years' worth of growth—assuming the state would ever grow again like it once had.

I went over to talk with Bob Gillespie, the head of the local Chamber of Commerce, whose house is in The Village at El Dorado. A metal sculpture of wild horses stands out front on John Wayne Highway as a monument to this subdivision, considered one of the better ones. The entrance road leads past a ceremonial row of palm trees and an artificial lake with four fountains jetting streams of water. Gillespie is a rumbling man with a gray ponytail who had worked as a bundler of mortgages— "yep, I used to be *that* guy," he acknowledged when we met—before switching to only individual deals, where he gets to meet every buyer to make sure they aren't squirrelly. He has worked in the lending business for forty-five years and remains bullish about the future of the town that sprang up overnight.

"We survived a category five financial hurricane here," he said. "Life goes on. You start over. Despite the fact that we're a bedroom community, you don't have to look further than the fact that we've got forty churches here. The level of volunteerism is very high. We're building a women's shelter." A small hospital, too, is on the way. The town happens to be one of the most educated in Arizona in terms of the rate of college degree acquisition. But despite these steps forward, Gillespie acknowledged that the pleasures of Maricopa are generally not shared ones. They are contained within the walls of the house, and that, he said, represents a fundamental change in American society more than it does any failing of the community.

"Movies are passé anymore," he told me. "You can sit in your air-conditioned home and watch DVDs on your sixty-two-inch plasma. Now certainly there's a percentage of the population that misses those things."

Nearly everyone I talked to in Maricopa had a variation on that idea.

It was a great place to live quietly and peacefully, but the happinesses were generally of the solitary variety. I went down to Pacana Park—the name means "pecans," though there are no trees like that in sight—to watch a soccer team practicing, and sat on the grass with a thirtyish dad named Perry Alexander. He and his wife and daughters had moved out from Lexington, Kentucky, so that he could take a job with a Chase Bank operations center near Sky Harbor International Airport. They bought their home in Maricopa with the understanding that they'd be able to trade up, and it hadn't worked out that way. Of the twenty-five homes on his cul-de-sac street, five are now empty.

"When we first moved here they were telling us there'd be a hundred thousand people here by 2012. Now you pass nothing but moving vans on your way out of town," he told me. "They move and they don't stay. We thought it was going to be a growing community. And it would have been, if the issue"—he meant the foreclosures—"didn't come up. But it's a real nice place, actually. No crime. The biggest issue is boredom. There is *nothing to do*. You don't have a sit-down restaurant. No movies, no shopping. You have to drive to Casa Grande to get any kind of entertainment. A lot of people here miss their families back home. Nobody I've met is from Arizona." He had started to get to know one guy on his block pretty well, but the fellow was transferred to Oregon within three months, and moved out.

Alexander decided he wasn't going to sit and watch his neighborhood deteriorate. He took it on himself to do yardwork on the houses sitting abandoned, without anyone asking. He pulls weeds out of the driveway cracks, clips the overgrown mesquite trees, clears the doorknobs of hanging advertisements, and makes the block look intact. Such freelance acts of tidying take place all over the city now. A volunteer group called Copa Cares has coordinated some of these outings, which double as a way for neighbors to meet one another, even as they tend to the properties of those who turned in their keys. For better or worse, the people who held on to their homes in Maricopa, and who also cared about building a life, were going to go about the halting work of creating a community in a town deliberately wiped clean of history, where making such new human connections was a bold act, even a radical one.

"I'm the kind of guy who loves feeling proud of my neighborhood," Bourquin told me at the city hall trailers, after a morning of cleaning up guk's mess. This had not necessarily been what he had envisioned at the beginning, but it was the promise he had bought, and he would see it through.

"You have to *want* to care about this place," he said.

ELEVEN

A BETTER PLACE

L ife got rough for Gabrielle in the second year of Barack Obama's
presidency. The administration rolled out its health-care plan, and
she told the newspapers she wouldn't take a position on it or cast
a vote until she heard from the citizens. She held three "town hall" meetings in the district designed to let people vent and opine, and they did so
in rowdy fashion. Protesters brandished signs showing Obama wearing
a monarch's crown. Hecklers interrupted her several times with catcalls,
grumblings, and boos. At Sahuaro High School she had to ask the crowd
to "be a little less rude," even though many there were trying just to listen
and were being drowned out. The former U.S. surgeon general, Richard
Carmona, went with her to another event and told the crowd he was disappointed in the shouting.

"Shut up!" somebody hollered at him from the audience.

On March 21, on a day when future House speaker John Boehner
would fume that the plan was "Armageddon," Gabrielle voted for it,
and the following day, in the early morning hours, somebody came and
smashed out the front window of her congressional office. "We've had
hundreds and hundreds of protesters over the last several months," she
told MSNBC. "Our office corner has become a place where the Tea Party

movement congregates, and the rhetoric is incredibly heated, not just the calls but the e-mails, the slurs."

She told me over the phone that she knew she might lose her seat because of the vote, and I told her I was never more proud of her. She had been put there to govern, not to pander. Doing what she thought was the right thing on this issue may have been going out in a blaze of glory, but it would have been because of genuine political courage instead of some other reason. That was probably framing it in melodramatic terms, but she did indeed buy herself an immediate problem for the fall.

Internal polling showed her trailing an unnamed Republican challenger by as much as ten points from the start. Later it came out that she wondered out loud to her husband, in a private moment, if somebody might not get upset enough about the health-care vote to shoot her at a public event.

Three Republicans lined up in the primary for the juicy chance to retire her—a chance very much like the one she'd gotten four years earlier—and the ablest of these was Jonathan Paton, a U of A graduate and U.S. Army veteran who had participated in the liberation of Iraq as an intelligence reservist. Paton held a state senate seat and the endorsement of Senator John McCain, and made a show of how he was the only one in the field who had the money, the experience, or the balls to defeat Gabrielle. He produced a television ad that took dead aim at her family's ownership of El Campo Tire and the perception that she was a silver-spoon elitist. "America has a deficit, but it's not just in dollars," said the voice-over. "It's a deficit of honesty and integrity in Washington. Self-serving politicians have forgotten who they work for." The camera then panned from left to right across the faces of Nancy Pelosi, Gabrielle Giffords, and Barack Obama. "Jonathan wasn't handed a company or a trust fund. He worked for everything he got."

The Arizona Democratic Party—with Gabrielle's approval—fired back with a campaign expressly designed to embarrass Paton and crown a voluble upstart named Jesse Kelly as the Republican nominee. This strategy had logical roots. Four years earlier the Republicans had effectively committed suicide by nominating Randy Graf, with his one-note immigration rants and his inability to tap into national sources of money. Paton had legislative experience and he had pipelines into the GOP establishment, which was more frightening in the spring of 2010 than a groundswell of Tea Party anger. But he had made the strategic error of doing some lobbying for "payday lending," which represents the murky depths of the banking business, preying on the desperate, foolish, or perhaps innumerate. Borrowers essentially mortgage their checks in exchange for advance cash, with usurious rates of interest. The ads labeled him as "payday Paton," a euphonious tag, as his name is pronounced PAY-ton.

Jesse Kelly was the knockdown candidate Gabrielle had wanted, just as she had wanted Randy Graf. He was a good-looking cipher with no record of public service and a propensity to blow hot, angry gas. But 2010 turned out to be an unusually forgiving year for just that kind of biography. The contours were right when it came to Jesse Kelly. He was six feet seven inches tall and not yet thirty years old, and he had served as a U.S. Marine in the invasion of Iraq. He was married to a woman who had gone to the U of A on a gymnastics scholarship, and they had a young child. Check on photogenic family values; check on military cred. He had grown up in Bozeman, Montana, the well-to-do son of a sewer contractor. He dropped out of Montana Tech after his first year in favor of the Marine Corps, and then came to work in the Tucson office as a project manager for his father's pipeline and sewer business, Don Kelly Construction. Kelly had zero record of elective office, and therefore no votes to attack and no enemies made. He was the prototypical Man from Nowhere. And he found a willing audience.

His rhetoric about the Mexican border crossers was nearly as strident as what he said about taxes, especially when he spoke to friendly audiences. On July 17, he held a Tea Party event at the Gadsden Hotel, an atmospheric old pile on the main street in the border town of Douglas, a onetime smelter town for Phelps Dodge whose underground was cut to lace with drug mule tunnels, and the same town where a handgun had fallen out of an angry man's pants at one of Gabrielle's Congress on Your Corner events at a Safeway a few months before. Kelly got a head of rhetorical steam going, and then compared illegal border crossers to terrorists.

"I led a squad of infantry marines during the Iraq invasion," he told the crowd. "Believe it or not, there is terrorism out there, even though this administration doesn't want to acknowledge it, and they want to kill everybody in this country. Unless we kill them first, they're going to. That's the reality of life. That's a harsh reality, but that is the reality. It's not a problem we can wish away and pray it goes away. They are committed. We need to be equally as committed. It's no different than the problem we face right down south here on the border."

He also talked contemptuously about the American government. "Believe me, you will never again in your life have a government this putrid over you. Never will you have a House this radical, a Senate this radical—you might have a president this radical—because you can't get worse than this. This is rock bottom. You can only get better. We see it. We see it right now. And that's what we like in Washington—is a love of this nation, quite frankly. They don't love America. And I am challenging their patriotism. And I know we have press here. Write that down."

Knowledge of process or policy was never a factor in that summer's Republican primary, which seemed more like a competition among normally reasonable men to utter the most extreme statements possible about the dire state of the country. Kelly was uniquely gifted in this area. He was as comfortable as an auctioneer at the microphone and possessed of a commanding marine baritone, and he had the innate musician's telepathy for the psychology from a particular crowd, feeding their own energy back to them with amplified juice. He stuck to his message, mostly, though when he tried to improvise, the results were bizarre. At a June 14 debate in Sierra Vista he tried to make a pun about a corporate logo that took a nasty turn: "Now, green jobs are working at John Deere. That's where green jobs are. It's not letting the government take over the energy sector, control your lightbulbs, control your windows. The land of the free is where we're supposed be living here. And these people want to control your toilets. They want to control the water pressure in your toilet. Stay out of my toilet, Gabrielle Giffords, all right?"

In an interview with Jim Nintzel in the *Tucson Weekly* Kelly had responded enthusiastically to the idea that Social Security ought to be eliminated. "If you have any ideas on that, I'm all ears," he told Nintzel. "I would love to eliminate the program. I'd love to take steps to let people opt in and opt out of it. Privatize it." This was what the base voters wanted to hear. Arizona's primaries tend to reward the orotund, and Kelly won by a decisive seven points.

White House chief of staff Rahm Emanuel called Gabrielle the night of the primary and, after quick congratulations for Paton's defeat, offered a blunt summary of what she needed to do next: *Put your foot on the guy's fucking throat and don't give him an inch.* Indeed, her media consultants uncorked an ad that night that pointed out his desire to "privatize" Social Security—a position that may have been ideologically pristine within his base but was jarring to the unaligned seniors that he would have to win over in order to secure victory. They were upset about the economy, and many had doubts about Gabrielle because of her health-care vote, but the recession had shown them how fragile the capital markets could be, and they were petrified about losing their rent money. Home foreclosures, too, had gone up by a factor of six since the time she first went to Congress.

Her campaign manager, Rodd McLeod, put out a memo in which he said that Gabrielle's prospects had "brightened considerably" because of Kelly's victory. "As Mr. Kelly's own words will demonstrate," wrote McLeod, "he is an ideologue with no interest in governing; he is hostile to moderate voters, to the middle class, and to the poor; he has embraced radical positions at every turn; he is not running for Congress to improve life for the people of Southern Arizona; he is running to eliminate Social Security, Medicare and the minimum wage."

But the poll numbers told a different story. Kelly was virtually tied with her and looking credible with uncommitted independents.

I assumed from a distance that the Republicans had essentially purified themselves to death by choosing Kelly and that Gabrielle would cruise right over him. And so it surprised me to get a call from her soon after the primary. She asked if I was free to lend some backup aid in the Tucson campaign office. "We're looking *aroooound* for you," she said, an ironic laugh hiding a serious request. She was happy to be fighting an undisciplined opponent, but there was a real chance that the spirit of the times could defeat her. It would take only a baby's touch of additional momentum: another small drop in the employment rate, or a new initiative from the White House that might play in Arizona as an outrage. I had been absorbed in writing a new book, but the thought of Gabrielle losing this seat for the health-care vote was not a happy one. Neither was the thought that the face of Arizona might be the glib anger of Jesse Kelly. And foremost of all, she was my friend, and she was asking for help. We didn't really talk the way we used to back when she was in the legislature, but it didn't matter. I put my work on pause, took a cross-country Amtrak train out in late September, and took residence in my old bedroom in Shadow Hills, with the same black clock-radio from Sears I had listened to as a junior high school student.

I was given a bare desk in the communications room and helped polish a few speeches that Gabrielle delivered to small audiences. When that material ran out, I worked the phone banks. But there was not much pleasure in it this time around. The staff seemed to be of a more battle-hardened Washington breed than the DIY bunch of four years earlier. The core message was less about bringing change to America than it was about holding the line and pointing out what a frightening representative Jesse Kelly would make. A corresponding part of the strategy was to make senior citizens believe that Kelly was going to strip them of all their benefits, which he would, of course, have no power to do as a congressional neophyte, but his thoughtless government-is-the-devil rhetoric made it easy to simply rebroadcast his more avenging statements and let them speak for themselves. I didn't blame Gabrielle for this. The dumbest move any politician can make is to stand still and be clubbed to death without response. Coasting above the fray was not an option.

Gabrielle's political consulting firm, Ralston Lapp, chewed at Kelly's credibility with televised bites. Anyone with a kid in school was given reason to be worried. At a forum a woman had asked him: "I'm wondering what your views on public education are and how you would move to fixing that?" And he had answered: "I can tell you what I think the federal government's role in education is, and that is none. Absolutely none. These federal mandates they put on schools, and they put on states, it does nothing but crush us. Why is Gabrielle Giffords running our local schools?" This quickly became a chiaroscuro television ad for Giffords in which Kelly is repeatedly heard saying, "*None. Absolutely none.*"

One of the weirdest statements Kelly made, characteristic of his zeal, was at a rally in the massive corporate housing community of Saddlebrooke. He took a question from a woman about a recent outbreak of salmonella poisoning from tainted eggs. "Who's protecting us?" she wanted to know. "That's the thing, ma'am," he replied. "It's our job to protect ourselves. Because no one else is going to look out for your best interests except for you."

This was a crystallization of everything he had been saying: Every man for himself. The government should stop meddling with companies who want to sell poisoned eggs. A press release went out almost immediately. Gabrielle took a beating for dealing out a beating. "Giffords just another career politician?" wondered a headline on a staff editorial complaining about the attack ads in *Inside Tucson Business*. The debate between her and Kelly at the University of Arizona student union was punctuated by hoots and catcalls from both sides. READ MY LIPSTICK: FIRE GIFFORDS! read one placard outside. Other signs began to crop up on the roadsides. GABBY CUT MY MEDICARE!

Some people took the nastiness to a new level. Roger Salzberger kept a GIFFORDS FOR CONGRESS sign in his front yard and aimed the landscape lights in such a way that it would be illuminated. He woke up one morning to find the lights smashed and a single word scrawled in marker across the campaign sign: "*slut.*"

I saw almost nothing of Gabrielle during those weeks and kept my head down with picayune tasks, feeling unsuited to the rigid bare-knuckle brawl that the race had become. When I asked her about how it felt to be so publicly vilified, she shrugged it off and changed the sub-ject. Rodd McLeod was capably running the show, and he was, as ever, as tranquil and inscrutable as a buddha. With no speeches left to write, I went down once more to Bisbee and rapped on doors and made phone calls all day long, trying to rouse the uninspired out to vote. As the sun went down on the evening of November 3, I finished up the last knock-ings in the San Jose neighborhood and drove up to the party at the Mar-riott University Park ballroom, where Gabrielle was encircled three-deep by a jungle of boom mikes and cameras.

Gabe Zimmerman was there on the far fringes, watching discreetly, and we briefly caught up. He was engaged to his girlfriend, Kelly O'Brien, a nurse from Yuma, and he had bought her a diamond ring that was certified not to have been mined in a conflict zone. He had taken her on a predawn jog and proposed to her with it at the base of A Mountain, the old Cuk Son for which the city had been named.

The official results weren't in by the 10:00 P.M. newscasts—in fact, it would take three more days for Gabrielle's victory to be counted to everybody's satisfaction—but it was clear from the precinct patterns that we were going to squeak this one out. Not nearly so fortunate were the Democrats on the state legislature level, who had almost all been slaugh-tered. I caught a plane the next morning without proper good-byes, feeling a mixture of relieved and moody. I didn't like what I had seen.

Arizona seemed caught in a sickness that had only been aggravated by the worst elements of its substructure, which was really just a tele-scoped version of some of the recent dysfunctions in the American sub-structure: the chilly disconnected neighborhoods; the televised anger; the hysteria about immigrants; the delicate economy tied to reckless growth; the way otherwise good people were so ready to devour one another's entrails when things got tough.

It wasn't just in Arizona. The 2010 election cycle had been the most antagonistic of recent years, according to a Wesleyan University study of nationwide races. Just 26 percent of the ads had been designed to show-case positive attributes. The rest were either black-and-white contrasts or outright attacks. I had read of an experiment in social stress in which rats of differing strengths were placed together in a close-quartered cage, which always provoked a fight. The loser experienced what the research-ers called "social defeat" and withdrew into sullenness, showing feeble interest in playing on running wheels or inside tubes. Humiliation had driven them into corners. My home state had felt a bit like that—the noise and the economic pressure and the isolation were becoming unbear-able, and instead of working together to solve the root problems, people were instead looking for enemies, clawing and biting one another into submission, though they were innocent.

A sense of just-sublimated brutality was in the air—that hunger for a burst of cleansing rage to renew the human spirit, that fatal crucify-ing desire that western historian Richard Slotkin called "regeneration through violence."

Gabrielle phoned a few weeks later. She was downbeat herself. The campaign had been the nastiest of her career, and she would be returning to Congress in the minority, which would make it nearly impossible to pass any kind of bill that wasn't a fluffy cosponsorship. The fumes of the Tea Party would be suffusing much of what was going to happen. Jesse Kelly would probably run against her again, perhaps with more cash and less tomfoolery, and it was uncertain if the president would recover his popularity enough in southern Arizona to lift her tide by 2012. I told her about some of my discouragements with the campaign, and she acknowl-edged it had been rough. "Well, you won," I remember saying. "And that's the important thing." But she would have to make adjustments. In a symbolic gesture, she voted for the Georgia Democrat John Lewis to be the minority leader instead of Nancy Pelosi, whom she personally liked but who had become an attack-ad liability for her back home. She and Mark and her parents were going on a trip to Rome over the Christmas holiday, and we would miss each other in Tucson, but we made vague plans to have dinner in D.C. in February. I congratulated her again. And we said our good-byes on an otherwise unremarkable catch-up conversation.

I looked at my phone bill later on. That conversation was on the twenty-first of November, a Sunday evening at the time of year when it gets dark early, and nine days before Jared Loughner went to buy a Glock 19 pistol from the Sportsman's Warehouse.

❋

Gabrielle's life was saved by a combination of medical skill and extraordinary good luck. Intern Daniel Hernandez had the presence of mind to sit her up against the wall of the Safeway so she would not choke on her own blood, and clerks from the store brought out clean smocks from the meat counter to put direct pressure on the wounds. Emergency calls flooded the 911 center almost as soon as the fifteen-second attack was over, and EMTs were at the bloody mess of the Safeway entrance within twelve minutes of the first shot. A decision was made to put Gabrielle into an ambulance rather than wait for a helicopter to scramble. This proved to be a critical decision, as the drive to University Medical Center took only thirteen minutes. The roads were relatively empty on a Saturday morning. So was the emergency room at University Medical Center, where trauma surgeon Dr. Randall Friese gave her extraordinary attention.

First he grabbed her hand and said what he always says to victims, "You're in the hospital. We are going to care for you. Please squeeze my hand." She did, grunting softly, trying to speak. Then he inserted an IV, administered an anesthetic, and called in the chief of neurosurgery, Dr. Michael Lemole. "That would be a special thing for her," he told a reporter later. "I wouldn't have done that if it were a regular patient, because one neurosurgeon could do the operation. That to my mind was a political thing, and I wanted another neurosurgeon, particularly the chief neurosurgeon." Dr. Peter Rhee was also called in; he had been out for a three-mile morning jog when he got a text message saying that ten people were being treated for gunshot wounds. Rhee jogged home and showed up at the hospital still in his running shorts.

Gabrielle's wound was what Rhee and Lemole called "through and through"—a clean entry and exit wound. They did not want to risk an MRI, because that machine uses magnets and there were likely tiny slivers from the bullet still lodged in her brain. Causing them to dance or twinge would have caused even more damage. A CAT scan, however, showed that the angle of the shot was high across the top of the left hemisphere and not into the life-regulating territory closer to the middle. No major arteries had been clipped, and little bleeding had actually taken place. They removed a portion of her skull to relieve swelling and picked out some dead brain tissue and bone fragments.

Rhee had seen many injuries like this; he had served for twenty-four years as a U.S. Navy surgeon and treated hundreds of combat head wounds in Iraq and Afghanistan. So he knew that only between 5 percent and 10 percent of their victims could survive a similar wound.

The little girl, Christina-Taylor Green, arrived unconscious with a devastating wound to the chest. She had been unresponsive to nearly fifteen minutes of cardiopulmonary resuscitation. Doctors could not find a vein to pierce, because the blood loss had been so great. Friese performed an immediate thoracotomy. He went to squeeze her heart, trying to get it to beat, and found it almost empty. Direct filling with an IV couldn't save her.

A vein near Ron Barber's groin had been severed, and while he was completely conscious and worrying about everyone else, his own life was in danger. Suzi Hileman, who had been hit six times, was at major risk for uncontrolled internal bleeding and was X-rayed before going into surgery.

A false report that Gabrielle was dead made it onto the air at National Public Radio, and a few other media outlets cautiously reported that as well. NPR had to walk it back forty-five minutes later, after the hospital confirmed that she was in surgery and Giffords staffers had insisted that their boss was still alive. Her husband, astronaut Mark Kelly, had to hear it on the private plane from Houston, streaking toward Tucson. Confusion reigned. A local television anchor said Gabrielle was shot "at a rally for her supporters"—a curious event to be taking place months after the election.

I heard about the shooting via phone that morning when I was sitting in my apartment in New York, and my first call was to Gabe to make sure he was okay. I left a message on his voice mail. Five hours later, I learned he was dead. Shot in the head. And Gabrielle "shot in the head at point-blank range."

Nothing at all prepares you for those clinical police words when it is applied to people you know and care about.

Seventeen other people shot for no reason at all, including a nine-year-old girl shot dead. Putting a bullet into another person is a decisive and irrevocable statement: *We don't want you anymore. We want you erased from the earth.* Some self-appointed avenging judge had made this verdict, and it could not be contradicted. *But he didn't even know her*, I remember thinking.

When the false death report on National Public Radio was set straight, and Rhee and Lemole gave their news conference saying Gabrielle would absolutely live through the day, I started looking for a flight to Tucson. The first Web videos from Jared Loughner were spooky and disgusting; I couldn't watch them for long. When the news slowed after midnight I drank four straight scotches with a friend and sat on the lip of the bathtub and cried without restraint for her and Gabe. *He put a hole in her head*, I kept thinking. *A hole in her head, and Gabe's.*

I wished then with all my heart that we had lost the election. I would have made Jesse Kelly president on the spot if it meant that there wouldn't have been a Congress on Your Corner at the Safeway.

The next several days passed in a distended haze, the hours on shuffle. The international press swarmed down on landscapes that had been familiar to me all my life, now the tableau for a terrible opera. It was the backdrop for every major newscast for a week. NBC News paid thousands of dollars to rent a house on a nearby dirt bluff on the other side of Ina Road and built a stage in its backyard for a nice overview of the parking lot. I had driven past that Safeway site—La Toscana Village—perhaps more than ten thousand times in my life. My adolescent braces had been installed and tightened by an orthodontist across the street. Though it was about three miles from the family home in Shadow Hills, I have never once passed by without the aid of a car.

My mother shopped there twice weekly and knew some of the clerks by sight, though not by name. She and my father had been out running an errand farther down Ina Road earlier in the morning. If they had needed some more milk, or a lightbulb, or a few avocados for guacamole, they would have stopped, noticed the signs, and surely decided to say hello to Gabrielle. Then they would have been killed for pleasure, another two of Loughner's trophies. I felt the chill that nearly everyone perceived in those first several hours: the fineness of the border between living and dying, and how we are so dulled in believing it is an iron cord and not as fragile as a spider's thread.

I wandered through those first few days like an automaton, not knowing what to say or do, and spent an inordinate amount of time looking at the Santa Catalina Mountains, visualizing the canyons that I had hiked there and wishing that I could disappear into them for a week to listen to the wind and watch lizards crawl on the rocks and hear nobody speak at all. The galaxy turned around the gravitational hub of a police-guarded suite at University Medical Center, our wounded queen, a small and inscrutable body, lying perfectly still.

The congressional office at the corner of Pima and Swam became a sweat chamber of activity. A conference room next door was quickly rented out to handle the overflow of interns, volunteers, and orphaned campaign staff who had flown to Tucson following a homing instinct. The lobby to the office had a giant horse's saddle on display and a revolving knot of people talking in funeral groups. Gabe Zimmerman's office near the back was left unused, his case of Diet Dr Pepper untouched. The outer door was hung with a note saying that packages could not be accepted. A permanent sign near the jamb said: IT IS UNLAWFUL TO CARRY A FIREARM INTO A FEDERAL FACILITY, TITLE 18, PART 1, CHAPTER 44, SECTION 30. This had been the same office that had had its windows smashed during the health-care debate. A few brave constituents came in to sign the guest book and offer hugs to Joni Jones, the gracious office manager. Sagging aluminum cradles of hot lunches came delivered from local restaurants that, like us, just wanted to do something that might be useful. The young staffers flown in from the D.C. office tapped their BlackBerrys as if programming a panel in their chests. That tender and excellent combination of stay-up-all-night energy, nervous ambition, high self-regard, and unquestioning obedience makes for a stack of waterproof policy papers and meticulous spreadsheets. Washington would grind to a halt without them.

I stood around and watched all the journalists tromp through—a lot of local reporters that I recognized and a flotilla of national and foreign correspondents that I didn't at all. The Safeway shootings had become an international obsession and would remain so for most of the month. It did not hurt at all that Gabrielle happened to have been physically attractive. There are few stories that resonate in the human subconscious more than a young, beautiful woman in danger, and Gabrielle's improbable survival advanced the story into the realm of Universal Mythos.

The journalists were all as hushed and respectful as we were, perhaps even more so, given the guilt of their necessarily invasive work. The trapezoid courtyard of the office plaza felt like a sunny cemetery that week. A uniformed Tucson police officer stood at the metal gate outside, psychological comfort. There was an inert fountain painted a garish blue on the inside.

I opened my laptop in the conference room, wrote a few e-mails for the reconstituted communications team, helped go through some of the letters that had cascaded in. Gabrielle would have wanted every address logged and every note to receive a corresponding thank-you letter. They filled at least a dozen postal bins, bearing postmarks from everywhere, but mostly from within southern Arizona. The rule of thumb for Congress is that for every thoughtful person who writes you a letter about an issue, there are probably one thousand more who feel the same way and stayed silent. Hundreds had come in from other American elected officials and foreign governments, on expensive stationery with raised seals.

The get-well cards were a torrent of optimism and sorrow. Those from children occasionally had the feel of having been encouraged by parents or teachers, perhaps as a lesson in civics. Others seemed like their own simple expressions of projected grief. Their leader was not an unapproachable statue in a marble suit but a vulnerable human being who bled and cried and might get better. I learned later that some of the letters from kids included crumpled wads of lunch money. A curving stucco wall outside had been decorated for the last four years with the legend GABRIELLE GIFFORDS, UNITED STATES CONGRESS. Now this low structure with planters had become one of three impromptu shrines that had instantly materialized around the city. There was a pile of flowers and cards beneath one of the Italianate arches at Safeway. And an astonishingly huge array of candles, flowers, balloons, cards, pictures, and plush toys on the front lawn of University Medical Center, where the national television satellite trucks surrounded them like a praetorian guard. A man with a violin had taken to playing in the violet light before sunset, and people linked hands to pray among the offerings. The UMC staff had used stone markers to create little paths through the cards and flowers. It resembled a road version of El Tiradito, the shrine to an outcast. The flowering of atonement was a spectacle, a thorn caught in the subconscious, especially in spite of—or perhaps because of—how badly Gabrielle had been treated just two months before. Tucson stopped for a week in the same way the nation stopped for a week after September 11.

We all knew that the impromptu memorials would eventually have to be dismantled, the letters filed away in an archive, the candles blown out, the balloons tossed away. These splashes of color on the hospital lawn and on the office corner were all necessarily ephemeral.

The Safeway at La Toscana Village reopened exactly one week after the shootings, the parking lot clear of police cars and FBI agents. The blood had been washed away and the plate glass windows replaced. A moment of silence was held at 10:00 A.M. to honor the victims. The grocery store put a metal sawhorse under one of the Italianate arches as a designated pull spot for all the flowers and cards and candles that people dropped off there. LaArnie Lucas, the human resources manager, called it "a center of healing." I watched people go into the Safeway, buy plastic cones of flowers from the section called POETRY IN BLOOM and silently drop them at the sawhorse. A woman crossed herself. "Years down the road, I knew I'd kick myself in the butt if I didn't come down here during the height of grief," a man named Mike Santa Cruz told me. Another visitor was the Reverend John Kitagawa, the pastor of St. Philip's in the Foothills Episcopal Church, which John Murphey had built in the twenties to serve the Beverly Hills of Tucson and its new wealthy residents.

"It's important for people to come here as part of the healing process," he said. "That's the shock of the whole thing. Most of the people here on that morning were doing their normal routines." I asked him why he and his wife had come, and he paused and said: "We needed milk. That was the deciding factor."

In the second week of Gabrielle's stay in intensive care I assigned myself the task of finding a home for the piles of stuffed animals that were mounting out near the corner. The skies were high and hard, but I worried about a frost or a rain shower that might get them wet. I talked it over with some of the Washington staff, and we agreed that the best alternative would be to donate them to a charity. An obvious one was Casa de los Niños, the local shelter for abused and neglected children. We also chose the UMC pediatrics unit as well as the other big hospital in midtown, Tucson Medical Center. A few phone calls sealed the deal. Casa de Los Niños and TMC were thrilled. It was one way to be in touch with what was happening: to have another small connection to the death and resurrection myth in their hometown. UMC had to beg off taking anything but the animals that were still in their store packaging because of infection protocols. Sick kids couldn't be clutching teddy bears that somebody might have sneezed into. It made sense, and we could still make a delivery. We had at least twenty pristine brown bears wrapped in plastic that somebody—I never found out who—had delivered in a giant crate. Now I went to gather up the rest from the street corner. Alongside them were notes laid out in the weak winter sun, addressed to nobody in particular.

Beginning today, treat everyone you meet as if they were going to be dead by midnight. Give them all the care, kindness and understanding you can muster.

I tried to thread gently between the candles and the construction-paper messages on my way to pick up the first armload of animals. There was a tiger at rest, a bear with outstretched sausage arms, a knuckle-dragging gorilla with big teeth. I tried to look tall and official, as this probably looked like a sacrilegious or perhaps larcenous activity to the handful of people milling about the corner. But nobody came forward and asked me where I was going with the toys. I took them into the conference room and laid the first load on a folding table.

We were targeted, we were hit but we will not be destroyed!!!

Here was the remarkable thing that I began to notice after a few armloads: Only a few stuffed animals came with signed notes. The vast majority—probably 95 percent—had been deposited with no written message at all, and those that were weren't signed with anyone's name. The animal itself was the message. A number of them looked like tough old veterans. The fur had been rubbed off in places, or was a bit pilled. I wondered if empty-nest parents had raided them from their grown-up children's closets and left them here like orphans. Or perhaps children had given up their own stuffed toys to the wounded queen, choosing to give as best they could. A good number were brand-new, with manufacturer tags attached and their velour not yet grubbing. The toy stores and the stationary outlets in the malls must have made an unexpected mint during those awful weeks in January. Smiling balls of colored rayon and polyester mounted and mounted on the folding table. Hundreds of people had dealt with the news on the television this way.

Mr. Potato Head wants you to get better soon

Moving these toys probably would have been much easier with a Hefty garbage bag, or at least a couple of the dingy plastic U.S. postal bins, but that seemed disrespectful, as though I were removing trash. I also wanted to touch each one as I was taking it away. I'm not sure why. I harvested a tiger with a pink nose, a Dumbo with the Disneyland tag still attached, dozens of bears with hearts on their sweaters, a black dog in a Harley shirt, an orange lion, Ernie, Pinocchio, a Democrat Donkey and a Republican Elephant standing together happily in stars and stripes, a multicolored hippo out of a stoner's dream, a bear in a silver aviator's suit from a unit at Davis-Monthan Air Force Base, a Nurse Nancy with a message scrawled in black pen—"I'm watching over you as long as you need me"—a pink bear with a *hug me* heart, a red dog with a candy cane tail, a gray dinosaur, a yellow bird, Superman with his arm extended, Barney Rubble, a pink dolphin. A bear with a note: "My name is pie and I am nice to hug." A reindeer with a green hat. They were squeezed in the planter and underneath the signs. I accidentally stepped on several. Eventually I had to give up and bring out a postal bin. The sun was drooping. There were perhaps three hundred of them heaped on the tables, making black-threaded smiles to the ceiling.

Last Saturday they got up and ate breakfast. They considered what they would say to their Congresswoman. They made plans for later. And this

in an instant: their plans their voices were stopped—and Tucson was
changed forever

Two interns and I went over to the hospital the next day and started
in there, harvesting our way carefully through the maze. Only a few
people asked what we were doing or where we were going with these
bears, and we heard later that somebody snitched us off to hospital security. There were many more candles here. One of them splashed hot red
wax on my pants after I tipped it over. There were painted tiles, birds in
folded paper, somebody's wedding photo. And even more animals than
there had been on the corner, also lacking any written comment. The
sun poured down on all of us as I pulled them up and walked them to
the trunk of the car. In went the bear in the jester suit, the frog with
orange hair, a dog with the cap of the L.A. Dodgers, Betty Boop holding
a placard: GET WELL, GABBY! Mark Kelly told a reporter that he had
gone out to take a look at the memorial one evening and had selected a
small brown bear at random to bring up to his wife's bed, where it lay at
her side for the next several days, an emissary among multitudes.

Gabby we are sending you wish dust because we hope you feel better, we
wish you can feel our love and hope for your total recovery.

It is hard to discuss stuffed animals without sounding either ridiculous or lachrymose. They have an intrinsic pathos about them. They are
also difficult to throw away. Tossing one out is a bit like drowning a
trapped mouse in a backyard pool. These are soulless inanimate objects,
but they were made to be repositories of affection—reminders to a child
that the world is perhaps a warm place, not a cruel one, and that love
might be given without question. To forget about one or to throw one in
the trash is a memento mori, a reminder that we, too, could perhaps be
forgotten or thrown away. And there is the sadness of their faith: their
willingness to be picked up and held though the affection channeled
through them lasts for such a brief time, if at all. I had a friend once who

told me she hated receiving them for Christmas, because they would invariably grow old and break. Seeing them new and unstained made the inevitable breaking even sadder for her somehow.

Please heal, dear Gabrielle, and come back to us. We need you.

I felt myself crouched behind a wall of tears that month and was never really able to make myself cry again after the night of January 8, but this heap of stuffed animals that strangers had brought for Gabrielle was starting to bring me close to the wall again. I had cause to remember a poem that my mother had once paraphrased when I was about twelve years old, a poem she had learned from her own mother. I looked it up later; it was an extremely sentimental—and bleak—rhyme from a newspaper editor named Eugene Field who wrote in Chicago at the end of the nineteenth century. Here is most of it:

The little toy dog is covered with dust,
But sturdy and stanch he stands;
And the little toy soldier is red with rust,
And his musket moulds in his hands,
Time was when the little toy dog was new,
And the soldier was passing fair;
And that was the time when our Little Boy Blue
Kissed them and put them there.

Ay, faithful to Little Boy Blue they stand,
Each in the same old place—
Awaiting the touch of a little hand,
The smile of a little face;
And they wonder, as waiting the long years through
In the dust of that little chair,
What has become of our Little Boy Blue,
Since he kissed them and put them there.

I had originally thought this poem was about the cruelty of growing older. We gradually forget our imaginary friends and the complicated dramas of our superheroes, put childish things behind us and move on into the clarity and banalities of the adult world. "Little Boy Blue" wasn't coming around to play with the dog or the soldier anymore, or invest them with imagined life, because he had grown into a man and forgotten his own silly games, as I had left behind *Superstar Baseball* and my own stuffed toys. *When I was a child, I spake as a child, I thought as a child.* I later read that one of Field's sons had died very young and that the poem was actually about the literal death of the boy. He had given life to his belongings, but they were beyond biology. They could wait for his animating gaze forever.

There were just over nine hundred of them by my count when we finished harvesting. They filled two long folding tables and a good portion of the floor beneath them. An older woman came by with a minivan, and we loaded them in. Gabrielle's press team had sent e-mail alerts to all five local television stations and the networks, and we made a caravan going from Casa de Los Niños to UMC, where a bearded cameraman from NBC besieged me with questions that I had few answers for. The gift of the bears to orphaned and sick children would make cute B-roll for the breakfast shows, and it occurred to me again how strange life looks when a camera is pointed at it: how it automatically molds into a cartoon version of itself, like the bears. At the third and last delivery stop, at Tucson Medical Center, the hospital had arranged a half circle of kids recuperating in wheelchairs to say a big thank you in chorus for the bank of cameras. It was a ridiculous exercise. But it was something tangible.

You stay strong and we will be strong. We need to make this a better place.

Tucson was looking for ways to grieve and to make atonement, perhaps because everyone knew just how nasty the last election had been.

Hopeful messages went up on marquees all over town. BE KIND TO EACH OTHER said one outside the Boon Docks Lounge. Crowds jammed the McKale Center at the university to hear President Obama deliver a eulogy to the victims; some people had camped out the night before and waited more than twenty hours to hear him. He announced that Gabrielle had opened her eyes after being in a virtual coma for six days. "We recognize our own mortality," said the president, "and are reminded that in the fleeting time we have on this earth, what matters is not wealth, or status, or power, or fame—but rather, how well we have loved, and what small part we have played in bettering the lives of others." Two friends, Amanda Hutchinson, twenty, and Amanda Lopez, twenty-three, used Facebook to organize a Walk for Peace that terminated in the parking lot of Giffords's office. Hundreds of people joined in. A fourteen-year-old girl offered free hugs. An entrepreneur opened a hot-dog stand near the end of the march.

> *Vinnie Dogs, $3 original hotdog. $1 donated to the victims and families for every dog sold. Stay Strong Tucson! Gabby Opened Her Eyes, So Should We.*

Gabe Zimmerman's funeral in the courtyard of the Tucson Museum of Art was packed with those who knew him. House Speaker John Boehner sent a representative. Gabe had been the first congressional staffer in American history to be killed while in the line of duty. A friend of his from college recalled how he had always said, "We can change things if we work together." The Dalai Lama was quoted: "The best way to find yourself is to lose yourself in service to others." Gabe's close friend and colleague C. J. Karamargin stood up and recalled how Gabe and he had recently traveled to Washington and stood for a while at the Lincoln Memorial, where the Gettysburg Address was carved in big letters on the wall. He had read the words aloud, line by line.

On January 21, a day that marked an apogee of collective grief,

Gabrielle was moved to a rehabilitation center in Houston, Texas, and crowds lined the sidewalk down Campbell Avenue to see off the ambulance, which was led by a group of motorcycle riders from the local VFW. The route of the motorcade had been published in the *Arizona Daily Star*. Her staff told reporters that she smiled from her gurney when she heard the crowds cheering for her. That detail was important. They wanted a sign, any sign from her at all.

> *My family will not forget. We will do our part to ~~continue the fight against violence~~ promote peace.*

In the rear conference room of Gabrielle's office I talked with Ross Zimmerman, Gabe's father, a Midwesterner by birth and temperament, who had loved Gabe like a best friend. When Gabe would call him on the phone, Ross gave a customary greeting: "Sonster!" Gabe had always responded with a cheerful: "Daddy-O!" Ross was in deep shock and mourning, and his eyes were exhausted, but he told me he had no anger about the casual murder of his son. He said Jared Loughner was "a poor sick child" more deserving of pity than vengeance. He had lived in a world of his own construction and perceived grievances that were only illusions.

"I'm not angry, because there's nothing to be mad about here," said Ross. "I was angry for maybe the first hour, when I didn't know what was going on. And believe me, if I had been at the scene and in a position to do something, I would have done whatever was necessary to stop this happening—up to and including causing any necessary harm to that poor kid. But that's a different issue. This is like a bolt of lightning. It had nothing to do with Gabe. It wasn't personal. That kid didn't know Gabe existed. He just fixated on an authority figure associated with his poor sick problems with the world and wanted to cause harm to the authority figure and everybody around her.

"The roots of anger go back to a sense of perceived unfairness," Ross Zimmerman went on. "When you're growing up and have been brought up in such a way that doesn't map well to the real world, the pragmatic world, you want to build a story in your head, a model. . . . That's not adaptive. It's not real."

❋

I don't think that the atmosphere of twenty-first-century Arizona made this crime inevitable or was the motivating cause of it. There was only one responsible human party: Jared Lee Loughner, who is gravely mentally ill.

The much harder question to examine—which must be looked square in the face—is the context in which the shooting took place.

James Clarke's study of American assassination demonstrates that those who plot violence against politicians are generally suffering from mental illness, but they are *never* free of influences from the culture at large. They always come from a specific set of circumstances in a specific time. And even in a case of an illness like paranoid schizophrenia, the social context becomes worthy of scrutiny, not as a direct cause of violence but as an influencing factor: an aggravation. The overpowering influence of environmental context on human context has been a factor known to social scientists for generations. In the eighteenth century, the Earl of Chesterfield put it in a military context: "A light supper, a good night's sleep and a fine morning have often made a hero of the same man who, by indigestion, a restless night and a rainy morning would have proved a coward."

Loughner's feelings of existential helplessness were a distorted amplification of what surrounded him that year in Arizona: a lack of jobs, a lack of confidence in the future, an angry dialogue, a sense that politicians were ultimately to blame, and that only a courageous act of restoration could improve the outlook. Feelings of personal violation did not belong exclusively to him, nor did the desire to extract a type of comeuppance upon elected officials in the wake of a soured dream.

"Every time I hear that this is just about a single sick individual, that's so limiting, so naïve and almost condescending," said Dan Ranieri of La Frontera. "That bothers me the most. It defines a person just by an illness, and it absolves people of their responsibilities. This event happened because of the extremism and the isolation of Arizona. And you have to talk about both. Nobody is going to convince me that didn't help pull the trigger."

What is happening in Arizona today is a modern version of the philosophical struggle that was written into America's genetic code from the start. Ours is a nation that cherishes government by the common person, mutual interests pledged together as a sacred honor. Volunteerism and charity pervade the life of most communities. But this is a nation that also treasures the liberty of an individual, giving him the freedom to participate or withdraw from sight as he likes. This tension is worked out through local debates about the proper role of taxation in a slumping economy, the ease and availability of firearms, the right of a state to set its own immigration policies, the role of quality public education, the shape of the neighborhoods we choose to inhabit. How much of this can we solve on our own and how much of it will require pulling together and erasing differences? Can we overcome differences of race and income in the name of building a commonwealth?

Arizona's economy was founded on the ease of personal reinvention, which is a powerful American value. But in spite of the billion-dollar hydrology and the air-conditioning and the myth of constant reinvention, people do not end up shaping the place nearly as much as the place ends up shaping them. In pursuit of that dream of liberty and privacy we built for ourselves a repurposed paradise that catered to some of the most isolating and misanthropic urges in our natures: homes that dissolve into the desert; gated communities amputated from their surroundings; garages that face the street like a row of backsides; high walls; no porches.

In times of economic stagnation that fabric of physical disconnection translates into fear and despair. Arizona is a fractal here for the United States of America: a vanguard of economic uncertainty, inhumane politics, and an emphasis on extreme personal liberties at the expense of a concern for the larger welfare.

"There's a lot worth asking about how a state with so much promise has failed that promise—whether it's education or jobs," Jim Kolbe told me. "The state is broken in so many ways. There's a sizable lack of leadership in this state. There isn't an easy fix for this. There's no question that political positions have been captured by people on the right or left, and it isn't friendly to compromise."

The thirst for radical solutions can become ugly, Kolbe said. During his last congressional campaign, two years before he gave the seat up to Gabrielle, he ran against the immigration hard-liner Randy Graf and went down to the city of Sierra Vista to have a town hall on the subject of immigration. One man called out from the audience that he had a solution in mind: When they cross the border, shoot them. Most everyone who spends enough time in Arizona has a story like that, an overheard invitation to violence that is not a joke.

To wash our hands of an errant citizen like Jared Loughner—to push him away and think of him like a natural disaster that nobody could have stopped—is to engage in the worst kind of denial about the human influences that made him who he is, especially in the four drifting years before his final violent act. The prevailing dialogue in Arizona that autumn was that politicians were elitist devils out to bankrupt the country, and the gun was readily available at a Sportsman's Warehouse down the street. In the Tucson of 2011 Gabrielle Giffords was the physical manifestation of the government, and she was making herself available for anyone who cared to approach. A set of environmental conditions was in place that made such an extreme act of superhero individualism within the range of possibility. Loughner was not a tornado or an earthquake; he emerged from a specific human context.

There will be lifelong consequences for Jared Loughner, but there are also consequences for all of us that cannot be ignored. What is best in us ought to rise to this occasion and have the conversation about our responsibilities toward the strangers in our midst as we, as a nation, move forward into an uncertain century.

If there had been, for example, a law in Arizona that required just one hour of safety training before a handgun could be purchased, Jared Loughner would never have acquired the Glock. His disease was uncontrollable by that point, and even the most liberal gun-rights advocate in the world would not have put a pistol into his hands after looking into his eyes. Instead, all that stood between him and the means to kill six innocent people was a clerk at a Sportsman's Warehouse.

If there had been a federal ban on arm's-length magazines that carry thirty-three bullets, a ludicrous amount, Loughner probably would have been stopped before he killed so many people.

If more listeners realized that partisan talk radio is not a genuine public policy forum but a money-oriented business designed explicitly to attract an audience through gross exaggerations and invented grievances, elected leaders would not be so easily vilified and thought of as subhuman.

If the state's electoral system were configured in a way that rewarded those who tried to build coalitions and seek common ground instead of playing on the fears and resentments of the base, the quality of the state's governance would rise. A culture that prizes competence would be less welcoming of histrionic figures such as Sheriff Joe Arpaio.

If there were an understanding that the changing demographics of the state is a historic inevitability and that immigration from Mexico has to be seen as an economic reality, the chances of seeing a humane solution to the problem would be vastly improved.

If all those who enjoy Arizona for its natural beauty saw—as many did for a brief time after the Safeway shootings—that living in a place involves a spiritual connection to everybody else in that place, then perhaps those growing visibly ill like Jared Loughner might at least be noticed in their misery and some attempt made to do the right thing for them.

If Pima Community College had thought to warn the courts or outside law enforcement agencies that Jared Loughner clearly met the legal test of "persistently or acutely disabled," if not an active threat to himself or others, he probably would have had to appear before a county judge and been unable to buy the firearm.

And finally, if the state of Arizona could adequately fund its infrastructure for taking care of the mentally ill instead of pushing that basic public responsibility onto untrained private citizens, there would be a diminished likelihood that Loughner and unknown others like him could cause such immense damage and misery to innocent people.

I don't think these are choices that fall into the category of liberal or conservative beliefs. These are social dysfunctions that transcend politics. The proper role of Arizona's government would now be to ignore short-term political pressures and take the necessary steps to prevent further violence such as this, becoming a national example of unity rather than the ugly hothouse that has characterized its governance for the last five years.

The conversation that should have followed the Gabrielle Giffords shooting was like that reckoning with race and inequality that was supposed to have started after Hurricane Katrina struck New Orleans. But it never happened. Arizona has also procrastinated. The quality of the dialogue at the legislature after the shooting was a prominent sign of where the state's governmental values were really located.

In the first session after the event, and one year before the state's centennial, lawmakers had the opportunity to have a sober discussion about reforming the broken mental health system, stopping up the loopholes that give the mentally ill access to guns, prohibiting the sale of thirty-shot magazines that are useless for hunting, perhaps asking if there were possible ways to bridge the rhetorical canyons that had formed between opposing sides. Instead the Senate slashed funding for the mentally ill, sought to make it possible for people to carry guns onto college campuses, and tried to make it a crime for a doctor to treat a migrant without calling the police. They also deemed the Colt Single-Action Revolver the official state firearm. Leadership is broken in Arizona, and its citizens must look within for answers, at least for the present time.

Many things about Arizona were revealed in that legislative session.

But many other things were also revealed under the arches of the Safeway on January 8, 2011. A collection of ordinary citizens reacted with bravery and clarity. Husbands threw their arms over their wives, trying to shield them from the gunfire. Suzi Hileman made every possible attempt to protect Christina-Taylor Green. Bill Badger and Roger Salzberger both got to their feet in the melee and tackled Loughner, preventing him from killing more people, possibly in the aisles of the Safeway store or out amid traffic on Ina Road. Patricia Maisch grabbed for his dropped magazine. Daniel Hernandez probably saved Gabrielle's life by immediately sitting her up and preventing her from choking on her own blood. The EMTs and surgeons acted with precision. There were dozens more acts in that window of two hours that gave the event at La Toscana Village a heroic cast. The massive display of concern, shock, and grief in the days afterward showed that, especially in extremis, Arizona knew the enduring qualities of love and courage, even for people they did not know and perhaps never would.

The location of the event was wholly emblematic of the character of Gabrielle Giffords, and also of the rambling city she was attempting to serve. She had been wounded at La Toscana Village, a shadow of an actual village but one that functions as a lame sort of town square for northwest Tucson. Everybody going there drives there. It is a physical expression of a detached society severed from all meaningful history. But Gabrielle was seeking to reach out to strangers there in the antiseptic apron of the Safeway, to make Tucson live up to the kind of place that it wanted to be, to do her job and put a stitch on the social fissures, at least in the most effective way she knew.

She was in no position to fix the biggest problems, but through tiny incremental acts—the unglamorous chore of making people feel more invested in the government they owned—she could live out a method of making an imperfect place just a little bit more like the older mythic America that we all still wanted it to be, a real interdependent community of people joined in common purpose instead of a random assortment of leisure seekers and luxury consumers wanting to be left alone. There were no splashy gestures or extravagant promises in her grammar, only the business of getting things accomplished for the greatest number of people in a way that made sense. There was a reason she was so respected by those who knew her, and it had to do with what she believed and did in the days before January 8.

She taught me the difficult lesson that it is not enough to merely dwell in a place. You must make the decision to truly live in that place, take ownership of it, be a citizen of it, and play a part in the common good beyond your own front door.

Gabrielle was made of tougher mettle than anyone could have guessed. She awoke from her coma after six days, opened her eyes, gazed around the room in bewilderment, and touched the sore spot on her head. She recognized people almost immediately. When I was led in to see her in the intensive care unit several days later, she squeezed my hand and smiled at me with life in her eyes, and I felt strongly then that she would one day be whole again, herself. I knew that she would have absolutely hated the media carnival that had erupted around her; the obsessive attention to her health would have embarrassed her, and she would have tried to talk about the national interest instead, and what was best for the people of Tucson.

Within one month of the shooting she was speaking words, and within four months forming complete sentences, smiling, laughing, and initiating conversations—a remarkable feat for one who had been shot through the head at close range. The mere fact of her survival is a testament to her courage. I don't know at this writing if she will ever want to seek public office again. I certainly hope so. But that is ultimately her decision to make.

Arizona turns one hundred years old in 2012. The youngest state on the lower continent has emerged as the vanguard for a range of national discontents. Its social and economic fissures are carved deep, but they are not unbridgeable. What transpires in Arizona in the next several years will be of tremendous importance to the destiny of the United States, as it will prove whether the American dream of "one out of many" can endure and prevail. The example Gabrielle set on the morning of January 8—reaching out to strangers at the fringe of a Safeway—is not a bad place to begin again.

ACKNOWLEDGMENTS

This was a difficult book that could not have been written without the help of many others. Nothing would have happened at all were it not for the initial encouragement—even insistence—of Korey Riggs, a friend since high school. Another longtime friend, Marcia Ring, provided cru-cial support and contacts, as well as constant good cheer. Also helpful along the way were Daniel Benavidez, Judy Pasternak, T. P. McCabe, Jennifer Johnson, T. J. Jiran, Ted Conover, Greg Cullison, Kat Rodri-guez, Doug Merlino, Elyssa East, Brad Phillips, Grady Gammage, Steve Apkon, Brad Tyer, Sugi Ganeshananthan, Dan Egan, Tom Clynes, Jeff Stensrud, Laura Galloway, Ellen Dickinson, Emily Mabry, Jon McNa-mara, Mirea Pineda, and Rich Galant. I met wonderful people in my home state whom I might not have otherwise: Jack Jewett, Jan and Rick Kleiner, Dan Ranieri, Lydia Otero, Wyatt Bills, Neal Cash, Juanita Molina, Steve Nanini, Melissa Amado, Jacob Owens, Paul Eckerstrom, James Clarke, Roger Salzberger, Chris Herstam, Brian Flagg, Pancho Medina, Jon Miles, Emma Kleiner, Joni and Gary Jones, Ross Zimmer-man, Jim Kolbe, Sam Kleiner, Bill and Sallie Badger, and Arizona's gentlemanly state historian, Marshall Trimble. I am also grateful to my friends in the Arizona press corps, past and present, who offered insight, including Jill Jorden Spitz, Emily Bittner, Walt Nett, Jaimee Rose, David

Fitzsimmons, Dylan Smith, Donna Coletta, Tom Beal, Tom Lee, Dan Shearer, James Palka, and Phil Boas. Especially generous with their time and friendship were Jim Nintzel, Jason Ground, Michel Marizco, Amy Silverman, and Tony Davis. My grandmother Ann von Blume, born in Arizona three years after statehood, offered recollections of her working life at the capitol. I would like to acknowledge the Millay Colony for the Arts and the Mid-Atlantic Arts Foundation for material support. I owe tremendous thanks, as ever, to my literary agent, Brettne Bloom, and my amazing editor at Penguin, Kathryn Court. Tara Singh and Allison Lorentzen of Penguin offered invaluable editing suggestions. Kate Griggs did an outstanding job as production editor. Mary Martha Miles was ready with a kind word. Michael Downs passed along key advice: Write where the wound lies. Kevin Gass wouldn't let me quit. Kate Krauss offered extraordinary support. My parents, Tom and Joanne Zoellner, never doubted.

February–July 2011

NOTES

ONE: THE SAFEWAY

Page

2   **That same day:** www.weather.gov.

3   **Gabe Zimmerman had brought:** "Tucson Tragedy," a series written by Shaun McKinnon, reported by Ken Alltucker, Karina Bland, John Faherty, J. J. Hensley, Pat Kossan, Megan Neighbor, Dan Nowicki, Jaimee Rose, Dennis Wagner, and Amy B. Wang, *The Arizona Republic,* February 6–8, 2011.

3   **Hernandez grew up:** Ernesto Portillo, "Even as a Child, Daniel Hernandez Was Calm, Poised," *Arizona Daily Star,* January 16, 2011.

5   **"When you represent":** Mark Z. Barabak, Lisa Mascaro, and Robin Abcarian, "A Calm Voice in a Divided District," *Los Angeles Times,* January 8, 2011. Also in Dan Nowicki, "Protester with Gun Didn't Rattle Giffords," *The Arizona Republic,* August 16, 2009.

5   **A woman named:** "Tucson Tragedy," *The Arizona Republic.*

9   **"It was surreal":** Stephanie Innes, "Doc Was Feet from Giffords, Aided Others in 'Surreal' Scene," *Arizona Daily Star,* January 9, 2011.

9   **Randy Gardner:** "Those at the Scene Share Stories," *Arizona Daily Star,* January 16, 2011; Sam Dolnick, "Flashbacks and Lingering Questions for Survivors," *New York Times,* January 12, 2011.

9   **Three more bullets hit Mary Reed:** Quote given to KPHO television in Phoenix on January 11, 2011.

12 **In the confusion of the moment:** Zamudio was interviewed on the television show *Fox & Friends* on January 10, 2011.

13 **Suzi Hileman looked at her:** Karina Bland, "Tucson Shooting Victim Suzi Hileman Sorry She Could Not Save Girl," *The Arizona Republic*, January 21, 2011.

14 **Pima County sheriff's deputy:** Dan Barry et al., "Looking Behind the Mugshot Grin," *New York Times*, January 15, 2011.

15 **He was an unemployed:** Amy Gardner, David A. Fahrenthold, and Marc Fisher, "Loughner's Descent into a World of Fantasy," *Washington Post*, January 13, 2011.

16 **He began to tell his remaining friends:** Nick Baumann, "Loughner's Friend Explains Gunman's Grudge Against Giffords," http://www.motherjones.com, January 10, 2011.

16 **He grew angrier and angrier:** Rhonda Bodfield, "Polarizing Dupnik Weary of Spotlight," *Arizona Daily Star*, February 6, 2011.

19 **The resentments against Kennedy:** Warren Leslie, *Dallas Public and Private: Aspects of an American City* (originally published 1964; reissued by Southern Methodist University Press in 1998).

20 **"Later, the guilt we felt":** Lawrence Wright, "Was Dallas a City of Hate?," *D* magazine, November 1988.

TWO: REINVENTION

23 **Herbert Leggett:** Richard Nilsen, "Building History: A City Explodes," *The Arizona Republic*, August 8, 2011.

24 **The introduction of cheaper materials:** Thomas Sheridan, *Arizona: A History* (Tucson: University of Arizona Press, 1995); Grady Gammage, *Phoenix in Perspective: Reflections on Developing the Desert* (Tempe: Herberger Center for Design Excellence, 1999); Tucson Urban Planning and Design Department, "Tucson Post World War II Residential Subdivision Development: 1945–1967" (October 2007).

25 **These physical settings:** Center for the Future of Arizona, "The Arizona We Want" (2009), http://arizonafuture.org/az-we-want/index.html.

26 **The growth of starter communities:** Robert D. Putnam, *Bowling Alone: The Collapse and Revival of American Community* (New York: Simon & Schuster, 2000).

28 **Construction slowed to a crawl:** Betty Beard, "Growth Rate Slows Arizona's Recovery," *The Arizona Republic*, September 8, 2010; Adam Kress, "Foreclosures Up 208 Percent in Arizona, 81 Percent Nationwide in 2008," *Phoenix Business Journal*, January 15, 2009.

30 **The paranoia has ticked upward:** William Frey, "Will Arizona Be America's Future?" Washington, D.C.: Brookings Institution, April 28, 2010.

31 **The European influence:** Sheridan, *Arizona: A History.*

32 **A city of mud boxes:** J. Ross Browne, *Adventures in the Apache Country: A Tour Through Arizona and Sonora with notes on the silver regions of Nevada* (New York: Harper and Brothers, 1864).

33 **"a valley of wonderful fertility":** Michael F. Logan, *Desert Cities: The Environmental History of Phoenix and Tucson* (Pittsburgh: The University of Pittsburgh Press, 2006).

34 **Though the local attitude:** The story of the Camp Grant Massacre is expertly told in two recent books: Karl Jacoby, *Shadows at Dawn: A Borderlands Massacre and the Violence of History* (New York: Penguin Press, 2008); and Chip Colwell-Chanthaphonh, *Massacre at Camp Grant: Forgetting and Remembering Apache History* (Tucson: University of Arizona Press, 2007).

34 **Many of Arizona's penny newspapers:** Jacoby, *Shadows at Dawn.*

36 **The railroad did far more:** C. L. Sonnichsen, *The Life and Times of an American City* (Norman: University of Oklahoma Press, 1982); Lydia R. Otero, *La Calle: Spatial Conflict and Urban Renewal in a Southwest City* (Tucson: University of Arizona Press, 2010). The history of an American city has rarely been told so vividly, or heartbreakingly, as in Otero's work.

37 **The dam itself:** F. H. Newell, "Annual Report of the Reclamation Service," vol. 4, parts 1904–5, U.S. Geological Survey.

THREE: THE COUNTRYSIDE

40 **Shadow Hills had been carved out:** J. T. Fey et al., *Joesler and Murphey: An Architectural Legacy for Tucson* (Tucson: City of Tucson, Pima County, and the University of Arizona, 1994).

41 **The El Con:** Lydia R. Otero, *La Calle: Spatial Conflict and Urban Renewal in a Southwest City* (Tucson: University of Arizona Press, 2010); John Bret Harte, *Tucson: Portrait of a Desert Pueblo* (Woodland Hills, Calif.: Windsor Publishers, 1986).

47 **The city had been drunk with growth:** For an ongoing discussion of this phenomenon, see the consistently intelligent Arizona columns of Jon Talton, whose work appears regularly at www.roguecolumnist.typepad.com.

50 **He had taken over the tire business:** After the shooting I learned details of Gabrielle's family that I had never known before, including the name of her horse, from the excellent profile by Sheryl Gay Stolberg and William Yardley, "For Giffords, Tucson Roots Shaped Views," *New York Times.* See also Tom Beal, "Giffords' Way: Pragmatic Service," *Arizona Daily Star*, January 13, 2011.

FOUR: SELLING THE VILLAGE

53 **Nanini left Italy:** Vickie Thompson, *Across the Dry Rillito* (Tucson: Territorial Publishers, 1979).

55 **Sam didn't talk much:** The story about Sam Nanini and Al Capone comes from an undated compact disc of family history entitled "An Elegant Family Legacy," narrated by Steve Nanini. The columnist Westbrook Pegler also wrote about his suspected ties to organized crime in a syndicated column titled "More to Sam Nanini Than You Read," published August 6, 1952, in *The Milwaukee Sentinel*, among other places. See also Ovid Demaris, *Captive City* (New York: Lyle Stuart, 1969).

55 **Tucson was also the retirement:** Joe Salkowski, "Family Ties Show on Bonanno's 90th Birthday," *Arizona Daily Star*, January 16, 1995.

56 **None of this invented landscape:** Thomas Sheridan, *Arizona: A History* (Tucson: University of Arizona Press, 1995).

57 **"Motorola management feels":** Michael F. Logan, *Desert Cities: The Environmental History of Phoenix and Tucson* (Pittsburgh: The University of Pittsburgh Press, 2006).

57 **The graying gentry:** The comment was made to Roy Kenneth Fleagle for a 1966 master's thesis, "Politics and Planning: Tucson Metropolitan Area," for the University of Arizona, and was quoted in Lydia Otero's *La Calle*.

58 **An official club summary:** http://skylinecountryclub.com/?page_id=173/.

58 **Sam Nanini founded:** An undated letter written by James Hughes on file at the Arizona Historic Society, Tucson, bearing the heading, "In Spite of Strong Opposition, Criticism and Ridicule, Sam Nanini Did the Impossible."

59 **"It's been crazy":** Thompson, *Across the Dry Rillito*.

59 **The big department stores:** Bonnie Henry, *Another Tucson* (Tucson: Arizona Daily Star, 1992); John Bret Harte, *Tucson: Portrait of a Desert Pueblo* (Woodland Hills, Calif.: Windsor Publishers, 1986).

59 **One of the only forces:** Thompson, *Across the Dry Rillito*.

61 **In this comfortable remove:** James Howard Kunstler, *The Geography of Nowhere* (New York: Simon & Schuster, 1993).

63 **El Tiradito is a shrine:** Trista Davis, "El Tiradito Shrine an Ode to Local Hispanic Folklore," *El Independente*, October 23, 2009.

66 **Even there her beliefs:** Andrea Stone, "Giffords Proud to Be Arizona's First Jewish Congresswoman," AOL News, January 10, 2011.

68 **She came out and took over:** Cheryl Kohout, "El Campo: Young Owner Changing the Tire Scene," *Inside Tucson Business*, October 20, 1997. See also Bob

Christman, "Families on a Roll—Youth Movement Gives Tire Firms New Acceleration," *Arizona Daily Star*, December 28, 1997.

69 **High-toned spa resorts:** Sheila Storm, "The Origins of Spa: It All Began at Canyon Ranch," *BizTucson*, February 27, 2009.

70 **At the corner of Oracle and Ina:** Ernie Hentsley, "La Toscana Anchors Still Plan to Build," *Arizona Daily Star*, April 22, 1991.

70 **Ownership soon passed:** Ernie Hentsley, "Firm with Hong Kong Ties Makes Inroads in Tucson," *Arizona Daily Star*, February 24, 1992.

71 **The Tuscany theme might:** Jaimee Rose, "Faux Tuscany! That's Almost Italian! Arizonans Put New Spin on Old-World Style," *The Arizona Republic*, May 4, 2002.

FIVE: CITIZENSHIP

82 **When the mine petered out:** Calvin Trillin, "Ground Floor," *The New Yorker*, March 3, 1975.

83 **Five hopefuls:** C. J. Karamargin, "Weiss May Seek Kolbe's Seat,"*Arizona Daily Star*, December 7, 2005.

87 **There had been:** Thomas Sheridan, *Arizona: A History* (Tucson: University of Arizona Press, 1995).

88 **Immigration was supposed to have been:** Daniel Scarpinato, "Congressional Contenders Start Run to November," *Arizona Daily Star*, September 17, 2006.

89 **The debates between them:** Daniel Scarpinato, "Weiss-Giffords Sparks Fly at Forum," *Arizona Daily Star*, July 14, 2006.

96 **He paid for one night:** "Tucson Tragedy," a series written by Shaun McKinnon, reported by Ken Alltucker, Karina Bland, John Faherty, J. J. Hensley, Pat Kossan, Megan Neighbor, Dan Nowicki, Jaimee Rose, Dennis Wagner, and Amy B. Wang, *The Arizona Republic*, February 6–8, 2011; Fernanda Echavarri, "Sheriff's Timeline Shows Loughner's Moves Before Shooting," *Arizona Daily Star*, January 15, 2011.

SIX: THE INFLUENCING MACHINE

98 **Scientists can only work off shadows:** E. Fuller Torrey, *Surviving Schizophrenia* (New York: HarperCollins, 2006).

98 **"a mental disorder":** http://health/nytimes.com/health/guides/disease/schizophrenia/overview.html.

99 **For centuries it was defined:** Gerald N. Grob, *The Mad Among Us: A History of the Care of America's Mentally Ill* (New York: The Free Press, 1994).

101 **There is a body of thought:** Ruthlessly picked apart in Torrey, *Surviving Schizophrenia*.

102 **There is evidence:** E. H. Hare, "Family Setting and the Urban Distribution of Schizophrenia," *British Journal of Psychiatry*, 1956; see also Ann Silversides, "Schizophrenia Linked to Urban Living," in a February 17, 2004, bulletin from the Canadian Medical Association, available at cmaj.ca.

102 **In 1933:** Viktor Tausk, "On the Origin of the 'Influencing Machine' in Schizophrenia," *Psychoanalytic Quarterly* (Spring 1933).

103 **Tausk's observations reveal:** Jerry Mander, *Four Arguments for the Elimination of Television* (New York: Harper Perennial, 1978).

103 **The surrounding environment:** Kwangiel Kim, "Delusions and Hallucinations in East Asians with Schizophrenia," *World Cultural Psychiatry Research Review* (December 2005).

105 **There was at least one student:** Jared Loughner's file of police contacts with the Pima Community College Department of Public Safety was obtained via a public records request to Pima Community College, Tucson, Arizona, and is contained on the compact disc "PCC Police Reports, 03/15/11."

115 **She let the weird young man:** Lynda Sorenson wrote down much of what happened to her on January 8 in an unpublished essay for a Pima College class called "When the Circus Comes to Town."

117 **What kind of parents:** Robert Anglen, "Portrait of Jared Loughner's Parents Emerges," *The Arizona Republic*, January 22, 2011.

120 **He had been arrested six days:** "Suspect Admits Safeway Store Holdup," an unbylined story accompanied by a photo in the *Arizona Daily Star*, July 17, 1952. Also reported in Anglen, "Portrait of Jared Loughner's Parents," and Amy Gardner, David A. Fahrenthold, and Marc Fisher, "Loughner's Descent into a World of Fantasy," *Washington Post*, January 13, 2011.

SEVEN: IT ALL PLAYS IN

123 **The state's committal laws:** Amy Silverman, "Arizona's Surprisingly Good Mental Health Laws Might Have Prevented Tragedy," *Phoenix New Times*, January 10, 2011.

125 **Brewer's own son:** Ginger Rough and J. J. Hensley, "Jan Brewer's Career Shaped by Son's Mental Illness," *The Arizona Republic*, September 14, 2010; Paul Rubin and Amy Silverman, "Jan Brewer's Criminally Insane Son and His Mysteriously Sealed File," *Phoenix New Times*, September 3, 2010.

127 **Just south of the building:** Zachary Lazar, *Evening's Empire: The Story of My Father's Murder* (New York: Little, Brown, 2009).

127 **In the English colonies:** Gerald N. Grob, *The Mad Among Us: A History of the Care of America's Mentally Ill* (New York: The Free Press, 1994). Also discussed in Pete Earley, *Crazy: A Father's Search Through America's Mental Health Madness* (New York: G. P. Putnam's Sons, 2006).

129 **The public mood began to sour:** Grob, ibid.

135 **The only real currency:** Anti-Defamation League report, "The Resurgence of the Sovereign Citizen Movement," August 9, 2010.

136 **Some have changed their names:** Kirk Johnson, Serge F. Kovaleski, Dan Frosch, and Eric Lipton, "Suspect's Odd Behavior Caused Growing Alarm," *New York Times*, January 9, 2011; also, Clyde Haberman, "Subjects and Verbs as Evil Plot," *New York Times*, January 13, 2011.

143 **The origins of modern talk radio:** Donald Godfrey and Frederic A. Leigh, eds., *Historical Dictionary of American Radio* (Westport, Conn.: Greenwood Press, 1998).

144 **Early in his career at WABC:** Interview available at http://youtube.com/watch?v=ELRmgJw8muw.

EIGHT: "I AM ARIZONA"

154 **Clarke developed:** James W. Clarke, *American Assassins: The Darker Side of Politics* (Princeton: Princeton University Press, 1990). See also James W. Clarke, "Tucson: How Culture Can Shape Killers," an article written for the Southern Poverty Law Center (January 2011).

154 **Yet one leaked detail:** Marc Lacey and Joseph Goldstein, "Man Charged in Tucson Shootings Had Researched Assassins, Official Says," *New York Times*, January 26, 2011.

157 **The only work he could find:** Lou Michel and Dan Herbeck, *American Terrorist: Timothy McVeigh and the Oklahoma City Bombing* (New York: HarperCollins, 2001).

165 **All this cost:** Yvonne Wingett Sanchez, "Joe Arpaio's Staff Misspent $99.5 Million, Budget Officials Say," *The Arizona Republic*, April 13, 2011.

166 **He had a miserable childhood:** Tom Zoellner, "Arpaio's Big Decision: Stay as Sheriff or Run for Governor," *The Arizona Republic*, March 3, 2002.

168 **The insane have a way of dying:** Reporters at *Phoenix New Times*, including, notably, John Doughtery and Ray Stern, have aggressively reported wretched

jail conditions for more than a decade. See also the *New Times* stories, John Dickerson, "Inhumanity Has a Price," December 20, 2007; and John Dickerson, "Was Juan Mendoza Farias Beaten to Death by Sheriff Joe Arpaio's Guards?," September 11, 2008.

NINE: IMMIGRANTS, GUNS, AND FEAR

172 **The online system called:** Flaws in the E-Verify program were detailed in a report entitled "Findings of the E-Verify Program Evaluation," prepared by the Rockville, Maryland, firm Westat for the U.S. Department of Homeland Security (December 2009).

173 **Putting up a wood frame:** Gabriela Rico, "Built on a Secret: Building Industry Depends on Illegal Labor," *Tucson Citizen*, November 19, 2003.

173 **The city of Tucson blatantly:** "Council Rebukes DATE Officials, Halts Booklet," *Tucson Daily Citizen*, March 29, 1977.

174 **Yet the hard numbers:** Pecuniary statistics came from the study by Judith Gans, "The Economic Impacts of Immigrants in Arizona," University of Arizona (2007).

176 **The tradition of using:** Thomas Sheridan, *Arizona: A History* (Tucson: University of Arizona Press, 1995).

177 **A plan approved:** U.S. Immigration and Naturalization Service, "Border Patrol Strategic Plan, 1994 and Beyond," approved by Commissioner Doris Meissner on August 8, 1994. The quote from Doris Meissner was given to *The Arizona Republic* and appears in Margaret Regan's powerful *The Death of Josseline: Immigration Stories from the Arizona Borderlands* (Boston: Beacon Press, 2010).

181 **The northern end:** Lydia R. Otero, *La Calle: Spatial Conflict and Urban Renewal in a Southwest City* (Tucson: University of Arizona Press, 2010).

183 **Underlying all the paranoia:** Tom Barry dissected racial fault lines in "Securing Arizona: What Americans Can Learn from Their Rogue State," *Boston Review* (March/April 2011). William Frey's data appears in a paper he wrote for the Brookings Institution, "Will Arizona Be America's Future?," April 28, 2010.

186 **Pearce is a grandnephew of:** His biography has been related in several *Arizona Republic* profiles, including Richard Ruelas, "Son's Shooting Drives Rep. Pearce's Efforts," February 7, 2005; Robbie Sherwood, "Pearce's Belief in 'The Rule of Law' Drove Him to Become a Co-Author of Proposition 200," July 10, 2005; and Gary Nelson, "Arizona Immigration Law Sponsor Russell Pearce Thrusts State into Political Storm," June 6, 2010.

187 **More than ideology:** Laura Sullivan's report about Russell Pearce's possible ties with ALEC ran on National Public Radio's *Morning Edition* on October 28, 2010.

188 **He wrote a book called:** Alexander Zaitchik, "Meet the Man Who Changed Glenn Beck's Life," Salon.com, September 16, 2009.

189 **the fate of these bills:** Alia Beard Rau, "5 Immigrant Bills Rejected," *The Arizona Republic*, March 18, 2011.

191 **A cultural quirk of the Arizona State Senate:** Debate is archived on video at http://azsenate.gov/video_audio.asp.

194 **Carrying a handgun:** Richard Allen Burns, "'This Is My Rifle, This Is My Gun . . .': Gunlore in the Military," *New Directions in Folklore,* an eJournal published in 2003. https://scholarworks.iu.edu/dspace/handle/2022/6906.

197 **State Senator Lori Klein:** Mary Jo Pitzl, "Lawmaker Carries Gun onto House Floor," *The Arizona Republic*, January 11, 2011. See also Luige del Puerto, "Klein Responds to Handgun Handling Criticism," *Arizona Capitol Times*, July 11, 2011.

197 **You can carry a concealed weapon:** Brady McCombs, "Why Arizona Is Called a Firearm-Friendly State," *Arizona Daily Star*, February 20, 2011. See also Dan Nowicki and Dennis Wagner, "Guns in Arizona: The Law, Lore and Lifestyle," *The Arizona Republic*, July 10, 2011.

204 **Arizona has:** Howard Fischer, "Brewer, Key Leaders See No Reason to Curb High-Capacity Ammo Clips," Capitol Media Services; ran in the *Arizona Daily Star*, January 16, 2011.

TEN: THE MEN FROM NOWHERE

209 **There was Richard C. Flower:** W. Scott Donaldson, "Arizona Mining Scams and Unassayable Ore Projects of the Late 20th Century," a paper for the Arizona Department of Mines and Mineral Resources (December 2002).

215 **Coughlin found a job:** Jeremy Duda, "Up Close with Charles Coughlin," *Arizona Capitol Times*, July 16, 2010.

217 **"Why would I apologize if I didn't say it?":** Dylan Smith, "Brewer Advisor Says Media Should Ask About Goddard's Sexuality," Tucsonsentinel.com, October 12, 2010.

222 **Some quick history:** Told in Pat Brock, *Reflections on a Desert Town*, a self-published 2007 book available at Maricopa City Hall.

223 **One durable rule of commuting:** Tom Vanderbilt, *Traffic: Why We Drive the Way We Do* (New York: Knopf, 2008).

227 **a depressing week:** Samantha M. Shapiro, "The Boomtown Mirage," *The New York Times Magazine*, August 6, 2008.

228 **Pinal County was full:** "The Future at Pinal," a report from Arizona State University's Morrison Institute for Public Policy (July 2007).

229 **But precious little evidence:** Dennis Wagner, "Stats Don't Support Pinal Sheriff Babeu's Statement on Trafficking," *The Arizona Republic*, April 10, 2011.

230 **Are such places doomed:** Christopher B. Leinberger, "The Next Slum?," *The Atlantic* (March 2008). See also Howard Fischer, "Vacant Housing Rampant in Arizona," Capitol Media Services; ran in the *Arizona Daily Star*, May 12, 2011.

ELEVEN: A BETTER PLACE

234 **Life got rough:** Stephanie Innes, "Crowd Attentive, Sometimes Rowdy," *Arizona Daily Star*, September 1, 2009.

236 **His rhetoric about:** Quotes from Jesse Kelly in this section came from a file of recorded media in the 2010 Congressional District 8 election.

238 **In an interview with Jim Nintzel:** Jim Nintzel, "Jesse Kelly on War, Health Care Reform, Federal Spending and the Rosemont Mine," *Tucson Weekly*, December 2, 2009.

242 **It wasn't just in Arizona:** Erika Franklin Fowler and Travis N. Rideout, "Advertising Trends in 2010," *The Forum* (January 2011).

242 **I had read of an experiment:** Full studies are by M. J. Watt, et al., "Adolescent Male Rats Exposed to Social Defeat Exhibit Altered Anxiety Behavior and Limbic Monoamines as Adults," *Behavioral Neuroscience* (June 2009); and P. Meerlo, et al., "Changes in Daily Rhythms of Body Temperature and Activity After a Single Social Defeat in Rats," *Physiology & Behavior* (May 1995).

242 **Richard Slotkin:** Richard Slotkin, *Regeneration Through Violence* (Middletown, Conn.: Wesleyan University Press, 1973).

243 **Gabrielle's life was saved:** "Tucson Tragedy," a series written by Shaun McKinnon, reported by Ken Alltucker, Karina Bland, John Faherty, J. J. Hensley, Pat Kossan, Megan Neighbor, Dan Nowicki, Jaimee Rose, Dennis Wagner, and Amy B. Wang, *The Arizona Republic,* February 6–8, 2011; Denise Grady and Jennifer Medina, "From Bloody Scene to E. R., Lifesaving Choices in Tucson," *New York Times*, January 14, 2011.

245 **I wished then:** Portions of the last chapter were adapted from Tom Zoellner, "A Close Friend's Wish for Gabby Giffords," CNN.com, January 18, 2011.

248 **The get-well cards:** Stephanie Innes, "A Place in Their Hearts," *Arizona Daily Star*, February 6, 2011.